A Future South Africa

Visions, Strategies and Realities

GENERAL EDITORS

PETER L. BERGER

BOBBY GODSELL

HUMAN & ROUSSEAU

TAFELBERG

© 1988 SABA Foundation
First published in 1988 jointly by
Human & Rousseau (Pty) Ltd, State House, 3-9 Rose Street
Cape Town; Atrium Building, 60 Glenwood Road, Pretoria
and Tafelberg Publishers Ltd, 28 Wale Street, Cape Town
Set in 10.5 on 13 pt Monotype Lasercomp Plantin
Printed and bound by National Book Printers, Goodwood, Cape
First edition 1988, second impression 1988

ISBN 0 624 02617 5

Contents

Afrikanervolkswag (The Afrikaner People's Guard) (58); the South
African Bureau of Racial Affairs (SABRA) (58); Die Vereniging van
Oranjewerkers (The Society of Orange Workers) (58); Toekomsgesprek
(Forum for the Future) (58); The Stallard Foundation (59); Die Afrika-
ner-Weerstandsbeweging (The Afrikaner Resistance Movement)
(AWB) (59); Die Blanke Bevrydingsbeweging (The White Liberation
Movement) (BBB) (61)

3 Exile and resistance: the African National
Congress, the South African Communist Party
and the Pan Africanist Congress

HERIBERT ADAM

4 The politics of internal resistance groupings

PAULUS ZULU

5 The incrementalists
ANN BERNSTEIN AND BOBBY GODSELL

6 The economics of conflict and negotiation
PIETER LE ROUX

Addenda

Preface

This research project, which was entitled 'South Africa Beyond Apartheid', had its origins in the belief of a group of South Africans and North Americans that the debate about the nature of change in South Africa should be deepened. This group, concerned that the debate is often characterised more by passion than by enlightenment, believed that there was a need both for a more faithful description of contemporary realities and a more reflective presentation of future possibilities.

The group (whose full membership is set out in Appendix 1) was in an important sense self-recruited. Its members share four basic beliefs about South Africa:

- Apartheid is morally reprehensible and should be abolished.
- It should be replaced by a democracy and not a tyranny.
- In the process of transition the productive capacity of the economy should not be destroyed.
- The costs of transition, especially in human terms, should be kept to the minimum.

Beyond these four broadly defined and shared convictions, the group has a diversity of opinions and levels of commitment. These have greatly enriched the research project. They have also precluded us from making policy recommendations, which was never our intention. Instead we have tried to produce faithful description, clarification and, we hope, some insight.

The project's intended audience is all those concerned with the future of South Africa, and especially those who share the four beliefs set out above. From the very start, project members were open about what they were doing. At the group's first meeting, a one-page 'charter' was agreed upon (this is set out in Appendix 2). This was shown to all the individuals and groups who took part in the research. The research findings have been made available to any group who requested them during the course of the project. (Many such briefings have taken place.)

The project's first task was to identify the key 'actors' whose visions and strategies are crucial to the pattern which change will take in South Africa. The term 'actor' as used here includes important organisations (such as political parties and movements), institutions (such as governments, churches and universities) and categories (such as 'youth'). Particular care has been taken to check the group's understanding of the nature, future visions and strategic logic of each actor researched with authoritative proponents of that actor's point of view. The actors identified by the group are listed below. Inevitably, no such list can be comprehensive, and some actors have been researched in greater detail then others.

Funding for this project was raised from corporate and philanthropic sources both in South Africa and the United States. (A list of these donors is included in Appendix 3.) The principle that costs incurred in South Africa were to be met from funds generated in South Africa, whilst American costs were to be met with American funds, was observed. Trusts were created in each country to ensure that the project was faithfully executed, and that the funds were properly expended. Control over the research process, however, remained entirely in the hands of the group itself.

The project adopted a simple methodology. Firstly, some twenty-five key actors were identified both in South Africa and the United States. In South Africa these consisted of:

- White right-wing groups (researched by *Helen Zille*).
- The state and the National Party (researched by *Lawrence Schlemmer*).
- The state as an economic actor/agent (researched by *Pieter le Roux*).
- State security agencies (researched by *Bobby Godsell*).
- The Labour Party (researched by *Helen Zille*).
- Inkatha (researched by *Vicki Cadman* and *Bobby Godsell*).
- The business community (researched by *Ann Bernstein*).
- The Progressive Federal Party (researched by *Bobby Godsell*).

- Black political groups – internal and external (researched by *Heribert Adam*).
- Resistance groups in Natal and the Eastern Cape, as well as the United Democratic Front and its affiliates (researched by *Paulus Zulu*).
- Resistance groups in the Transvaal as well as AZAPO and the National Forum (researched by *Vincent Maphai*).
- Educational and religious actors (researched by *James Leatt*).
- Black professional organisations (researched by *Reuel Khoza*).
- Trade unions (researched by *Bobby Godsell*).

In the United States the actors researched were:
- 'Washington' (researched by *Helen Kitchen*).
- The United States business community (researched by *David Hauck*).
- State and city legislators (researched by *David Hauck*).
- Anti-apartheid groups (researched by *Shelley Green*).
- United States colleges (researched by *Ronald Goldman*).
- Religious actors (researched by *Richard Neuhaus*).

Other aspects of the 'world' also researched were:
- The frontline states: Angola and Mozambique (researched by *John Marcum*).
- The frontline states: Zimbabwe and the BLS (Botswana, Lesotho, Swaziland) territories (researched by *Michael Spicer*).
- Europe (researched by *Michael Spicer*).

All of these actors were researched as to their nature, their future vision of South African society and their 'core' strategies to achieve this desired future. The project chairman, *Peter Berger*, produced a schema to guide this research. (This is presented in Appendix 4.)

Secondly, these actors, their visions and 'strategic logic' were subjected to a critique by their researchers in the light of contemporary South African 'realities'. Again *Peter Berger* provided an analytic schema for this 'reality testing', which is included in this report as Appendix 5. We hope to be able to publish the individual research papers, as they constitute a valuable overview of contemporary South African politics.

The third phase of the project was the preparation of this report. For this purpose the twenty-five actors were grouped into five categories. The first four represent competing strategic logic in South Africa, as pursued by:

The South African government (Chapter 1), written by *Lawrence Schlemmer*.

The right wing in South Africa (Chapter 2), written by *Helen Zille*.

A description of resistance in exile (Chapter 3) written by *Heribert Adam*.

A description of internally based resistance groups (Chapter 4) written by *Paulus Zulu*.

Actors broadly grouped together as 'incrementalists' (Chapter 5) written jointly by *Ann Bernstein* and *Bobby Godsell*.

A chapter (Chapter 6) which examines critical economic decisions, written by *Pieter le Roux*.

A seventh chapter, which has been given the title of 'The United States and the World'. This has been written jointly by *Helen Kitchen*, *John Marcum* and *Michael Spicer*.

Chapter 8 attempts to place South Africa in a comparative context. This chapter has been written jointly by *Peter Berger* and *Bobby Godsell*, who are also the book's general editors.

It cannot be stated too strongly that this research project has the character of a debate. Perhaps it can best be understood as a colloquium spanning two continents and continuing over a period of two years. As the word colloquium implies, it represented an exchange of views. The group itself does not have a unified view of the South African problem, neither of the past, the present nor the future. All that unites the group are the four common beliefs mentioned above (and even these produce widely differing interpretations within the group). The second uniting characteristic is a belief in the value of reflection and reason.

It is both impossible and undesirable to be neutral or 'objective' about South Africa. It is a land whose problems produce passionate commitment and beliefs amongst its citizens and those from beyond its borders who become entangled in its affairs. It is hoped that this book clearly illustrates some of the dimensions of difference and debate. In questions ranging from the meta-theoretical (such as approaches to social order and social change) to the empirical (such as the nature of 'street violence') members of the group hold widely differing views. These differences have enriched the research process, resulting in a more faithful reflection of the divergent positions of the actors themselves – a reflection which would have been impossible for some key actors if the group had shared a unified perspective. These differences have also caused this to be a book without a concluding chapter. The concluding chapter will be written by South Africans themselves, helped or hindered by those beyond this country's borders who are concerned about her destiny.

An exercise of this breadth, spanning two continents, some twenty-three researchers and continuing over two years accumulates a significant burden of gratitude. Four types of assistance require particular acknowledgement.

Our sincere thanks are extended to the following:

Firstly, those who funded this venture in both generosity and faith. Not only did they make the funds possible to conduct this research, but they also gave the team full freedom to pursue their objectives as they saw fit. Responsibility for the report vests fully within the group, but creating the possibility of such a report is the action of the funders.

Secondly, a New York City and a Johannesburg law firm, Shearman & Sterling and Webber Wentzel & Company, respectively, who provided legal and administrative services on a *pro bono publico* basis. In particular, profound thanks are due to *Stephen A. Oxman* in New York and *Carveth Geach* and *Ronny Napier* in Johannesburg who gave their time, efforts and especially their wise counsel.

Further acknowledgement is due to all those individuals who gave significant amounts of time and effort in helping group members understand the nature, vision and strategic logic of their organisation. Indeed, the openness of individuals and organisations, particularly those inside South Africa, to the pedestrian demands of reason and research is itself a source of hope for that country's future.

The programme administrators (*Bonnie McShane, Liz van Niekerk, Charles Carter* and *Annette McKenzie*) without whose efforts this bi-national effort could never have succeeded.

In the end the existence of the book is a tribute to the diligence, patience and endurance of *Liz van Niekerk.*

Margaret Hitge helped convert academic jargon into accessible prose. A team of editors at Human & Rousseau and Tafelberg under the leadership of *Koos Human* and *Danie van Niekerk* completed the metamorphosis from a collection of academic papers into a book.

1 South Africa's National Party government

LAWRENCE SCHLEMMER

Introduction: analysis versus letting the apartheid state off the hook[1]

At a press conference held in Dakar, Senegal during the July 1987 visit by a number of South Africans to meet ANC (African National Congress) representatives, a senior ANC member took exception to a remark by a South African academic that 'apartheid' had developed over centuries of South African history. Whether this was true or not, the ANC member retorted, one should not let the apartheid government 'off the hook'.

This conversation illustrates a major difficulty in describing and analysing South Africa's National Party government. Most social scientists in South Africa and abroad are totally opposed to a government which bases its rationale and programme on a formal classification of the South African population in terms of race groups. This author is no exception. Yet these moral concerns should not preclude analysis.

The tendency to regard what is frequently referred to as 'the apartheid regime' as a unique instance of official racism frequently carries with it the inclination to be wary of or even to refrain from an analysis which might indicate that the South African political structure is a variant of patterns which have occurred throughout world history. There is often a feeling that the evil of apartheid dare not be cloaked by approaches which regard (in political terms) the National Party politicians as part of the human race.

On the contrary, however, efforts directed at change in South Africa can only be properly pursued if the factors which underlie the resilience of the National Party are fully understood and taken into account. If some of these factors are universal political proclivities, or perhaps even attributes regarded as positive in other governments, they have to be faced and incorporated into an over-all analysis. Even for those implacably opposed and hostile to the South African government, a realistic assessment of its positive or universal features can only serve to refine their strategies.

The concept of 'crisis in government' is also relevant here. It has become widespread in critiques of the South African government to refer to the crisis of the state. Yet, as Berger and Godsell suggest in Chapter 8, this crisis may be chronic. If this is true, it is not a crisis of survival, or perhaps not even a crisis at all. Nevertheless, it is almost as if social scientists in South Africa are expected to keep the concept of crisis alive, if for no other reason than to protect the morale of those in radical opposition to the government. However, if the label 'crisis' is not fully justified, it will inevitably produce opposition stances which are either over-optimistic or naive and, in both cases, faulty. In part, apartheid may owe its resilience to dec-ades of academic and journalistic analysis which, because of not fully acknowledging certain positive features of the South African government, have predicted an imminent collapse of the state.

In this chapter the author has attempted to describe and analyse, as objectively as possible, the nature of the South African govern-ment, its visions for the future and how it intends achieving its aims. In some ways the analysis may appear discouraging to government opponents. This is not intended. Indeed, it is hoped that the analysis may assist in formulating programmes for change beyond apartheid.

The beginnings of change?

Archetypal apartheid was developed to its epitome in the period under Verwoerd. It represented a brutal, massive but almost heroic attempt on the part of the then ethnically solidary National Party of the time to secure a correspondence between nation and territo-ry for whites by imposing an order much more incisive than race segregation. It was the period of the grand experiment: dividing South Africa into homelands, called national states, by using a full barrage of legislative, economic and administrative strategies. It might have succeeded at that stage of black politicisation and international sympathy had it not been for other major elements in the tradition of government: paternalism; a disregard of the interests and aspirations of the subjugated peoples and the all-pervasive conviction that the most developed nation deserved the lion's share of resources. The most significant event in the failure of grand apartheid was the rejection by the Verwoerd government of those aspects of the report of the Tomlinson Commission (1955) which estimated the extent of the resources which had to be deployed to make grand apartheid succeed.

However, a number of policy reforms and adaptations have been introduced (particularly since September 1978) which, taken together, leave no doubt that a departure from traditional policy commitments has occurred.

To many the reforms noted below cannot be expected to win any praise or sympathy for the government, since the structures so reformed can be regarded as having been an insult to humanity in the first place. Nevertheless, they are slowly transforming South Africa from a society more rigidly segregated than any other in the world to one in which black South Africans can begin to participate in some of the benefits of a modern urban society. Changes have included the formal desegregation of sport, the granting of full trade union rights to blacks, the acknowledgement of permanent residence and citizenship rights for blacks in the common area together with provisions for full property rights, the abolition of the laws prohibiting marriage and intimate relations between the races and a gradual opening of university education to all races.

More complex reforms, controversial in some respects but which nevertheless illustrate the trend, include the following:

- The government's regional development policy is now formulated and implemented within nine major demarcations which traverse the boundaries of the homelands. This indicates that economic and socio-demographic interdependence between so-called white and black areas is being increasingly emphasised, as opposed to the former policy of attempting to promote as great a degree as possible of separation and autonomy.
- Consistent with the shift away from an emphasis on separation,

the government has very recently promulgated legislation at the request of KwaZulu and the province of Natal which makes provision for a joint executive authority and associated administrative functions to deal with matters of common interest to the two regions. The principle may be extended to other provinces where black and common areas are juxtaposed.

- Also within a framework of interdependence the new Regional Services Councils which provide for multiracial metropolitan authorities to deal with the provision of bulk services are a very controversial reform. The representation on these councils, which is nominated by racially separate municipal authorities, is claimed to entrench apartheid at the third tier of government, to reinforce the influence of the wealthier white local authorities through a system of weighted representation based on consumption of services, and to impose new tax burdens on metropolitan industry which will not apply to industry in decentralised areas. On the other hand, the RSCs represent a type of advance in a political context because they, along with the joint homeland-provincial executive, are among the first multiracial bodies with more than advisory functions to have been established since 1948.
- The establishment of fully fledged black urban local authorities, with status and powers fully comparable to those of white local government, has (despite fundamental problems of funding and political legitimacy surrounding the councils) reflected the government's departure from the old principle that blacks have a temporary and rightless status outside of the homelands.
- A shift, with similar connotations, has been the lifting of the so-called coloured labour preference regulations for the areas of the Western Cape.
- Another move has been the repeal of the Prohibition of Political Interference Act which, in the past, prevented multiracial membership of formal political parties.
- A dramatic departure from an established policy has been the legislation in 1986 to abolish influx control applicable to the black population. The legislation in some ways tightens controls on squatting and avoids addressing the issue of the Group Areas Act, and therefore falls short of allowing completely unfettered physi-

cal mobility for the population at large. It is a significant reform nevertheless, since people of all races permanently resident in the common areas and non-independent homelands are now subject to the same controls on movement between cities and regions, and have the same identity documents and hence, in principle, a common citizenship. The government no longer has the power to remove people from one part of the country to another on ideological grounds by sheer administrative fiat.

– A reform which, like many others, has ambiguous elements is the recent change in the structure and powers of second tier or provincial government. On the one hand it involved the withdrawal of the representative status of provincial authorities in favour of nominated provincial executive councillors, thus reinforcing the power of the central executive. On the other hand, however, African, coloured and Indian nominees have been included in these bodies which have important devolved functions, particularly in the fields of planning, education, health, local government and racial zoning.

– A highly controversial 'reform', which helped to precipitate the violent protests which swept the country between 1984 and 1986, was the introduction of the tricameral parliament. Its most significant characteristic by far was the exclusion of the African majority. It also contains provisions which allow the majority party in the white chamber, through its control of the President's Council, to override the potential veto of the coloured and Indian houses. This parliament is not a departure from apartheid in terms of its intrinsic constitutional provisions. However, this development makes provision, in the normal process of legislation, for 'concurrent' approval of bills by coloureds and Indians as well as whites, thus qualifying white political hegemony to a certain extent. This introduces a new 'theme' into National Party rule – that of power-sharing. It has also introduced a new mechanism into the legislative process – that of the Parliamentary Standing Committee – as a means of promoting a working consensus between the three chambers before legislation is put to the vote in the three houses.

– The government has fully accepted the necessity for incorporating the African population into the political system at the level of parliamentary decision-making. This has only recently been given some formal substance by the publication of the National Council Bill which provides for an interim structure of high formal status, fully multiracial in composition, to prepare for the inclusion of Africans in the political system, probably by means of the ultimate establishment of a Council of State.

– During the run-up to the May 1987 election, an earlier proposal for accommodating urban African politics within a framework of 'city states' was strongly revived. The idea is that several black townships in a region be combined into an equivalent of a self-governing state, with considerable powers and enhanced constitutional status, presumably to enjoy eventual representation in the Council of State.

In summary, it is clear that the policy of major territorial separation in the political and social spheres and of exclusive and autonomous nation status for whites in the common area of the Republic of South Africa has largely been abandoned. The line of resistance to change has been drawn back to the issue of power as such, and to the sphere of white 'community' interests, as opposed to national life. The white residential areas with their associated services and facilities are the areas in which the most important privileges associated with white lifestyle are enjoyed. Obviously the all-white voting constituency is also the power base of the government, and racial group areas and the Population Registration Act are the foundations of both the white power base and whites' privileged and relatively exclusive lifestyle.

At the time of final editing, the State President had just taken one cautious step further in accepting a recommendation of the President's Council (1987) that a new category of mixed or 'grey' areas be accepted alongside ethnically-segregated residence. Although the scope of the opening of residential areas is expected to be largely limited to those suburbs in which informal integration has already occurred, the new policy will establish a precedent in the sense of a formal acknowledgement of a 'common' or nonracial sphere of social life. The precedent will also establish a contradictory situation in regard to franchise arrangements in the new open areas, and as such will create pressures for further policy adjustments, some in respect of important political institutions. The government promoted the new departure in policy in adverts in national newspapers with the major theme of 'Live and let live'.

Together with the abandonment of major territorial separation, a new basis for the government's constitutional planning has emerged which makes a distinction between community (or 'own') affairs and general affairs. This distinction is at the heart of the new constitution of the tricameral parliament. It is a device for separating the issues connected with white community living (own affairs) from major overriding government functions (general affairs). Power-sharing is seen to be advantageous for planning in the context of general affairs, and is not a threat to the more intimate concerns of whites in a community context.

Thus the system has shifted from socio-geographic apartheid to a separation of spheres of interest along racial lines. The concept of the white nation has given way to the concept of the autonomy and lifestyle of white communities within a 'multiracial nation'. A policy of non-territorial race-federation biased towards white power has emerged as the dominant basis of policy at present.

Key aspects of the nature of present National Party policy can be deduced from Mr P. W. Botha's address to parliament immediately after winning the 6 May 1987 white general election with an increased overall majority. The following extracts from his speech indicate how this party leader interpreted the renewed mandate:

"... (the mandate) confirms the government's point of departure that security, order and stability in all of our communities are preconditions for reform and that the proponents of radicalism and violence will have to renounce that course before they may participate in constitutional processes . . . it involves a clear endorsement of the point of view that a group approach has to be accepted in the expansion of our democratic system and the stabilisation of our communities . . . it reiterates that South Africans themselves, and not the outside world, will decide the country's future . . . It is not possible in a multicultural country like the Republic of South Africa to talk about the protection of *individual* rights unless one talks about the protection of *minority* rights at the same time . . . it is (also) impossible to talk about the protection of minority *rights* unless one talks about the protection of minority *groups* at the same time. . . . it is also not possible to talk about the protection of minority groups and the prevention of domination unless groups enjoy statutory recognition and the relationship among them is regulated constitutionally . . . Constitutional development cannot take place in isolation, but has to be preceded and accompanied by economic and social processes to create the conditions in which renewal may be continued on the basis of security . . . our challenge lies in narrowing the gap between the first world and the third world without lowering standards in South Africa . . . At the same time the government will ensure that safety and security will enjoy the highest priority because without them development and progress are not possible . . . In dealing with our country's problems there is no room for ill-considered instant solutions born out of fear, panic and surrender."

These quotations illustrate five keynote features of the government programme: its group basis, the first world/third world distinction within South Africa, socio-economic reform, tough security and a rejection of outside pressures.

We turn now to an examination of the prospects for further shifts by the government in the short to medium term. Empirical evidence collected for this analysis was obtained from fifty-one formal interviews with National Party functionaries, members of parliament, cabinet ministers and deputy ministers as well as officials in the security agencies.[2] In addition, National Party literature, the debating points at party congresses in 1984 and 1985, press reports and other documentation were analysed.

The South African government's response to pressure

Since it is frequently assumed, inside South Africa and abroad, that coercive economic and political sanctions are the only certain way to achieve change, it is essential to consider the government's reactions to such pressures. Violent or coercive pressure as a factor of change could theoretically so overshadow or eclipse other processes that any further analysis would be redundant.

The major coercive pressures on the government are the recent widespread violent protests in the country, externally promoted sabotage and insurgency, the disinvestment campaign, cultural and sport boycotts, trade sanctions and diplomatic pressures. In considering the significance of these pressures it must be assumed that they will have some degree of effect. The question is whether or not their effects on the government are such as to make external and internal coercion the dominant dynamic in the change process from now on.

The violence which erupted fitfully in isolated places in 1983 and which gathered momentum after September 1984 and continued until late 1986 has not yet fully abated. It has necessitated the use of the army to assist the police on a scale unheard of for half a century, and has seriously depressed confidence in the economy. In the context of a lack of fundamental political rights for blacks, police and defence force action to quell the unrest is generally perceived by internal opposition groups as well as agencies abroad as a repression of legitimate activism and protest.

One must assume that the large scale of activism in the black townships has changed the government's assessment of the black political situation considerably. The government may persist in holding the view which was expressed by most of the people interviewed (and which is probably by no means entirely incorrect), that a majority of rank-and-file blacks do not have a revolutionary agenda. However, the capacity of mobilised township activists to persuade and/or coerce the masses (outside of KwaZulu and certain other homelands) into observing stayaways, strikes and consumer boycotts and into withdrawing support from more conservative community leaders has made an impression on the government. In the interviews it was indicated that senior civil servants and a member of the cabinet had even made some attempts to initiate discussions with black activists in the Eastern Cape.

In order to understand the potential effect of unrest on the government, one must understand the context of the black political mobilisation which underlies the violence. From early 1983 onwards, progressively more activism and militant rhetoric developed within extra-parliamentary organisations in the townships. This coincided with the establishment of the United Democratic Front. During 1983 various political observers fully expected the government to use its battery of security laws and controls to deflate the expanding balloon of militant rhetoric, but this did not occur. The *1983 Annual Survey of Race Relations* describes the shift: "In May (1983) it was suggested that the government might be 'easing up' on banning orders in response to criticism and pressure from Western countries. It was observed that no person had been banned since October 1982, that fifteen people whose banning orders had lapsed had not had them renewed and that several newly released political prisoners had not been banned, as had previously been a normal occurrence" (Cooper, 1984: 545). The government had shifted its position away from comprehensive repression towards partial repression under the impact of human rights protest in the media which had gained momentum after the 1976-1977 disturbances. This had also happened previously: the initial rise of the Black Consciousness Movement in the very early seventies was allowed to gain considerable momentum before the government imposed blanket repression. It delayed long enough for the movement to take root in black youth society, with dramatic results in 1976-1977.

A number of analysts of revolution (Muller, 1979; Gurr, 1970; Taylor, 1984) have argued that if a state has the resources, the loyalty of security personnel and the determination to impose blanket repression, almost any revolutionary challenge can be surmounted.

In the early seventies, and even more so in the eighties, the South African government did precisely what most analysts of revolution would have advised it to avoid. It eased repressive controls slightly, at a time when reforms were benefiting coloureds and Indians more than Africans, and when changes in aspirations stemming from socio-economic reforms were causing heightened 'relative deprivation'. Alternative outlets for political aspirations were virtually non-existent. The government probably did not make a strategic blunder, but eased controls partly out of a desire to strengthen links with the West at a time when the United States policy of 'constructive engagement' promised to be useful.

In part this easing of controls may also have been a consequence of an experiment in partial 'repressive tolerance'. A report in the *Sunday Times* (31 May 1987) based on 'security sources' argued that General Johann Coetzee (Commissioner of Police until 1987) had been blamed for being "too elaborate in his approach to extra-parliamentary groups . . . (thinking that) . . . by allowing the UDF to organise openly, the security forces could exploit tensions . . . and counter them more effectively". The report suggested that the security agencies had since reverted to their earlier and more effective direct approach.

An interview with officials in the National Intelligence Service clarified and confirmed the viewpoints expressed in the other interviews with regard to government responses to internal violence. The mass of black urban dwellers were not seen as intrinsically radical or militant – 'ideology is not a factor which counts in depth'. Many people in the black community were seen as having an identity crisis – an uncertainty about which political line to follow. In this situation activism, which was seen as being minutely planned by underground organisations, created a bandwagon effect which drew large numbers of supporters, tipping the balance in favour of the activists. The State of Emergency was necessary to counter this effect. Establishing negotiations also created an opposite pole. Security action was described as almost clinically necessary in the short run, although political expression in a future dispensation was seen as the answer in the longer run.

No-one who was interviewed either stated directly or indicated even covert signs of basic survival anxiety. The point was made by one minister that white communities were only very indirectly affected. The dominant position was that the unrest was either impeding the programme of reform or affecting the sense of security of supporters and others. Hence violence is having its effects at a level of threat to the state *below* that which the state would regard as critical for its survival. Violence does not appear to have pushed the government to the limits of its political or security resources.

The effects of external pressure are equally difficult to assess.

Some noteworthy successes can, however, be claimed. There is little doubt that the desegregation of sport was immensely facilitated by the well-orchestrated pressures originally mounted by Peter Hain and subsequently expanded by many other overseas bodies. The abolition of the Masters and Servants Act was also preceded by specific legal action on the part of American trade unions which would have affected the direct export of coal. These were not crucial issues for the government, however. Past achievements of pressure lobbies do not offer persuasive proof that the government will respond positively to pressure on issues perceived to be of major significance for its power base.

The interviews revealed that there was far less concern about external economic pressures than about internal violence. Not one of the members of parliament (MPs) interviewed spontaneously mentioned sanctions as a problem when asked to indicate the major challenges and issues facing the party. In 1984 and 1985, at the Transvaal and Natal congresses of the National Party, the issue of South Africa's external image, which broadly encompasses the divestment issue, was raised only once each year, much less frequently than the issue of unrest. Divestment is obviously an issue of concern at cabinet level because it relates to an economic system-need of the country. Even in the interviews at cabinet level, however, divestment was mentioned spontaneously by only one deputy minister.

Professor Jan Lombard, Deputy Governor of the Reserve Bank, has argued very convincingly that the problem of capital availability for productive investment is fundamentally a matter of internal investor confidence, and that the foreign sanctions issue is, comparatively speaking, a marginal consideration (Lombard, 1986: 41-42).

The interviews and other contacts at government level leave an overwhelming impression that the South African cabinet is attempting to orchestrate responses to widely divergent internal demands, as well as to organic influences from within its own support structures, so that any specially accommodating response to divestment pressure is very unlikely indeed. One very important factor is that there are influential businessmen within the National Party itself who are committed to the belief that a policy of economic independence, including direct controls on imports, enhanced exchange control mechanisms, and direct government intervention in productive investment would be the most reliable path to economic recovery and growth (*Financial Mail*, 30 May 1986). Dr Aidan Edwards, Chairman of the State President's Advisory Council for Technology, has also suggested that limited divestment could 'push local industry into a higher gear' (*Business Day*, 3 June 1987).

Furthermore, any accusation that the government is dancing to the tune of the pressure groups abroad carries severe penalties for the government. These far outweigh what are perceived to be the uncertain benefits of responding to the agendas of lobbies in foreign countries. The emergence of the Conservative Party as official opposition after the May election will increase the penalties. 'Outside world be damned' was the way one National Party functionary from Pretoria summed up feelings on sanctions. As one MP put it: 'Frightened people do not talk of reform.'

Nevertheless, it would be a great oversimplification to suggest that the pressure strategies of township protest, insurgency or external sanctions have no effect on the South African government. Their effects are, however, mediated by a range of other factors, some of which may have the capacity to transform coercive pressure into an extremely counterproductive result.

The interest base of the National Party and the influence of the business sector

In one of the interviews with a high-ranking salaried official in the National Party, we were assured that it is a principle of the party to rely mainly on many small donations from members and supporters rather than on large corporate or business grants. On the other hand, there have been campaigns in the recent past which were directed at the business community, under the patronage of the leader of the party, which according to all accounts were successful. One must assume that the party is not averse to corporate funding. At the same time the National Party is clearly not elite-based, and member-participation in activity and financial-support drives remains important.

Another indication of the party's interest base is the socio-economic distribution of its voting constituency. In February 1986 the following comparison between party supporters emerged from a nation-wide political opinion poll conducted for the author by Market and Opinion Surveys (Pty) Ltd.

Table 1 : Household income rating by party support : February 1986

Household Income	PFP	NP	HNP/CP
Upper-middle	38%	20%	10%
Middle	43%	45%	49%
Lower-middle/Lower	19%	35%	41%
Population	(n 335)	(n 801)	(n 262)

The percentage distributions show quite clearly that the National Party support base still tends to be somewhat inclined towards the lower socio-economic levels. These estimates also display in a very crude fashion the extent to which the National Party has to attempt to balance upper middle-class, middle- and working-class interests, a problem which its two major opposition groups share to a much lesser extent.

A large body of literature which has appeared in recent times argues that apartheid is crucially concerned with the conditions for (private) capital accumulation. Obviously any government has to act to protect and promote the interests of institutions which are functionally important in determining overall national welfare. It therefore proves very little by way of ideological orientation if a government promotes industrial growth (whether public or private), or nurtures agencies such as business corporations whose profits contribute substantially to fiscal revenue. Much more specific mutual interests and ideologies have to be established in order to prove that apartheid is geared to the service of capital.

In the interviews with parliamentarians and ministers, very careful note was taken of any mention of interest groups to which the politicians appeared to be sympathetic or sensitive. The vast majority of such references were to party supporters, the general white public at large and finally to the 'moderate' coloured, Indian and African communities to which many interviewees claimed to have some communication route. Business interests were not mentioned spontaneously at all. While small businessmen are often prominent in constituency politics, one MP declared that big business had 'little to offer'. In some of the interviews with ministers the author suggested the possibility of a more structured relationship between the private sector and the government as partners in reform initiatives. The reaction was highly cautious. The government seems not to wish to become subject to intensively organised private sector pressures. When interviewed, most people spoke, either directly or by implication, of a need to balance a variety of interest groups within the party. No-one suggested that the large corporate sector had a singular influence on the government.

Interesting case studies of the relationship between lobbies and the government can be found in the KwaZulu-Natal unity issue and in the matter of the abolition of influx control laws, which are frequently regarded as a success for the private sector lobby.

Despite an obvious desire to accommodate the KwaZulu leadership in order to draw it into constitutional negotiations at central level, and despite strong business backing and participation, the government has responded more negatively than positively to the Buthelezi Commission (Schreiner, 1982) and the KwaZulu-Natal Indaba proposals, to the extent that analysts in a Marxist tradition such as Southall (1982) were perplexed by the government's rejection of a well-organised 'capitalist' campaign.

Much of the activity of business lobbies in pursuit of the abolition of influx control has been described elsewhere (Giliomee and Schlemmer, 1985). The conclusion was that the opposition of private industry to the influx control laws was as complete and emphatic as any position by a very significant interest group was and could be. The reform took place, but only after the government had delayed moving on the issue and had considered the problem in the greatest detail in terms of its own perceived priorities and needs, first through the Grosskopf Committee of 1981, then through the Hoexter Commission into legal reform of 1984, and finally by means of the President's Council Investigation into Urbanisation of 1985-1986.

Furthermore, a nation-wide survey of white opinion by Market and Opinion Surveys (Pty) Ltd had shown in February 1986 that only nine per cent of Afrikaners and substantially fewer National Party supporters considered the retention of influx control laws to be essential. A prominent expert, Dr P. Smit, who was a member of the Human Sciences Research Council at the time and was also a government advisor on urbanisation, had been recommending the repeal of the laws. The fact that the influx control system was no longer functioning effectively is also significant. In 1984 Cabinet Minister Koornhof had admitted that 40 per cent of Africans in the Western Cape were 'illegal'.

The pattern of events which led to the repeal of the influx control laws would suggest that the government can be responsive to private sector influence, but only where such influence is in agreement with expert opinion, where there is substantial acceptance of the reform measure within the government's own support groups, *and* after its own enquiries have provided evidence and a rationale for the reform.

In general terms, the impression is that from 1979 onwards the Botha administration has to some extent courted the corporate sector, as evidenced by major joint conferences (Carlton Conferences 1 and 2 and the Good Hope Conference), but not so much in order to identify private sector concerns and respond to them as to secure the co-operation of a sector with large resources for solving development problems. At the time of writing, the State President, in an address to the annual general meeting of the Afrikaanse Handelsinstituut (Chamber of Commerce) in Bloemfontein, warned businessmen not to interfere in political issues about which he felt they were generally poorly informed. They were directed to the State President's Economic Advisory Committee as the proper channel for influencing government.

While there are many joint government actions and interests

which are in agreement with the interests of capital (which will continue to be selectively cited by Marxist scholars), the government position prevails where the interests diverge. There is no evidence from any of the interviews, or in any action or response by the government, that the National Party is a handmaiden to capital.

It has also frequently been argued that the National Party is the handmaiden to agricultural capital. There certainly was a time when farmers were a vital segment of the party's support base. With steady urbanisation and a decline in the number of white farmers (from 116 000 in 1950 to approximately 65 000 in 1986), this is no longer the case. Farm debt is currently a major problem, and farming incomes on average are only some 20 per cent above debt repayments (*SA News Summary*, 2nd Quarter, 1985). There are at present great tensions between farmers and the government. The government is currently granting relief only to those farmers who can prove their efficiency. As one MP who was interviewed put it: "We have been afraid of white farmers far too long – we must be prepared to lose votes."

The civil service, on the other hand, is probably more vital to the party than business or agriculture, because it has a collective capacity for much greater coherence of mobilisation. The same would apply to the teaching profession. In any society with deeply held political convictions, a government is not likely to ignore the modal views of a large, cohesive public sector comprising nearly 40 per cent of the white labour force.

If one were to try to seek proof from specific examples, one could establish specific interconnections of ideology and interest between the National Party and just about any formation in white and nonracial politics in South Africa. On balance, however, the National Party is increasingly the party of the centre-conservative, urban middle and lower middle classes in both the private and especially the public sectors. As such, it represents the larger mass of relative privilege in the white community. To seek any more devious or specific alignments of interest would be to force the analysis outside the bounds of plausibility and commonly perceived reality.

The National Party and Afrikaner ethnicity

The National Party is frequently referred to as the party of Afrikaner nationalism. In a classification of discussion points at the 1984 and 1985 National Party congresses, however, we could identify only one which related specifically to Afrikaans culture and that referred to the importance of Christian nationalism. In the interviews with politicians, which were all conducted in Afrikaans, not one interviewee mentioned threats to, or the future of, Afrikaans and its related culture as being among their most pressing problems or pertinent issues. Party officials in Natal, where Afrikaners are in a minority and hence more likely than elsewhere to develop a sense of threatened ethnicity, overwhelmingly endorsed an amalgamation of Afrikaans- and English-speaking 'moderates'. They considered that the barriers had fallen and that English-speaking support was now a permanent and integral part of the National Party structure.

Interviews with party officials in the Transvaal suggested a greater prominence for specifically Afrikaans culture, but their statements were always qualified. Afrikaans culture was seen as part and parcel of a broader, Western culture, or it was noted that culture could not be protected by law or politics. The observation was also made that the National Party was committed to protecting and promoting all cultural heritages.

These views are in agreement with the realities and requirements of the present situation in which white politics are dominant in the society. As Afrikaners are nearly a two-thirds majority in the voting population, a 'centre' party will always automatically cater for Afrikaans interests, and the less these are emphasised the more easily coalitions in the 'centre' of white politics can be promoted.

Adam (1979) has argued that ever since the failure of grand apartheid, the National Party has had to 'disguise' its central commitment to Afrikaans culture in order to adopt more pragmatic policies, for which it needed English-speaking support to counterbalance the defection of committed Afrikaner Nationalists. Minister Heunis is quoted as saying: "It is in the long-term interest that the Afrikaner should always have the privilege of the leadership role" (Giliomee, 1983: 26-35). The interviews conducted for the present study suggest that the 'disguise' is working so well that an Afrikaans-English support coalition is now taken for granted as desirable and necessary.

English-speaking South Africans have also displayed a remarkably consistent pattern of rallying to the National Party in times when it appeared to be in most need of support for reform or under external threat (Schlemmer, 1983: 11). This tendency was manifested once again in the most recent white election. According to Mr Con Botha, Director of Information for the National Party, the defection of some 30 per cent of Progressive Federal Party (PFP) supporters and up to 75 per cent of New Republic Party (NRP) supporters means that the support base of the National Party now corresponds to the ratio of Afrikaans- to English-speakers in the electorate. Certainly, the National Party can no longer be called an ethnic body in the sphere of white politics.[3]

These comments refer specifically to the manifest or effective posture of the party at the present time. They do not discount an underlying cohesion derived from Afrikaner nationalism as a primary white political dynamic, nor the probability that ethnic fervour will re-emerge if threatened. Currently, however, the manifest ideology of the party is that of white community unity within a multinational context.

The National Party and white self-determination

With this issue one comes much closer to the core of the National Party charter. The earlier excerpts from the State President's speech to parliament are apposite. The issue was tested in a well-publicised conflict of views at cabinet level between the leader of the National Party in the Transvaal, Minister F. W. de Klerk, and Foreign Minister Pik Botha. The latter had claimed that as long as suitable constitutional means of protecting minority rights could be identified, then the 'sting' of racial categorisation should be removed (*Citizen*, 7 February 1986). Minister De Klerk, on the other hand, had said that voluntary group association would lead to chaos and confusion (*The Argus*, 5 February 1986). The State President entered the debate to say that Minister De Klerk had interpreted him most correctly on minority rights (*Star*, 8 February 1986).

The interviews suggested that the principle of political self-determination for racially defined communities is still supported by a clear majority in the party, and very strongly so by party functionaries. While a relatively limited proportion of caucus members would place their bottom line at no more than minority *protection*, the prevailing commitment is to minority autonomy and *at least* equal co-determination for whites along with others in national affairs. The impression was gained that the cabinet's stand was rather more firm on the issue of power than that of many MPs, among whom a few fairly modest views on power aspirations for whites were encountered. Only one cabinet minister who was interviewed predicted the possibility of the government moving away from separate racial voting.

The emerging future position will not simply be one of minority protection – it will make provision at least for white participation and co-determination in all major affairs of state. The white political 'subsociety' will be protected, as the post-election speech of the State President, quoted earlier, so firmly promises.

The first world in Africa

In the interviews careful attention was given to what has been indicated as the most basic goal of National Party politics: the nature of white community self-determination and national co-determination. It is certainly not ethnic culture, as the previous section has suggested. It is also not a 'capitalist' economy – capitalism or a free market system was mentioned spontaneously in conversation by one English-speaking deputy minister only. Socialism and communism are feared not because of their specific implications for the mode of production (the state has never hesitated to establish public corporations), but for their threat to religion and to the popular privileges and lifestyles enjoyed by whites.

Amidst all the variations in position within the National Party, there is a unifying core of emphasis on the concept of a European standard and way of life, mythical or otherwise. This is expressed in various ways (as will become evident below), but it is what whites in general perceive as 'white culture'. In the past the National Party with its fundamental dedication to this issue has been comfortably aligned with the majority sentiment in the empowered white voting minority in South Africa.

A major feature of the government's concern with white interests is the comprehensive way in which such interests are seen. While the concern is obviously sectional, the variety of issues and interests referred to in the interviews makes it clear that the National Party is concerned with an entire *subsociety*.

This is not to suggest that a subsociety is an objective reality. It is after all the product of the institutional privileges of a group. The *perception* of a subsociety is part of a powerful motive, however. It corresponds to what earlier writers have referred to as corporate group organisation (Kuper and Smith, 1969; Smith, 1965).

The most articulate National Party spokesmen, such as Mr Albert Nothnagel, MP, described white interests as including the following: a combination of lifestyle, a sense of origin and identity, the psychological satisfaction of an in-group community life, standards of public order, behaviour and respectability and sufficient control over the allocation of resources and the maintenance of security to ensure the continuation of these benefits.

One senior MP summed up the major interest of white Nationalists as being "security and standards – there is a great fear (among whites) that a third world situation will arise in their own areas". Another senior MP and deputy minister close to the core of National Party thinking gave the central concern a more ethnic flavour but also stressed the composite character of its ideology by listing Western values, Christian values, life views, community cohesion, material security, a familiar and recognisable environment, a strong economy, property rights, an objective legal system and the protection of established institutions in general. These everyday or popular interests would be taken for granted in any typical Western society. In South Africa, however, they are clearly much more consciously experienced as constituting a first world sub-society within a third world continent.

Commenting on the 1987 election results, Ken Owen, editor of *Business Day* (8 May 1987) defined this concept very clearly by stating that white voters, in contemplating their insecurity ". . . blame 'them' . . . the outsiders, the third world hordes moving inexorably into the cities and the once manicured first world sub-urbs". These attributes of daily life are the 'bottom line', and the notion is almost totally pervasive that a degree of racial exclusivity in a situation with a predominance of third world people, whether it is formally or informally achieved, is the only certain way to maintain the pattern.

The role of the security agencies[4]

A consideration of the nature and strength of the South African security system is essential to this assessment. Were the govern-ment to perceive itself, or be perceived, as weak and unable to impose legislative and administrative authority, a completely dif-ferent set of prospects for change would exist than those based on the assumption of strength and the ability to impose authority if and when required.

THE SIZE AND COMPOSITION OF THE SECURITY SERVICES

The size of the South African Defence Force (SADF) is almost 430 000 if full-time and part-time, reserves and paramilitary per-sonnel are combined. Full-timers comprise less than one-third of the count but they render nearly 87 per cent of the service (*Inter-national Institute for Strategic Studies*, 1986: 106-107).

The South African Police, which recently combined with the Railway Police, has a force of some 62 000 men and women. In addition there are some 17 000 reserves. The full-time force is set to expand to some 80 000 within the next few years (*Sunday Times*, 31 May 1987).

There are three major intelligence agencies: Military Intelligence, the Security Police and the National Intelligence Service (NIS) located in the office of the State President.

The State Security Council (SSC) forms the focal point of a national security management system. Its statutory membership consists of the State President (its chairman), the Ministers of Defence, Foreign Affairs, Justice and Law and Order, and the senior civil servants of these departments. Additional co-opted members appear to be the Ministers of Finance, Constitutional Development and Co-operation and Development. Other ministers and senior officials attend by invitation. The SSC has a secretariat of about 45, drawn from a range of government departments, predominantly from the National Intelligence Service.

Grundy (1983) has argued for a *primus inter pares* status for the SSC on the grounds that it is chaired by the State President himself. It is the only cabinet committee established by law with a fixed membership, and it has much wider terms of reference than the other three committees.

Furthermore, Geldenhuys (1986c) notes that the SSC has a much larger secretariat and supportive organisational structure (see below). Attendance is by invitation only, other than for standing or co-opted members (unlike the other three committees) and its decisions are not widely disclosed within the government, as is the case with other cabinet committees.

Supporting the SSC is a structure of Inter-Departmental Committees (IDCs) and Joint Management Centres (JMCs). The IDCs (14 or 15 in number) cover areas of common interest in the national security field which would affect more than one government department, such as the departments of political action, transport, science and technology, and culture.

Joint Management Centres, instituted in the early 1980s, provide co-ordination between security agencies at a regional level. Nine regions are demarcated (corresponding with Defence Force Command Areas) as well as four covering "certain South African countries, including one for Namibia" (Geldenhuys, 1986c). Although JMCs have no executive powers, they appear to be a 'grey' area, where national security management intrudes into the affairs of local government structures.

Recently, Joint Management Centres (JMCs), sub-JMCs and 'mini'-JMCs have been mobilised at all levels down to street committees, to "counter the ANC and UDF (African National Congress and United Democratic Front) on its own turf with its own methods" (*Business Day*, 12 November 1986). Interviews conducted with various relevant politicians, however, indicated that the local activities of the JMCs and sub-JMCs are not directed at particular individuals or groups for security action (this occurs independently of the JMCs). The goals are rather to target influences in order to identify grievances and problems, to mobilise and co-ordinate civil departments for the provision of short-term solutions, and to mobilise campaigns among local people in order to promote stability and co-operation.[5] An informal conversation with a senior member of Military Intelligence gave the impression that the military would ideally like to reduce its role in the JMCs.

What does seem clear, nevertheless, is that the mechanisms created at present are characteristic of societies which perceive themselves to be besieged or under attack.

SOUTH AFRICAN SECURITY AGENCIES
IN COMPARATIVE PERSPECTIVE

Whilst every effort has been made to obtain the most meaningful and accurate comparative statistics, some reservations should be registered. A degree of hidden expenditure is often alleged, particularly in regard to military expenditure statistics and most often with regard to the production and procurement of armaments. Whilst such hidden expenditure is probably not unique to South Africa, it might distort some of the comparisons.

South Africa's defence force is neither particularly large, nor particularly expensive in a world context. It is of course dwarfed by the superpowers (106 400 full-time members as opposed to the Soviet Union's 5 300 000 and the United States' 2 100 000). Its force is modest in comparison with other major NATO powers (West Germany's 478 000 and the United Kingdom's 329 200).

A comparison with members of the old Commonwealth such as Canada (83 000) and Australia (70 400) provides one important standard of contrast. South Africa maintains a larger permanent defence force than either of these former dominion territories. A third area of comparison is that of other high-conflict countries: here South Africa's army is smaller than Israel's (142 000) and much smaller than Taïwan's (444 000). The contrast with two other developing countries provides further perspective: Brazil (276 000) and Cuba (161 500). On the African continent Egypt (445 000), Ethiopia (217 000), Algeria (170 000) and Morocco (149 000) exceed the full-time South African army, and Nigeria (94 000) is roughly on a par with it.

As a percentage of total government spending, South Africa's military expenditure at 13,4 per cent (1983) is exceeded by the United States (29,6 per cent), Taiwan (25,9 per cent), Israel (24,9 per cent) and West Germany (23,2 per cent). It is on a par with Britain (13,7 per cent) and ahead of Canada, Australia, Brazil and Cuba (9,8 per cent, 9,8 per cent, 7,5 per cent and 7,2 per cent respectively). In Africa, Mozambique (34,2 per cent), Ethiopia (27,5 per cent), Angola (22 per cent in 1982) and Zimbabwe (16,7 per cent) comfortably exceed South Africa's relative government spending on defence.

South Africa faces two types of military opponent: the guerrilla wings of South Africa's two liberation movements, the ANC and the PAC (Pan Africanist Congress), and (hypothetically) the conventional armies of African states which could decide to attack the present government militarily.

Reliable estimates of the strength of the ANC's and PAC's military wings (Umkhonto we Sizwe and Poqo respectively) do not exist. The range of estimates for the ANC varies from a 20 000 high to a 3 000 low (Lodge, 1986). A recent estimate of 6 000 is probably the best guide. Estimates of the strength of Umkhonto we Sizwe are made more difficult by the fact that its members are now trained inside South Africa. A telephone interview with a member of the ANC in Lusaka failed to confirm the above figures. Estimates for the PAC are even more elusive, but all commentators agree that its military resources are much smaller than those of the ANC (*Defence White Paper*, 1986: 13).

Clearly, forces of such size do not pose a serious conventional threat to a defence force of the extent and sophistication of the South African Defence Force. A small force of well-trained and well-equipped guerrillas can achieve no more than significant *symbolic* victories (such as the attacks on the Sasol II plant and the Koeberg Nuclear Power station indicate), as well as increasing the costs of security surveillance.

Shortly before assuming office in the Reagan Administration in 1979, Chester Crocker wrote: "By almost any conventional index of national military power, the Republic of South Africa continues to tower over any current or foreseeable African opponent or coalition" (Crocker, 1979: 71).

Since then nothing has occurred to alter this view, despite a significant build-up of sophisticated weaponry in neighbouring states. Indeed the sophistication of the South African armaments industry has increased. What was until recently South Africa's major strategic 'gap' has been partly filled by upgrading its older Mirage fighter jets to become the more competitive 'Cheetahs'. A recently published strategic atlas concludes that "the frontline states (Tanzania, Botswana, Zambia, Mozambique, Angola) have no means of changing the status quo" (Chaliand and Rageau, 1985).

As regards relative police force size, South Africa has been an underpoliced society for some time. In June 1984, Minister Vlok indicated that there were 1,4 policemen per 1 000 of the population (*Financial Mail*, 12 April 1985). This compared with roughly 2,3 per 1 000 in the United Kingdom, 2,7 in Israel, 2,6 in West Germany, 4,4 in Ulster and 5,7 in Algeria (*International Institute for Strategic Studies*, 1984). There are in fact only a handful of countries with a lower figure for police per 1 000 members of the population than South Africa. South Africa's current strength has recently risen to roughly 2,0 per 1 000 and an increase to 3,0 per 1 000 in 1995 is planned (Bennett, 1985: 6-8). At present there is also an active programme for the training of municipal policemen for duty in African townships, the so-called *kitskonstabels* (instant policemen).

THE ROLE OF THE SECURITY AGENCIES
IN THE POLITICAL PROCESS

The question at the heart of this assessment is: to what extent and in which ways will the security agencies reinforce the present system or alternatively influence the process of political change away from the present political order?

In this context, the prospect of a military coup is frequently raised in 'dinner table' debates about South Africa's future. It is usually suggested that right-wing fears of reform going too far might motivate such a coup, although some years ago the idea of a left-wing De Gaulle pattern of intervention was also fashionable. This possibility is not supported by any serious analysis, and South Africa's military have neither the inclination nor the opportunity to seize political power.

A much more serious argument is made for growing military influence (to the point of dominance or a covert coup) in political decision-making in contemporary South Africa. The most developed thesis of this kind is Frankel's *Pretoria's Praetorians* (1984). In this work Frankel argues that a significant *militarisation* of both society and polity has already occurred, and that the conditions for *military intervention* (direct or indirect) can be envisaged.

Praetorianism has been defined as "a situation where the military class of a given society exercises independent political power within it by virtue of an actual or threatened use of force" (*Encyclopedia of the Social Sciences*). Reviewers have claimed that Frankel does not make a convincing case for such a state existing now or in the foreseeable future (Baynham, 1985; Du Toit, 1985; and Seegers, 1986b).

An important precondition for a praetorian role, as noted by both Nunn (1976) and Baynham (1985), is the presence of weaknesses, inefficiency and illegitimacy in central political institutions. Whilst it can be convincingly argued that South Africa's present political regime lacks legitimacy among the disenfranchised, it does not lack legitimacy among the military. Nor can the most important political structures be described as weak. The military must compete for influence with other government departments, with parliament and with the National Party.

Whilst an argument can be made for growing military influence in state affairs, this argument cannot be carried with any conviction to the point where the military are viewed as the dominant political lobby. This is not, however, to ignore the role of the State Security

Council in the political decision-making process (see below), but the SSC is a body in which politicians take responsibility for decisions. The growing *general* influence of the military is often inferred from the alleged destabilisation of surrounding states. While this type of incident is evidence either of conflicting directions or, more probably, of a dual agenda in the government, it does not necessarily attest to the military's ability to dominate the polity.

The militarisation argument is also often advanced by inference from the military's growing size and from its monopoly of resources. However, it has already been observed that South Africa's armed forces are not particularly large in comparative perspective, nor particularly expensive (given the earlier qualification in this regard). Furthermore, the case for dramatic growth is unconvincing. The defence force budget, in real terms, has decreased by 3,2 per cent in contrast to a general state expenditure increase of 22 per cent (*1986 Defence White Paper*: 9). However, a significant part of defence expenditure is disguised. In the budget for 1988 defence expenditure will increase by 30 per cent, but as a percentage of state expenditure it will decrease from 14,7 per cent in 1987 to 14,3 per cent in 1988.

Even more significant is the fact that during 1985 full-time manpower in the defence force was decreased by 4,5 per cent and part-time service requirements were reduced by 1 288 000 man-days (*1986 Defence White Paper*: 29). There is also no indication of any intention to extend the current period of basic service from its present 24 month level (*1986 Defence White Paper*: 13).

None of the above should be seen as an argument for South Africa's defence force being as large or as expensive as it is. It points simply to the fact that the available evidence suggests that it is not becoming bigger or more expensive at the present time.

A major underlying influence of the intelligence agencies may exist in their role in defining the 'enemy'. It is common knowledge that the ANC is highly stereotyped, indeed even demonised, in government communications. The potential danger that this holds was emphasised by the call made by the former Security Police Major Craig Williamson for a more sophisticated approach by the polity to the ANC (Williamson, 1986).

34

In contrast to this it should perhaps be noted that informal conversations with politicians suggest that the subject of possible legalisation of the 'nationalist' wing of the ANC is sometimes discussed. Other matters under examination include speculation on the coherence of this liberation movement and on likely future interactions between it and 'moderate' internal groups. Possibly the definition of the enemy occurs at two levels – on a short-term action level, and on a longer-term strategic level; the latter perhaps much more vaguely formulated.

THE JUNE 1986 STATE OF EMERGENCY
The State of Emergency of 12 June 1986 has extended the role of the security services in national affairs significantly and deserves some specific discussion. This latest State of Emergency applies countrywide, whereas the 1985 proclamation applied to only one-third of South Africa's 133 magisterial districts. Its definition of offences is more far-reaching: it has introduced prepublication censorship for the first time in South Africa's 'peacetime' history, and it gives very great powers and discretion to even fairly junior members of the security forces.

The State of Emergency has meant that in some areas with a high tendency towards unrest, defence force units, security policemen and riot squads have taken over normal community policing functions.

In the eleven months following the declaration of the State of Emergency, some 25 000 people were detained, according to the monitoring agency of the Progressive Federal Party and the Detainees' Parents' Support Committee. Of these, the majority have been released. The Minister of Law and Order gave a figure of some 4 200 people still detained on 15 April 1987, of which 34 per cent were eighteen years or younger (*Weekly Mail*, 22-29 May 1987), but hundreds, particularly children, have subsequently been released (*Weekly Mail*, 29 May-4 June 1987). The State of Emergency seems to be proving successful in suppressing unrest and in reducing the need for security action. One indication of this is the reduction in the number of fatalities from political violence.

The following figures on deaths, recorded by the South African

Institute of Race Relations, reveal a sharp downward trend in fatalities after the measures in the State of Emergency took effect (*SAIRR News*, April 1987).

Table 2: Deaths in political violence

September 1984 – February 1985	- 188
March 1985 – August 1985	- 492
September 1985 – February 1986	- 565
March 1986 – August 1986	- 955
September 1986 – February 1987	- 187

Subsequent to the above figures the incidence of fatalities due to political unrest has been significantly raised by violent confrontations between the UDF and Inkatha in the Pietermaritzburg region. This phenomenon, arising from a struggle for political dominance in hitherto under-mobilised townships, is highly particular in its significance, however, and does not gainsay the overall trend referred to above. Some aspects of the more general conflict, such as a rent boycott in Transvaal townships, have tended to persist until time of final editing and reflect the fact that despite the successful repression referred to above the situation is not quiescent.

One may expect further action against some organisations in an attempt to reinforce the measures adopted in the State of Emergency. In his post-election speech the State President suggested that external funding of extra-parliamentary political organisations would be prohibited, and the Minister of Home Affairs has imposed controls on the alternative press (mainly publications by various extra-parliamentary organisations such as the UDF (United Democratic Front), but probably also including some semi-academic journals).

VISIONS OF THE FUTURE

The military are commonly and correctly credited with an important role as originators in the development of reform strategies. For some time military leaders have defined the challenge to the state as

36

80 per cent political and 20 per cent military. The present Chief of the Defence Force, General Jannie Geldenhuys, noted in an interview that change was taking place, and that the defence force had a positive contribution to make towards a process of constitutional, lawful and peaceful change.

P. W. Botha's 15 years as Minister of Defence are often cited as one of the reasons for his reformist policies. Certainly Botha referred to multiracial co-operation in the defence force as one of the reasons why South African society must 'adapt or die', in his first major policy speech in Upington in 1979. The senior leaders of the South African police also appear to see strategic benefits in reform. For example, General Coetzee (former head of the police), states in a published work: "What is true, is that a dynamic policy in regard to change firstly makes the RSA a target that is difficult to pin down, and secondly disturbs the strategies of its enemies . . ." (Coetzee, 1981: 76).

This is not to suggest that both the military and the police, or even all levels within them, are equally enthusiastic about all aspects of the government's reform incentives. However, at least they do not appear to represent a consistent ideological impediment to reform.

Current priorities and constraints

INITIATIVES FOR CHANGE

Almost without exception, the politicians in the National Party who were interviewed saw the challenge of commencing negotiations with black leaders concerning incorporation into the political process as the greatest single issue facing government. Security and economic issues loomed large, but they were frequently linked to the matter of black willingness to negotiate. As far as could be determined, the modal position is a genuine commitment to power-sharing, but within a system in which whites as a group would retain at least the right to equal co-determination. The State President has recently assumed personal responsibility for exploring the possibility of such negotiations and had a deputy minister

(Stoffel van der Merwe) reporting to him directly on this issue. More than one government department is actually engaged at present in attempts to facilitate talks with the full spectrum of black political groups, including the UDF.

The strong promotion, both during and after the election campaigns, of the multiracial statutory National Council has already tended to shift the emergent constitutional government model beyond a multicameral system, and it appears that a review of constitutional thinking will now take place. There were subtle indications in the interviews of growing dissatisfaction with the tricameral system as a means of achieving consensus and orderly government.

The interviews left the author with the impression that the broad *idea* of continuing evolutionary reform and change has become part of the popular wisdom and political culture of the National Party government. The following are some typical examples of 'keynote' statements: "A white power monopoly has become intolerable . . ." (Minister Heunis, *Hansard*, 8 May 1985). "Many things have occurred in the past for which some of us must now ask forgiveness" (Heunis, *Hansard*, 1 February 1985). "I think we went too far with certain measures under the apartheid principle. We made a mistake" (State President, *Hansard*, 21 April 1986). "Any system aimed at keeping some of its participants in a subordinate position through clever or devious means is doomed to failure. It must be visibly and honestly just and equitable towards everybody" (Minister F. W. de Klerk, *Hansard*, 27 March 1986).

CONSTRAINTS ON CHANGE: THE WHITE RIGHT WING

In the May election the right-wing Conservative Party, which is the product of a split away from the NP in 1982, established itself as the official opposition in the white chamber, with 22 seats. Had it entered into an election pact with the other right-wing party, the HNP (Herstigte Nasionale Party), it would have gained roughly another eight seats. The two right-wing parties combined achieved 30 per cent of the vote compared with 17 per cent of the vote gained by parties to the left of the NP. Furthermore, up to 16 additional seats held by the NP are marginal and vulnerable to right-wing gains in a future general election.

Against this inhibiting influence, one must consider that the opposition role of the CP in parliament will tend to crystallise differences between its position and that of the NP. Furthermore, part of the vulnerability of the NP is felt within the party to lie in the fact that it has not produced a viable power-sharing model. A development and consolidation of its policy will reduce the effect of criticism from the Right, as reflected in statements during interviews such as: "The NP must perform dynamically, then the right wing will become irrelevant", and "The threat from the Right is a symptom of uncertainty". Nationalists interviewed seem to think that the CP is not a 'growing factor', as one put it.

It is also relevant that the promising performance of three independent candidates to the left of the party has demonstrated their capacity to draw support away from the left flank of the NP. As a trio they drew some 17 per cent more votes than PFP candidates would have (at the PFP's 1981 strength). These votes came from so-called *verligte* (enlightened) Nationalists. Hence the party realises that it dare not watch its right flank only. An analysis by this author (Schlemmer, 1987a) and by Swilling (1987b) suggests that a broad movement towards reform is still occurring, despite popular perceptions of the 1987 election.

Dr Willem de Klerk, a well-informed ex-editor, argued at a post-election seminar of ASSOCOM (Association of Chambers of Commerce and Industry) on 8 May 1987 that the NP will be inhibited by the Right, but will not 'move to the right'.

NEGATIVE PRESSURES ON THE GOVERNMENT

Another possibly serious constraint on reform is the demoralising effect of the refusal by black community leaders to participate openly in discussions and negotiations with the government. This was a factor facilitating racial polarisation in Rhodesia in the 1960s and 1970s (Lewis, 1987) and it could have the same effect in South Africa. While some black community spokesmen loosely associated with the progressive extra-parliamentary groups have had clandestine meetings with the government and recently more openly with the President's Council, the lack of any public success inhibits the government from making effective rejoinders to a variety of accusations that neither the white nor the black populations want the reforms offered by the National Party. Interviews with parliamentarians also revealed a danger that the absence of any rewards for the party in its attempts to commence negotiations with blacks erodes morale and depresses enthusiasm for change or experimentation. The renewed mandate of the party in the May election, as well as its success in curbing black protest, may, however, counter this somewhat.

A factor identified by a deputy minister who is a well-known former academic and researcher is related to this. His comments in an interview suggest that the earlier United States' policy of 'constructive engagement', despite international perceptions of its failure, had opened up hopes of international recognition, and had drawn the government along a reform trajectory faster than it would otherwise have gone. By the same token, the switch to a negative policy of sanctions had deflated the mood of change and progress. He was convinced, however, that the impetus for reform would slowly build up again.

Concluding assessment

THE NATURE OF THE NATIONAL PARTY GOVERNMENT: INDIGENOUS POST-COLONIALISM

The evidence from all the interviews suggests that the National Party government is in a process in which a comprehensive range of interests within the white segment of South African society are becoming reconciled and acted upon. These interests are not predominantly class-based, ethnically based or currently primarily focused on Afrikaner nationalism, although culture is obviously a factor in the mix of elements.

Within the party there is a diversity of ideological positions. Dr Willem de Klerk, former editor of the largest Afrikaans newspaper, and brother of a cabinet minister, sums up the party caucus as 22 per cent left of centre or *verlig* (enlightened/concerned with quicker reform), 60 per cent 'middle' and some 18 per cent conservative and resistant to reform.

These facts taken together confirm a view argued hypothetically in the introduction, that the National Party government is very largely synonymous with the whites' self-concept of their being a 'European settler' segment of South African society which has become indigenous – a 'subsociety' – rather than one with a particular nationalism, ethnicity or class interest. It shares this very basic political position with the Conservative Party (albeit with a very different agenda for action) and it is worth noting that 82 per cent of whites who voted in the May 1987 election aligned themselves with the 'subsociety' ideology in their voting (52 per cent NP and 30 per cent CP or HNP). Whatever its implications, it is a political position which appears to be unshakeable among whites in the short to medium terms.

The dynamics of white corporate interests are such, however, that they need not have been focused around race. A broadly analogous formation is that of the non-Catholic Ulstermen, who are not racially distinguished from other Irish, but were also settlers in an earlier period of history and have a perception of cultural links with Scotland or England. It may be absolutely true of its effects, but it is nevertheless oversimplified to regard the South African system as institutionalised racism.

The interviews with members of parliament and ministers strongly confirmed the white 'subsociety' model of the South African system. One after another the respondents could suggest no major single dimension of interest which supported the commitment to white self-determination. The repeated mention of a combination of elements as the basis of National Party ideology and policy was striking.

The basic mobilising identity among the white 'settler' groups is that of being a fragment of Europe, in the way best described by Hartz (1984). This sense of having an origin in Western Europe appears to be more pertinent than the specific cultural interests of either Afrikaans or English linguistic subcategories (Schlemmer, forthcoming). The social identity of the European fragment or segment is deeply, if sometimes subtly, imbued with a consciousness of being associated with a 'superior' civilisation. Hence, as in all other colonial or former colonial situations, relationships with the indigenous people are tinged at best by pervasive paternalism and social distance. The perception, and to a very great extent the reality, of a conflict of interests is not simply between classes and ethnic or racial interests, but between a first world and a third world social order. In the collective fears of whites, the third world within the country is associated with a lack of sophistication, disorder and lower standards. The perverted vision of a future under majority rule most frequently conjured up among rank-and-file whites is one of irregularities of administration, loiterers in parks, dirt in the streets, a lack of public discipline and power-hungry politicians with a fateful sway over slavishly adoring masses. The fact that none of these images is confined to the third world, and that all are gross oversimplifications, does not alter the power of the perception.

The cleavage between the indigenous peoples and the settler group in this type of society is among the deepest of all social divisions. The opposed groups are multibonded by class differences, perceptions of origin, cultural features and political interests, and rather than being subgroups, they emerge as subsocieties. The political hegemony of the settler-colonist class, and the nature of the resultant conflict in which the subject classes tend to develop a very high-key and uncompromising mobilising rhetoric with promises of a comprehensive displacement of the old order, tend to reinforce the dire perceptions of threats to their own rule which are held by the settler communities.

Theories of this type of plural society have tended to fall into obscurity in recent years, partly because colonial systems have been displaced in most parts of the third world. The earlier writings of Furnivall (1948), Smith (1965) and Kuper and Smith (1969) are worth referring to, however.

As with most colonial plural societies, the basic structure of the system is initially established by territorial conquest. The social differences between the victors and the vanquished subsequently prevent comprehensive absorption of the vanquished into the social system of the dominant group. This is particularly the case if the vanquished outnumber the settler colonists. An early pattern of dominant and subject societies within the same territory emerges. This deeply influences subsequent development, even though the interdependence of the two systems increases over a period of time. The system is akin to one of 'nations' interacting within the same territory with highly crystallised, almost caste-like status differences between them.

In the resulting system, relations between the ruler group and the subject communities are characterised by a great emphasis on control and paternalistic administration, behaviourally analogous in some ways to a permanent foreign occupation of an indigenous territory. In the South African case even the fact that the Afrikaans group has itself been exposed to British colonial domination, and the reality that there is no single European society of reference for South African whites, has not altered the deep-seated consciousness among whites of their being the bearers of a superior, non-African system which requires a pervasive imposition of controls on the indigenous peoples.

Furnivall (1948) was the first to point out that in the colonial plural societies which he studied, the economy is integrated (albeit stratified), in contrast to the separated social life of the different communities. An obvious consequence of the social and political dominance of the settler group is that the material disadvantage of the indigenous peoples is perpetuated. This class inequality is a central element, but unlike the propositions of the Marxist theories, material inequality does not condition social and political relations but vice versa. Socio-political dominance perpetuates privilege.

A particularly powerful dynamic is established if, as part of its ethnic self-identification or nationalism after the early conquest of territory, one segment develops an identification with the territory as its 'own'. Walker Connor (1978) quotes a well-known definition of a nation as including ". . . a strong group sense of belonging, associated with a particular territory considered to be peculiarly its own". This dynamic has been a fundamental feature of South African history.

The indigenous settlers of the old white Rhodesia represented a subsociety very similar to that in South Africa. This particular example tends to suggest that the element of specifically Afrikaner ethnic interests is by no means the sole factor underlying white dominance.

It must be considered, however, that Afrikaans nationalism is in a sense largely dormant at this point because its status is demographically guaranteed, as it were, within a system of white power mobilisation. If, however, white identity were to be fundamentally threatened, Afrikaans nationalism would re-emerge as a strong factor. In that sense the notion among whites of being a type of subsociety is ultimately reinforced by Afrikaans nationalism (Schlemmer, forthcoming).

POLICY ORIENTATION: SEPARATION, DOMINATION OR CONCILIATION?

The evidence reviewed suggests that the present NP government is in a (prolonged) phase of transition from its earlier commitment to securing a territorially defined 'nation-state' for whites (separate development) towards a form of co-existence or parallelism within the same geographic domain. Although the concept has been on the political agenda since 1977, the May 1987 election finally gave the National Party a mandate to work towards the central representation of blacks, outside the politically and economically marginal homelands. Currently, in the National Party view, the interests of whites have to be articulated in a politically more abstract and complex way than that of territorial hegemony. To many the shift may be hardly perceptible. However, the most significant division in white politics, to judge from the 1987 election, is between the concept of 'subsociety within territory' (Conservative Party) and 'subsociety independent of territory' (National Party). Although the roughly 20 to 25 per cent left-of-centre minority in the National Party may come to consider relaxing or phasing out the constitutional definition of groups or communities, the majority commitment to this principle is very powerful in the party at this stage.

CIVILIAN RULE VERSUS SECURITY IN A DEEPLY DIVIDED SOCIETY

However one may conceptualise the current phase, it remains in effect a form of racial hegemony, in which a coercive security is an inevitable condition for the survival of the system. The strength and effectiveness of the security system are of major importance in any assessment of the regime. A government in which coercive security plays such a prominent role is in ever-present danger of its agenda being usurped by the very tools which it uses for survival. The review of the security agencies, however, does not suggest that this is occurring. It suggests instead what Swilling (1987a) has called a 'dual state' strategy – a form of carefully orchestrated parallelism between a political process and security action. According to this view, which accords with our evidence, the civil political agenda continues to assign roles to the security agencies.

The review strongly suggests that the security agencies have little or no reason to seize power or to mount a major political challenge to present cabinet priorities. The security elites have not acquired superordinate political status and they do not determine or influence state policy in spheres outside those relevant to security control. Particularly in the light of massive white electoral support for the security objectives, there is, in effect, no need for either a seizure or militarisation of the political process. Political and security goals are mutually compatible.

In this regard, it is significant that the most recent and pervasive security initiative, the Joint Management Centres, are under the overall control of a civilian politician with no security background (Deputy Minister Roelf Meyer). Their special role appears to be one of political and social action in the pursuit of security goals. This, theoretically, could have occurred without the security agencies; their particular function seems to be the efficient co-ordination of sluggish and poorly co-ordinated civilian bureaucracies.

This is not to suggest that the State Security Council does not have a very considerable influence within the arena of political policy. The civilian state has so defined its goals and priorities that keynote advice from the security agencies probably follows automatically. In addition, the security agencies have important implicit roles in the political process. The way in which they define resistance movements limits the extent to which the government will be prepared to negotiate with these movements. Furthermore, the effectiveness of the security agencies in suppressing dissent in the society undermines these movements' leverage for change, which might otherwise be considerable. It must be noted, however, that the deputy minister who was assigned to the State President's office to give special attention to the constitutional incorporation of black people has firmly committed himself to negotiation with even the most radical movements (*Rapport*, 7 June 1987 – quoting Dr Stoffel van der Merwe).

One of the most significant conclusions that can be drawn about the security agencies is their capacity to expand. Even with a 30 per cent escalation in the security vote in the 1988 budget, security expenditure as a proportion of GDP is constant and fairly low by international and African standards. This point is frequently made by informed observers.[6]

Furthermore, as a consequence of the recent violent protests, the security management system has become much more sophisticated and pervasive. The Joint Management Centres and the rapid training of additional police personnel for black areas are the two most prominent examples. It would seem that the state, if anything, is busy strengthening its control over the internal security situation and, if need be, could augment its resources in this area very significantly in the future.

PROSPECTS FOR CHANGE

Given the strengthening of security resources, the deeply entrenched ethic akin to indigenous colonialism in the white voting constituency, the 1987 election results and a firm policy commitment to a constitutional system based on racial groups, what prospects exist for the ending of apartheid? Extreme pessimism in this regard is understandable.

There are nevertheless indications that a gradual process of change which will take the governmental system beyond its present constraints will occur. Some of these indications are given below.

– Our interviews showed evidence of an active policy debate within the NP caucus. Although there was widespread feeling that the cabinet was frequently unresponsive to the ideas proposed in the caucus, it would be surprising if a changing consensus in a parliamentary support group did not permeate through to the executive over a period of time, particularly after a change in top leadership.

— It also seemed clear from the interviews that the present policy position of the party is seen by growing numbers within party ranks as a makeshift compromise between political realities and the ideal of white community self-determination. As a compromise it is less compelling and less able to command commitment than alternative models to the left and right, and therefore is not likely to become an ideology as encapsulating as Verwoerdian separate development was.

— Important developments which will influence the National Party at all levels are occurring in the Dutch Reformed churches, in particular the decision of the 1986 Synod of the Nederduitse Gereformeerde Kerk that apartheid was 'unbiblical'. This important decision has stripped apartheid of any last vestige of moral legitimacy in a formal sense, among Afrikaners to the left of the right-wing parties.[7]

— The most 'progressive' members of the caucus and the executive appear to be among the most able intellects in the party, hence recent promotions have favoured the change-oriented wing of the party. Over the past 18 months at least a dozen so-called 'new Nats' have either achieved deputy ministerships or chairmanships of standing committees.[8]

— Furthermore, the electoral support base of the National Party (particularly since it increased its English-speaking support in the May 1987 election), has most probably shifted to the left of the present executive.

— One aspect of its earlier commitment to the grand design of separate states which the National Party has not entirely lost is the intrinsic attraction of a possible solution to the black constitutional issue which meets the requirements of universal legitimacy. The interviews with some of the more significant political thinkers suggested that purely co-optive techniques for securing black participation would be an unattractive last resort. Hope of achieving a negotiated solution which would be manifestly legitimate in the eyes of most blacks runs strongly in the party caucus, and Dr Stoffel van der Merwe, who until recently had a key role in the attempts to stimulate negotiation, was adamant that a legitimate solution had to be found.

- While the system functions as an elaborate form of constitutional and institutional racism, political motivation in government is generally not overtly racist or exploitative. At policy level there is no evidence of systematic intentions to damage the socio-economic circumstances of blacks in order to advance the privilege of whites (although many constraints imposed on blacks in the interests of white political and social autonomy undoubtedly have this effect). For example, from the interviews it would seem that there is considerable acceptance among National Party decision-makers that high inflation and its associated 'fiscal drag' enable some redistribution of income from whites to blacks to occur indirectly and gradually (some would say by stealth). The priorities in the most recent (1988) budget maintain this emphasis (*Financial Mail*, 5 June 1987). To quote one example only, whereas the white 'own affairs' budget increased by 8 per cent, homelands budgets increased by 70 per cent.[9]
- The new Regional Services Councils are a particular example of redistributive policy, albeit within an ethnic framework and a context of white definition of black needs.[10]
- There was evidence from the more analytical members of the National Party caucus that, while the government will continue to respond negatively to direct pressures from abroad, a positive response to more sympathetic external co-operation for change could be rekindled. It is significant that the entire National Party rationale is the maintenance of a Western subsystem. It is therefore likely that opportunities to co-operate with Western initiatives which acknowledge fundamental local commitments will be grasped.
- Perhaps the most certain reason why further policy adaptations will occur is that, after having dispensed with the politics of grand territorial designs, the practical realities of governing and developing a racially mixed order have to be taken seriously. This shift was fundamental to the abolition of influx control and other recent reforms. Like most conservative governments without a coherent game plan, South African policy is on the slippery slope of precedent, and this, irrespective of abstract policy decisions, will produce change via the unintended consequences of

earlier measures. The recent acceptance by government of the principle of open areas, no matter how limited in scope such areas may be, fundamentally contradicts the present implicit political model and racial 'subsocieties'. It opens the way, therefore, for a steady erosion of the presently dominant sphere of white social exclusivity in South Africa.

There are a range of powerful constraints on change. On balance, however, their effect will not be such as to counteract the processes outlined above.

STRATEGIES OF POWER-SHARING

As already indicated, considerable state energies relating to a new constitutional dispensation within its framework are currently directed at initiating a process of negotiation with black community leaders. Given the firm structure within which a new constitution is likely to be acceptable to the government, it is not likely that many visible and celebrated black leaders will enter into formal negotiations in the near future. How does the government intend dealing with this problem?

From the interviews the following thinking has emerged:

— Firstly, the assumption is made that by dampening the climate of protest, confrontation and revolutionary expectations, greater realism and a willingness to accept compromises compatible with the governmental framework will grow among black opinion-formers.
— Secondly, the government is not in a great hurry. The responsible deputy minister has declared that the State of Emergency could last for three years or more, if such a period were necessary to restore a balanced political climate in the country (*Citizen*, 19 March 1987).
— Thirdly, the government appears to be increasing its efforts in the direction of socio-economic reform, on the assumption that the alleviation of grievances and an improvement of the quality of life in black areas will incline black community forces towards a less resistant position.

49

- The impression is gained that, *if all else fails*, a strategy of co-opting black personalities into the statutory National Council and giving them resources with which to dispense patronage will create a political impetus which in due course will draw other blacks into co-operation with the government.

A future beyond apartheid

In the light of the conclusions above, and those reached in other chapters in this volume, an early mutual compromise between the government and internal or external resistance movements is highly unlikely. It is more probable that the co-optive strategy referred to above will be followed initially. This course of events has frequently been predicted and has been referred to as 'multiracial autocracy' by former leader of the PFP, Dr Van Zyl Slabbert, and as 'multiracial fascism' by Peregrine Worsthorne. The evidence from the interviews, however, is that the government will continue, during a period of authoritarian multiracial rule, to introduce gradual reforms and to seek increased legitimacy and popular black participation. Thus a slow, stop-start mutation of the system of government towards multiracial incorporation and socio-economic reform, accompanied by the maintenance of a racially defined order in one form or another, all transpiring in a climate of barely suppressed dissent in the country at large, appears to be the most likely scenario for the foreseeable future.

As already suggested, one aspect of this mutation, stimulated particularly by the recent acceptance of (limited) multiracial residential areas, will probably be the formalisation of overall policy around the concept of parallelism between an 'open' order and a sphere of group interests and organisation. The goal of freedom of association, currently impossible, could well be accommodated in such a parallel order, which will also allow for freedom of dissociation. This principle could extend to constitutional thinking in due course.

Given these probabilities, one is left with painful choices as to how they should be evaluated. From the perspective of black democratic movements and from a traditional liberal perspective, the complex causality behind the South African state system is of little relevance. The justified perception will be of a continuation of the policy of racial preference as a basis for allocating and sharing power: in other words, apartheid and racism. The more variations that are introduced to accommodate black participation, and the more socio-economic reforms that are introduced to bolster the process, the more they will be viewed simply as more devious ways of protecting apartheid, or of sharing power without sacrificing domination.

There will be unquestionable validity in this evaluation. This author can adduce no evidence to contradict its formal correctness, especially within a moral framework which rejects a formal allocation of roles and powers on the basis of so disreputable a criterion as race.

There is, however, an alternative way of perceiving and evaluating the outcome, which is offered not as a prescription but simply in an attempt to address the political stalemate and the increasing and understandable, but probably futile anger which the first view encourages. This view would proceed from the following assumptions:

1 That the basic tenet of white politics – that of protecting a putatively 'western' socio-political subsystem – is thoroughly entrenched. If the present government were to fragment, say under the impact of extreme pressure or of disaffection on its left wing, the centre would probably recombine or enter into coalition with right-wing formations in order to continue to represent this set of interests.

2 That the basis of government in white constituency politics and its relative independence of special interest groups make it highly resistant to pressure and external persuasion in any event.

3 That the now well-tested strength, adaptability and capacity for growth in the repressive machinery of state security will ensure the survival of the system for some considerable time to come, excluding the unlikely event of an armed superpower invasion.

4 That in the interim, if the economy permits, objective conditions for the majority of South Africans will not worsen. Socio-economic reform and cautious socio-political reform will proceed apace.

5 That the constitution of white hegemony involves processes somewhat more benign in socio-economic terms and far more complex and self-reinforcing than crude racism. It is also relevant to consider that if the driving motive were crude racism, the system could not be managed with the degree of self-conviction, determination and morale that the South African state displays.

6 That there is considerable debate within the National Party and, particularly after the retirement of the present leadership in the next few years, greater opportunities will exist for influencing the debate.

These assumptions do not involve moral acceptance of the order, nor do they for one moment imply a relaxation of criticism of its effects. They might, however, indicate a different strategy from the first form of evaluation.

The second and more complex evaluation presented above most certainly implies that an advance on the present stalemate will require more than moral exhortation, punitive sanctions or even the pressure of violent confrontation. In particular it would suggest a need for creative strategies which would, without sacrificing the universal legitimacy of the nonracial democratic goal, take serious account of the forbidding resilience of the corporate interests represented by the South African government and the fact that *one* of the keys to a future without apartheid is the debate within the government itself.

Nevertheless, it also still implies that, notwithstanding the resilience of the present state form, the legitimacy of the South African government will continue to be questioned by the overseas community and by most South Africans. Fundamental uncertainty regarding the future will persist, affecting investor confidence in particular and hence the ability of the economy to expand faster than population growth. The most basic question is not whether there will be chaos and revolution, but whether or not a resolution to South Africa's conflict can be found which will ensure a future of acceptable quality for all.

The challenge is daunting. The government's gradual reforms have brought it to a threshold. Beyond this the issues of real power and white 'subsociety' self-determination are starkly exposed. Can this threshold be crossed?

One route would involve the eventual acceptance by significant black leadership of the idea of a 'race-federation' or some other form of 'bi-communalism' in government, as Giliomee (1987) has described it. Such a shift would allow meaningful negotiation to take place concerning relative sharing of power and a demarcation of power domains and could indeed formally result in a system with characteristics such as a rotating state presidency and very substantial black control of the fiscal process and government expenditure.

While this has proved to be possible in some other divided societies, such as Lebanon, Switzerland and Belgium, the geographic interpenetration of South Africa's peoples in the developed common area of the country, and the huge socio-economic differences between white and black, prevent the sense of ethnic autonomy, self-reliance and pride from developing among blacks, which has made this solution appropriate elsewhere. Generally, the entire history of black protest has been directed at control over, or inclusion and integration into, the institutions of the dominant white subsociety, rather than at autonomy.

One therefore has to consider whether there is any alternative to the government's framework which could represent a compromise between the two positions. This would imply at the very least a broadening of the National Party framework to allow for a less formalised accommodation of the ethnic claims of the white segment. The alternative could encompass some form of voluntary association, but it would most certainly have to avoid statutory race classification, while incorporating the principle of majoritarianism for the basic franchise.

This is not likely to be possible at a broad national level within a reasonable period. Quite apart from the fact that there would be formidable, and possibly destructive resistance from at least a third of the white voters, such a compromise most probably implies that the National Party would lose all or much of its executive power, through losing its dominant power base. The government's rejection of the KwaZulu-Natal Indaba proposals and the recent constitutional proposals put forward by the Democratic Turnhalle Alliance for Namibia is strongly indicative of its present stance. Both sets of proposals incorporate basic majoritarianism, with ethnic representation based only in second chambers.

The indications are, therefore, that a constitutional stalemate, with some co-opting of blacks, is likely to continue for a long time until the mounting costs of repression force the government to back down, unless some other route to an acceptable compromise can be found. Such a route may very well have to avoid confronting the issue of the National Party's broad national power base in the first instance.

A general impression gleaned during the interviews with members of government, despite the current rejection of the KwaZulu-Natal Indaba, is that the route to political change which will evoke least resistance will be along the lines of local or regional devolution.

Negotiation initiatives in certain metropolitan areas or in regions such as the Eastern Cape, the Western Cape, and, of course, Natal could at least allow the formidable impediment of statutory race classification to be relaxed in some parts of the country. A fundamental break with apartheid in such areas need not affect the government's broad national power base in the first instance, or directly confront the right-wing strongholds in the Transvaal and Orange Free State. In some areas it could also be reconciled with the government's Regional Services Councils or the embryo concept of city states, avoiding, however, the starkly racial character of the developments as currently proposed.

This route, as a means of starting to cross the threshold of core political apartheid, will be no easy passage. Powerful interests within both the government and the resistance movements will perceive it as a wedge which will eventually divide their power, or potential power. It is also likely to be considered by influential sections of the international community as an untidy and ineffectual compromise.

Untidy it will most certainly be, but the benefits of this course of development, or something akin to it, can only be appreciated in comparison with the alternatives – continuing stalemate or revolutionary upheaval, neither of which can yield a satisfactory resolution for the present generation of South Africans.

2 The right wing in South African politics[1]

HELEN ZILLE

Introduction

Most analysts and activists absorbed in South African politics believe that the demise of apartheid is inevitable; a foregone conclusion if not yet an accomplished fact. On this unstated premise they construct theories and develop strategies to expedite the transition and the reconstruction of our society beyond apartheid.

Until recently, most observers effectively ignored the growing number of white South Africans dedicated to reconstructing and implementing partition, often in a form more radical than was ever envisaged by apartheid's original architects.

This perception changed somewhat on 6 May 1987. The outcome of the House of Assembly election on that day showed that even the government's halting reform programme (let alone the struggle for a radically transformed political economy) has elicited the resistance of at least the 610 516 voters who supported right-wing candidates. The right-wing vote accounted for 29,62 per cent of the votes cast and constituted a 25 per cent swing away from the National Party's 1981 electoral support base.[2] Most right-wing voters supported the Conservative Party, enabling it to win 22 seats and become the official opposition at its first attempt, five years after its formation. In their opposition to the Botha administration's limited reforms, these voters provided a foretaste of the response that can be expected if meaningful political change occurs in the years ahead.

The right wing's election performance surprised almost everyone except right-wing statisticians and strategists. Nor were they particularly pleased with the outcome. The election, they argue, was held in the worst possible circumstances for the feuding parties of the Right, the Herstigte Nasionale Party and the Conservative

55

Party. In addition, the government's tough security clamp-down under the State of Emergency had done much to restore its image and waning credibility among conservative voters. Had reformist commitments dominated the government's election platform, right-wing election statisticians believe that a united Right could easily have taken between forty and fifty seats. (Even under the prevailing circumstances, an election pact between the CP and HNP would have given the Right at least ten additional seats.)[3] Nevertheless they consider that the election was an important breakthrough, giving the CP the structural base it needs to double its seats by the next general election, as white South Africans increasingly realise that black resistance cannot be bought off by reform but will continue to force a never-ending series of concessions that will inevitably lead to majority rule.

The organisations described

The organisations of the Right are pledged to resist the process of change, either by capturing power in time to reverse it, or at least by building a support base so formidable that no attempted political solution can be implemented without their consent.

'The right wing' is a blanket political term which covers a wide range of organisations with different policies and strategies. For the purpose of this study the term is used to define those organisations that describe themselves as right wing opponents of the South African government.

THE HERSTIGTE NASIONALE PARTY

The HNP is the oldest and most conservative of all right-wing groups. It was established in 1969 by four members of parliament expelled from the National Party for opposing a deviation in the Vorster government's sports policy. The HNP adheres unwaveringly to the original apartheid tenets established by Dr H. F. Verwoerd during the 1960s. The HNP waited 17 years to win its first seat, Sasolburg, in a 1985 by-election, but lost it in the 1987 election when the party was effectively crushed at the polls. The HNP still retains a small core of support, drawn mainly from the declining ranks of the disillusioned and alienated white working class who were dropped from the government's protection and patronage during the 1970s. There is also a hard core of ideologues epitomised by the party's leader, Jaap Marais, who nurse an abiding grudge against the Conservative Party leadership for continuing their support for the government after the 1969 split, undermining the right-wing cause and allowing the NP to retain conservative credibility while moving to the left.

THE CONSERVATIVE PARTY

The Conservative Party (CP) was established on 20 March 1982 after 16 conservative Nationalist members of parliament rejected the then Prime Minister P. W. Botha's use of the phrase 'healthy power sharing'. From its inception, the CP has provided conservatives with a political home more acceptable than the HNP with its image of extremism and fanaticism. The CP immediately became the rallying point for many smaller conservative groups with widely divergent policies and strategies. Most right-wing extra-parliamentary organisations supported the CP in the May 1987 election.

The CP's support is concentrated mainly in rural and urban working-class and lower middle-class constituencies, but the party also draws between 15 and 25 per cent of voter support in some Afrikaans middle-class and upper middle-class constituencies.[4] The CP also claims the support of at least 57 per cent of public servants in the Transvaal.[5] The CP considers the public service – comprising 40 per cent of all economically active Afrikaners – to be its greatest actual and potential source of support.

The CP is supported by a range of different organisations with varying policies. These groups have come together in a tactical alliance because they consider the electoral defeat of the National Party to be their primary objective. This would re-establish the principle of partition as the only constitutional solution for South Africa. Thereafter, each organisation believes that it will be able to prove that its model of partition is the most viable.

DIE AFRIKANERVOLKSWAG
(THE AFRIKANER PEOPLE'S GUARD)

This organisation was formed in May 1984 to engage the right-wing struggle at a cultural level. The Volkswag's purpose is to draw Afrikaners together in a cultural organisation as the bedrock of the political struggle. The basic unit of Volkswag membership is the family, and the organisation is open to Afrikaner families who subscribe to its principles and policy. Its current membership is approximately 7 000 families.

THE SOUTH AFRICAN BUREAU OF RACIAL AFFAIRS (SABRA)

SABRA is an academic research group, established in 1948 as the National Party's counter to the liberal South African Institute of Race Relations. SABRA maintained a close liaison with the government until SABRA researchers officially rejected the 1983 version of the tricameral constitution. The organisation is now a right-wing think-tank primarily engaged in examining alternative models of partition.

DIE VERENIGING VAN ORANJEWERKERS
(THE SOCIETY OF ORANGE WORKERS)

Founded in June 1980, this organisation takes its name from the House of Orange in the Netherlands, which has strong symbolic significance for Afrikaner Nationalists. The organisation grew out of a research project conducted by a SABRA subcommittee to investigate the viability of establishing areas within South Africa to be inhabited and worked solely by whites. The Oranjewerkers Society, which has some 2 500 members, believes that apartheid in its original conception did not go far enough to ensure the self-determination of whites, who must now work and develop their own *volksland* (national state). They are attempting to mobilise white support for the idea.

TOEKOMSGESPREK (FORUM FOR THE FUTURE)

This organisation, established in 1983, represents a right-wing attempt to establish an alternative to the Nationalist-dominated Broederbond (Bond of Brothers). It is a secret organisation with membership by invitation only, which aims to infiltrate all spheres of society in order to establish a strong and co-ordinated right-wing presence. In recent months right-wingers have mounted a concerted strategy to infiltrate civic associations, voluntary organisations, school committees and agricultural co-operatives in order to promote the right-wing cause within them, with a long-term objective of controlling them.[6] It is difficult to establish the extent to which Toekomsgesprek has co-ordinated this strategy.

THE STALLARD FOUNDATION

Established in 1985, the Stallard Foundation is the only right-wing organisation directed specifically at English-speaking South Africans. It describes itself as an 'issue-oriented forum', which promotes conservative philosophy and policies, sponsors conferences and seminars, hosts conservative foreign visitors, and opposes reform. It has approximately 1 000 paid-up members and a mailing list of 25 000.

DIE AFRIKANER-WEERSTANDSBEWEGING
(THE AFRIKANER RESISTANCE MOVEMENT) (AWB)

While most right-wing organisations are still prepared to limit themselves to legal and constitutional processes to achieve their aims, the AWB is actively preparing for the eventuality that Afrikaners may lose control of the political process and is committed to fighting back to regain it. Its leader, Mr Eugène Terre'Blanche, refuses to divulge the size of the organisation. Estimates by specialist observers are that the AWB, which was established in 1973, has between 5 000 and 9 000 signed-up members, 150 000 supporters who attend the organisation's meetings, and about 500 000 tacit sympathisers.[7] Terre'Blanche contends that the organisation's signed-up membership is 'far higher' but that the other estimates of its support are broadly correct. Other estimates of the AWB's membership range from 50 000 (*Sunday Times*, 11 May 1986) to 150 000 (author's interview, Derby-Lewis, November 1986). The organisation owes much of its size and support to its leader's charismatic demagoguery, and like Terre'Blanche, many AWB followers are open admirers of Nazism and Fascism.

Although the AWB is also registered as a political party – the Blanke Volkstaatparty (White Nation-State party) – it does not operate as a political party. However, in the May 1987 election the AWB began to assert its influence in party politics by supporting the CP in a strategic move to promote its own policies. According to Terre'Blanche, four of the victorious CP candidates are AWB members. "Without our support the CP would not have become the official opposition," notes Terre'Blanche (interview, June 1987).

The AWB's organisational structure is based on Burgerrade (Citizens' Councils), the equivalent of the political party's local branches. All the Burgerraad leaders in a specific region form the Streekraad (Regional Council) and their leaders in turn sit on the Hoofraad (Chief Council).

The organisation has also established paramilitary Brandwagte (outposts/guards) in every large town outside the Cape Province. It is actively recruiting Brandwag members among men who have completed their military service, with the aim of turning the Brandwagte into a 'force of thousands'. Although the AWB does not arm Brandwag members, it encourages them to carry their own firearms (interview, Terre'Blanche, June 1987).

The Brandwagte's main purpose is to crush a possible black uprising (even if this occurs on a sporadic or localised basis) if government forces are unable or unwilling to do so. The Brandwagte have also embarked on a concerted 'hearts and minds' campaign in the rural areas, where they are always available to help out in a community crisis such as a major veld fire. In this way the AWB hopes to build up a reputation as a "friend and ally that Afrikaners can rely on in times of trouble" (interview, Terre'Blanche, June 1987). The *Stormvalke* (literally storm falcons) are the elite paramilitary youth wing of the AWB modelled on the *Stormjaers* of the *Ossewa-Brandwag*.

Although Terre'Blanche denies that the AWB has already embarked on a course of violent resistance, the government-supporting press has attempted to link the AWB with acts of vigilantism (for example, *Rapport*, 23 February 1986).

The AWB supports a particular model of partition which differs radically from the traditional apartheid model. (This is discussed in more detail below.) The AWB aims to capture power in its proposed *volkstaat* (nation state), after which it will establish a government of technocrats in a one-party state (interview, Terre'Blanche, June 1987).

DIE BLANKE BEVRYDINGSBEWEGING
(THE WHITE LIBERATION MOVEMENT) (BBB)

This organisation, established in 1985, is led by its founder, Professor P. C. Schabort, a biochemist formerly of the Rand Afrikaans University. Schabort refuses to disclose the BBB's membership figures but it is generally believed in right-wing circles that the organisation is a small, if vocal, group. Schabort says that active membership recruitment only commenced in June 1987, with impressive results.

He describes the organisation as 'openly racist' and 'to the right of the AWB' (interview, August 1987). "We believe in the genetic superiority of the white race, and we believe it is the duty of the white race to stop the natural increase and the decadence of the black races from destroying this planet." The BBB differs from other right-wing organisations in that it attempts to establish links with international right-wing organisations to engage in a global struggle "for the survival of the white race and of this planet".

Domestically, the BBB's policy is based on 'total partition' in terms of which every black person will be "repatriated to a homeland, by violence if necessary".

Common perspectives

The organisations of the Right are often deeply divided on issues of policy, strategy and tactics. Nevertheless, they share certain ideological, socio-political and philosophical perceptions. This 'cognitive map' provides the broad parameters within which they formulate their goals, identify their enemies and forge their actions. The central tenets of this shared world-view – as well as some key differences – are set out below. This section draws heavily on the writings of Professors Carel Boshoff and Hercules Booysen, two of the right wing's most influential intellectuals. Boshoff, a former chairman of the Afrikaner Broederbond and the Federasie van Afrikaanse Kultuurverenigings (Federation of Afrikaans Cultural Societies), plays a leading role in most right-wing extra-parliamentary organisations. During the 1982/1983 split of Afrikaner nationalist institutions, Boshoff, a son-in-law of Dr Hendrik Verwoerd, championed the right-wing cause. He became the first chairman of the Afrikanervolkswag and retained his chairmanship of SABRA. He was a founding member of the Oranjewerkers and serves on its executive. In January 1988 he resigned his professorship in missionary science (*sendingwetenskap*) at the University of Pretoria to devote himself fully to extra-parliamentary politics.

Booysen is a professor of law at the University of South Africa, specialising in constitutional law. He is one of the most prolific conservative writers, constantly analysing developments, identifying trends and illuminating options for the right wing.

Although neither Boshoff nor Booysen's detailed policy proposals are universally supported by the Right, their articulation on the shared world-view is widely accepted as authoritative in what is generally an under-documented area.

In recent years there has been a growing body of progressive analysis on the South African right wing. Some of it is based on the assumption that the articulated ideology of the Right is little more than an elaborate and consciously formulated cover to advance the economic self-interest of whites.

While right-wing leaders openly acknowledge that economic factors (such as growing white unemployment) are important components of their political analysis and mobilising strategy, there is little evidence to suggest that economic interests are the sole (or even the primary) motivating force behind right-wing ideology. Ironically, several right-wing leaders stressed that whites would have to be prepared to make significant economic sacrifices to implement right-wing policies successfully. "We would rather be poor and free than rich in a common society," was how Boshoff described a commonly articulated view (interview, November 1986).

Nationalism is the guiding principle of the right wing. This nationalism is rooted in the belief that Afrikaners (together with some other white South Africans) form a distinct and separate nation. The right wing holds that any nation, large or small, has an unassailable right to 'self-determination' (Booysen, 1985a: 5).

Self-determination is defined as "the right to determine your own future, to govern yourself and to enjoy the fruits of your own labour and technical abilities, and to have your own country and fatherland" (Booysen, 1985a: 4). The right wing believes that this right is currently threatened as never before. Afrikaners (and South African whites in general) are facing the greatest moment of crisis in their history. Indeed, their position is unique in world history. "Never has a nation faced such a total, determined, international onslaught against its existence" (Booysen, 1981: 3).

The Right regards nationalism as the central dividing line in South African society. Most other social divisions (such as race, culture, language and religion) reinforce nationalistic barriers. But when social cleavages cut across each other, nationalism always predominates. Right-wingers often use the concept of class as an example: although race and class are often coterminous and mutually reinforcing in South Africa, this is not always so. There are, for example, white workers. Yet they overwhelmingly identify with their 'national group' (within which they are outnumbered by other classes with differing 'class interests') rather than with a broad working class (which cuts across nationalist boundaries).

All right-wing groups are, in varying degrees, prepared to assimilate people of a different language, tradition, religion and culture.[8] However, no right-wing organisation is prepared to compromise on the assimilation of other 'races', even if a group meets all the other requirements of a common 'nationhood'. The clearest example of this is the 'coloured' people who share the Afrikaners' language, culture, history, religion and traditions but are not considered eligible to become part of the nation. Booysen attempts to explain:

"The coloureds have never been acceptable to whites in the same political system, amongst other things because of their natural increase and the possibility that they could form alliances with opposition parties or other national groups which would damage the rights of whites to self-determination irrevocably" (Booysen, 1981: 1).

The English – who have a different language, culture, history, religion and tradition – are not considered a serious threat.

"The different white groups and particularly the Afrikaners and English have shown themselves prepared through the course of history to co-operate with each other in the same constitutional system. This co-operation did not occur without tension or conflict, but it was possible because of their common race and values and norms regarding the economy, politics and other spheres of life (*lewensverbande*). Co-operation has also occurred on an important condition, namely the maintenance, by the group itself, of its own language and traditions. Because of the existence of this condition, co-operation in the political sphere is possible and because of the nonacceptance of this condition by other race groups, (the possibility of) co-operation with them within one political system is excluded.

"Co-operation with the different white groups is also possible for another reason and that is that there is approximately a balance between them in respect of the numerical strength of their natural increase. The delicate balance between the white groups in number, their respective religious institutions, language and traditions will not easily be disturbed by political co-operation. Such a balance is absent with respect to the white groups on the one hand and the other race groups on the other and makes political co-operation with them within the same political system too dangerous to be considered seriously" (Booysen, 1981: 2).

While many conservatives use the word 'white' interchangeably with 'Afrikaner', extra-parliamentary organisations have shown a trend towards a more exclusive definition. They are actively promoting the concept of the *Boerevolk* (Boer/Afrikaner nation) that is entitled to a *volkstaat* (nation state).

Right-wingers argue that the Afrikaners have shown themselves willing to assimilate small groups of foreigners such as Germans, French and Portuguese, saying that "it is possible to assimilate up to 5 per cent of foreign blood without affecting a nation's identity" (Boshoff, C. 1985a: 4). "But it is physically impossible for the Afrikaner to assimilate blacks and to survive as a group with its own language, culture and traditions" (Booysen, 1985a: 10).

Although they acknowledge a strong 'race consciousness', most right-wing organisations, with the exception of the HNP and BBB, deny charges of racism.

"We reject racism as an attitude of life, but we also reject the accusation that a nation that wants to remain white is merely a bunch of racists" (Boshoff, C. interview, January 1986).

They believe that only people who have no contact with other races and have not personally felt the effects of cultural and racial differences can have no race consciousness.

"That is why a country like Sweden so easily prides itself on its lack of racialism. They don't have to take account of other races" (Booysen, 1985a: 13).

The Right considers racially determined nationalism to be a significant force, but not the primary force binding political groupings in South Africa. Ethnic nationalisms which cleave homogeneous racial groupings are the primary force binding groups with a common historical experience, language, religion and culture. Although various ethnic nationalisms can be subsumed under an umbrella of race consciousness to ward off an overwhelming threat to their continued existence (or to overthrow an oppressor), ethnic nationalism always reappears once the immediate crisis has been resolved. Thus Afrikaners and English-speaking whites may unite to ward off a threat to their 'survival' by black ethnic groups uniting to overthrow what they regard as a white oppressor. But that does not imply that either racial category has formed a solid national entity.

The right wing usually qualifies 'nationalism' with the word 'Christian'. Their Christianity is rooted in Calvinist Protestantism and this has a profound influence on their world-view. While they say that they do not believe they are a 'chosen people' in the sense of being superior beings with a destiny to rule others, they believe that their nationhood, forged over centuries in the furnace of struggle, was divinely ordained. Therefore the survival and maintenance of their nationhood also enjoy divine sanction.

"Nations owe their existence to God, the creator of heaven and earth. We find reference to nations from the first to the last book in the Bible . . . From this truth we conclude that the management of God's nations in God's world gives them rights and duties. According to the institution of God, work is a duty of each person and this is coupled with responsibility, stewardship, diligence and vigilance. It also demands respect for life, truth and justice. Of these duties, no nation in the world is exempt.

"But then a nation also has rights: the right to identity . . . the right to a fatherland . . . the right to self-determination" (*Volkswag Newsletter*, January/February 1986).

There are still isolated references to the belief that the white nation in Africa has a calling to spread 'Christianity and civilisation', but this is rapidly being replaced by the notion that Afrikanerdom's crisis is partially a result of self-neglect and over-involvement with the interests of others. The Right now places the primary emphasis on preserving the nationhood God ordained for them (Boshoff, C. 1985a and interview, January 1986; Booysen, 1985a: 3; Terre'-Blanche, 1984: 85).

A major contradiction that challenges the right wing is the conflict between their Christian principles and the political actions undertaken in the name of nationalism. The usual explanation is captured by Booysen:

"Some apartheid measures . . . that are seen by the outside world as highly immoral, are not primarily defended in conservative circles on moral or religious grounds. They are viewed as essential practical measures for the South African situation. Obviously it would be senseless for Britain or Sweden to introduce apartheid measures . . . In the South African situation they are indispensable for the protection of the interests of the Afrikaner . . . In the light of the factual situation and the strongly developed determination of the Afrikaner to survive, measures have been taken to ensure the continued existence of the Afrikaner as a separate nation – measures that are seen as morally justifiable and responsible by many Afrikaners" (Booysen, 1985a: 10).

Mr Z. B. du Toit, former editor of the HNP mouthpiece, *Die Afrikaner*, put it like this:

"Politics is about power, and for the Afrikaner that means survival. The whites cannot survive in a moral utopia. They must make sure that blacks live in black areas and they must apply influx control. It is not possible for us to live according to perfect standards. We live in an imperfect world. Freedom with justice is impossible. If we use justice and morality as the only yardstick we will sacrifice our survival" (interview, November 1986).

Calvinism also imbues Afrikaners with a respect for authority, rules, traditions and prescriptions – particularly those formulated by their forefathers.

Much of the right-wing revolt against the National Party grew from the conviction that government leaders were deviating from the political and moral prescriptions of their predecessors and had fallen prey to worldly pragmatism and materialism.

"The Afrikaner nation appreciates what his forefathers have established. He lives in faith and respects the world-view, traditions and prescriptions that are grounded in his faith . . . Our character and identity are determined by our spiritual procreation, which is the source of power for our struggle for survival, and we regard our spiritual heritage more highly than material gain" (Boshoff, 1985b: 4).

There are three main protestant Afrikaans churches. Of these, the Hervormde Kerk (Reformed Church) has maintained a strongly conservative tradition and racially exclusive membership. In contrast, the Nederduitse Gereformeerde Kerk (NGK) (Dutch Reformed Church) reflects all the tensions and conflicts of Afrikaner nationalism. It was the only major Afrikaner institution that remained intact during the 1982-1983 split, but the NGK's strained unity collapsed following the October 1986 synod's official endorsement of the controversial document, *Church and Society*, which rejected certain major tenets of apartheid. After futile attempts to have the endorsement rescinded, a conservative group under the leadership of Professor Willie Lubbe broke away and founded the Afrikaanse Protestantse Kerk (Afrikaans Protestant Church) on 27 June 1987. The new church grew faster than expected and by August 1987 had an estimated 60 parishes with 15 000 members – still minuscule compared with the estimated 1,5 million members of the NGK. However, certain influential right-wingers have remained with the NGK, opting for an 'internal opposition strategy' and establishing a group known as the Nederduitse Gereformeerde Bond to oppose reform from within.

Right-wingers believe that the debate around apartheid in the NGK – and particularly the church's split – potentially constitutes the 'greatest crisis that the Afrikaner has faced in the last 40 years'.

Du Toit explained it as follows:

"The Afrikaner is in a crisis because he always thought that apartheid was in accordance with the Bible. He could always say "the Bible says so and my clergyman says so". That is not so anymore. That has caused a terrible crisis of conscience because for his survival he needs apartheid, but now his clergyman is telling him it is a sin. If he accepts the value system that is now being propagated by some theologians, he will destroy himself, he cannot survive" (interview, November 1986).

CULTURE

Another major component of nationalism is 'culture'. Boshoff defines culture as "the way a person reacts to the situation in which he finds himself" (1985a: 1).

For the right wing, culture is an inclusive concept which covers every aspect of life. Each nation has its own culture of work and relaxation, economics and politics. Its culture is one of the major determinants of its nationhood.

Language gives verbal and written expression to a nation's culture. Afrikaans has an almost religious significance for the Afrikaner right wing. It is seen as the language which developed as a central component of their nationhood and which provides one of the major justifications for their right to be recognised as an independent nation.

Education is regarded as a means of transmitting a nation's culture (which includes religion, values and skills) from generation to generation. This cannot happen unless each national group has its own schools and educational institutions:

"If the Afrikaner wishes to survive as a cultural entity, he will jealously have to guard over the Christian-national character of the education, teaching and training of the youth. They must build on what they have inherited. We march into the future on their feet" (Treurnicht, *Patriot*, September 1985).

Boshoff describes the 'crisis of survival' facing Afrikaners as 'a crisis of culture' (*kultuurkrisis*). The Afrikaner has faced similar crises in the past: the Great Trek took place as a result of one such crisis. The Anglo-Boer War (*Tweede Vryheidsoorlog*) was a result of a threat to the Afrikaner's right to independent self-determination.

"And this is the crisis of the moment, the Afrikaner faces the threat of being swallowed up in his own space" (Boshoff, 1985a: 2).

Geographically defined space is repeatedly emphasised as the basic prerequisite of a nation wishing to secure its survival with its own culture, religion and language. The South African Bureau for Racial Affairs puts it like this:

"A nation must have its own country in order to survive. Only this gives it indisputable power to take its own decisions that cannot be frustrated by other nations. Every nation in the world owns, inhabits, works, preserves and governs its own country. The nation that does not is destroyed as a nation" (1985: 12).

A nation that does not have its own territorial base is scaled down to the status of a group – and in the case of the Afrikaners (and whites in general), a minority group. Thus the establishment of a country which is indisputably their own is the major political objective of the Right. It can only be achieved by a policy of partition.

PARTITION

While there is unanimity on the principle of partition, there is no agreement on a particular model. Indeed, the variety of partition proposals constitutes the major point of divergence between right-wing organisations. Those that support a particular partition model devote much time and energy to proving that other models are un-workable. Ironically, their collective critique constitutes a devastating dismissal of the policy of partition! While only a few still adhere rigidly to the original apartheid blueprint, they all agree that there are only two political alternatives for South Africa: political equality in a unitary state with one constitution (in which whites will be a dominated minority), or partition.[9] They reject constitutional formulae to protect the rights of minorities, which they say can only be temporary signposts on the road to majority rule. Of the two alternatives facing South Africa, partition is the only one which can bring peace to such a deeply divided society. They consider this to be a fact established by international precedent:

"As partition brought relative peace to Europe, Cyprus and the Indian subcontinent, so too will it bring peace to South Africa; partition led to the establishment of Europe as it is today; the partition of Cyprus into a Turkish and a Greek territory has brought peace, and the partitioning of the Indian subcontinent into Bangladesh, Pakistan and India has limited the continual bloodshed and violence. Extended to the Sikhs, peace will return once again to mainland India, at present torn by Sikh/Hindu conflict" (CP election pamphlet, 1985).

They believe that partition will eventually prove itself to be the only feasible constitutional option when all the conflicting nations in South Africa accept that this is the only way to achieve peace. The real question for them is not whether partition will come about, but how. It can either come about by agreement between nations, or by a protracted process of violence and counter-violence. All right-wing organisations are publicly committed to the pursuit of radical partition by constitutional means for as long as this option is available. If this is no longer an option, they reserve the right to change their tactics.

Yet the cause of partition would not be lost, they argue, even if a common constitutional system for all South Africans became a reality. Indeed, the right wing believes that such a development would expose the myth of 'the common society' living at peace, and reveal the fact that a single constitution promotes ceaseless conflict in a divided society. "If you really want the races to explode apart in separate political entities, promote integration," says Booysen (1985a: 13).

The right wing believes that the government's failure to bring about meaningful partition lies at the root of most of South Africa's political problems. The increasing anger and revolutionary resistance among blacks is a direct result of the heightened expectations arising from the perception that the government has lost its will to implement partition, and that the country is moving irrevocably in the direction of majority rule in a unitary state. They believe that blacks have the right to demand equal rights in a common system once the principle of a unitary state has been accepted. Had effective partition been timeously implemented, it would have been an accomplished political fact (as was the case with Lesotho and Swaziland), and expectations of a common society under majority rule would not have become a major issue. The government's failure to implement effective partition has resulted in a common economy with grave political implications.

The Right also blames the inadequate attempts at partition for the denial of democracy, justice and human rights in South Africa. These can only flourish in societies in which a community or group does not feel that its survival is in jeopardy. Democracy and human rights are most likely to be attained in a homogeneous society.

"The recognition and maintenance of human rights depend on healthy group relations. Human rights cannot be maintained where tension and friction between groups are the order of the day. Human rights are maintained more easily in a stable society than in one where a struggle for survival or power is in progress. By definition a homogeneous society lends itself to the maintenance of human rights . . .

"Democracy succeeds where a community or group feels safe and secure and where its survival is not in jeopardy. Therefore democracy, too, flourishes in a homogeneous society" (Booysen, 1985a: 5).

They argue that effective partition would also lead to the scrapping of social segregation and racial discrimination. Booysen comments:

"When the stage is reached where foreigners only constitute about 10 per cent of the white country's population, apartheid will be redundant, obsolete, and even ridiculous" (1985a: 3).

Here the right wing's consensus on partition ends. Only the HNP and a core section of the CP still support the original apartheid blueprint in terms of which 13 per cent of South Africa's land area was to be divided between the different 'black nations' to provide each with a separate 'country', thereby attempting to nullify black demands for political rights in the rest of South Africa.[10]

Supporters of Verwoerdian apartheid reject the contention (made by both left- and right-wing critics) that this policy has failed. It could have succeeded – and still can – they argue, if applied with sufficient resolve and vigour. The strategic focal point of their policy is the development of the agricultural sector within the 'homelands', the drastic curtailment of black employment in urban areas, stringent influx control and various mechanisms to enforce economic decentralisation in order to provide employment within or near 'homeland' boundaries. Their policy also involves large-scale demographic rearrangement to ensure that the 'national groups' are appropriately placed in order to make a policy of political partition viable. This will inevitably involve mass forced removals or what right-wingers call 'migration':

"Large-scale migration of people to solve political and cultural problems is nothing new in history. With the establishment of Israel in 1946-1948 about 700 000 Arabs left the area of the newly created state. The establishment of the separate states of India and Pakistan at the same time had the result that a two-way migration of about 14-18 million people took place from and to the respective states. After the Second World War the Allies decided that all Germans in Europe had to be moved to the two German territories, and this removal affected an estimated 9-10 million people. Our removal problems are really not the greatest in the light of history" (Booysen, 1981: 11).

A growing number of right-wingers reject this policy for a variety of reasons.

The Afrikaner-Weerstandsbeweging believes that Afrikaners have no legal or moral right to govern any land outside the Transvaal, Orange Free State and Northern Natal, which constituted the independent Boer Republics in the nineteenth century. This land was acquired by settlement and war 'as nations all over the world have acquired theirs' (interview, Terre'Blanche, January 1986). The Afrikaner's right to the land was internationally acknowledged in 1902 at the conclusion of the Anglo-Boer War (*Tweede Vryheidsoorlog*). The AWB argues that this area must form the reconstituted republic of the Boer nation.

This policy, in turn, is rejected by all the other partition-promoting organisations for one or more of the following reasons. Firstly, the AWB's partition model is based on history, not on the realities of the present. Secondly, it cannot solve the fundamental demographic problems inherent in the original apartheid model, among other things because the boundaries of the proposed *Boerevolkstaat* would incorporate Soweto, one of Africa's largest urban settlements. Demographically, Northern Natal is also predominantly black. In addition, the *volkstaat* would include many English-speaking liberals on the Witwatersrand who would oppose the re-establishment of the Boer Republics. Thirdly, the proposed *volkstaat* excludes conservatives living in other parts of the country.

The Oranjewerkers and many other right-wingers also increasingly reject the original Verwoerdian apartheid model of partition for a different set of reasons. They argue that in the first place it has proved impossible to establish the necessary economic infrastructure to encourage blacks to remain within or return to the 'homelands'. It will therefore be impossible for whites to become the demographic majority within the current boundaries of South Africa – an essential prerequisite for apartheid to work in the long term. Secondly, blacks overwhelmingly reject this model of partition, and a growing number are actively resisting the concept, making security and stability unattainable. And finally, whites will not be able to defend the present borders of South Africa indefinitely in an escalating war.

Interestingly, the Oranjewerkers accept some points of the liberal critique of 'grand apartheid', believing that it is immoral for a minority to dominate a majority within a common country. They also reject the inequitable division of land on which grand apartheid is based, as well as the mass forced removals by which the government sought to implement the policy. They believe that the only morally acceptable and viable way to implement partition is for its proponents to buy adjacent farms in designated rural areas. These would constitute 'growth points' with the potential of expanding into 'heartlands', providing a nucleus for the establishment of an independent country that will eventually incorporate about 25 per cent of South Africa's land area. Within these boundaries (as yet unspecified) an economy will have to be built from scratch, employing only white labour.

The Oranjewerkers have pinpointed three major regions for the development of 'growth points'. Top priority is accorded to the area that forms a 'half-moon' to the southeast of the Witwatersrand, within which the Oranjewerkers have already started to buy up land and develop the Eastern Transvaal village of Morgenzon. The second designated area lies around the Orange River border between the Orange Free State and the Northern Cape. The third area is centred on Mossel Bay in the Southern Cape.

This model is itself rejected by all the other partition-supporting organisations as 'entirely impractical'. Its critics point out that most Afrikaners with jobs, mortgage bonds, domestic help and other entrenched interests in existing urban areas are unlikely to pack their bags and trek to an underdeveloped area to start from scratch for the sake of ethnic purity. Nor will it be possible for a small group of people to start a viable economy in an area devoid of any economic resources or infrastructure (interviews, Uys, Du Toit, Terre'Blanche, January 1986; November 1986).

Supporters of the original apartheid model dismiss the notion that alternative models of partition could overcome the obstacles faced by the traditional version.

"Even if the boundaries of white South Africa shrink, will this save the whites? Will it satisfy the outside world? It will still be seen as an apartheid state. The ANC and the UDF will never accept it because it will be seen as the last bastion of the evil of apartheid. You see that is where these organisations (the AWB and the Oranjewerkers) are mistaken. They try to use a moral argument. They think that if they give the greatest part of South Africa to the blacks and pull themselves back into a small area where they try to be self-supporting, then the world will say that is all right; you have given up everything else, you can keep that little bit. But this issue has nothing to do with morality. It is a struggle for power" (interview, Du Toit, November 1986).

Thus the debate rages on. But despite their lack of agreement on the details, right-wingers are optimistic that the gradual scrapping of social segregation is likely to add considerably to the growth of the Right and make an increasing number of whites determined to implement a form of partition (Booysen, 1985a: 15).

"Fear is the driving force of white politics. That is why the right wing will keep growing. It offers whites the only solution that is acceptable to them" (interview, Du Toit, August 1987).

OPPOSITION TO REFORM

The Right remains implacably opposed to all the government's 'reform initiatives', particularly the tricameral constitution. They dismiss it as undemocratic, immoral, fraught with contradictions and a clear step in the direction of majority rule in a unitary state.

"Blacks have heard that they are native people of the RSA, who can remain here permanently, who have equal rights as regards work, homes, education, land ownership, local government and citizenship" (SABRA, 1985: 8).
". . . If a state consists of one land area, one authority and one population of which the members are all considered equal, it is a unitary state, irrespective of the words that may be used to disguise this fact" (SABRA, 1985: 7).

The Right believes that it is contradictory and immoral for the government to move towards a unitary state while trying to avoid majority rule.

"If you have once committed yourself to the position of equality in a unitary state, the crux of power must be placed squarely in the hands of the black majority. That is the only outcome that is morally justifiable" (SABRA, 1985: 6).

President Botha's opening address to parliament on 25 January 1985 contained the explicit promise of black participation in the highest government forums:

"The concessions that have already been made contain the promise of black political participation and power and black people have

76

reason to be impatient and angry if they are kept waiting outside the halls of power while complicated solutions are sought to entrench the power of whites, Indians and coloureds" (SABRA, 1985: 7).

Nor will complicated formulae succeed in protecting the rights of minorities. Constitutional guarantees are not worth the paper on which they are written.

"An artificial new constitution with group representation, guarantees, protection of rights and declarations of intent has never achieved anything anywhere in the world where populations have deep cultural divisions . . .

"The masses that desire power and are already prepared to use violence and risk their lives to achieve it, will not rest until they have made themselves felt in every village, hamlet and farm, unto the farthest outposts of this land" (SABRA, 1985: 7).

It is equally fallacious to believe that a black middle class can be bought off by reform: "To expect that a white government can win the unconditional support of blacks against black revolutionaries is really naive", comments Booysen (1981: 7).

REFORM AND REVOLUTION
Right-wing organisations all support and quote Professor M.T.W. Arnheim, a Witwatersrand University academic and proponent of the thesis that reform will encourage rather than prevent revolution.

"It is commonly supposed that reform and revolution are opposites, which is why reform is so often invoked as the way to prevent revolution. But this assumption is exactly the opposite of the truth" (Arnheim, 1985b).[11]

Arnheim argues that reform is 'senseless and indeed suicidal' for South African whites because it catapults black aspirations and expectations sky-high, seriously aggravating their sense of relative deprivation. This is the surest road to revolution. "The young revolutionaries are actually better off than their elders but feel more deprived."

He describes Britain's Reform Acts, beginning in 1832, as the one example in history 'where reform did not lead to revolution' but argues that a similar course is not open to the South African government.

"Reform can be a moderating influence in a homogeneous society but not in a society divided by racial, cultural or religious differences. This is one of the chief reasons why reform is doomed to failure in South Africa" (op. cit.).

In Britain, the new lower middle-class voters wanted to join the privileged strata of society, argues Arnheim. They seized the opportunity enfranchisement offered, and some new voters actually became Tories who, far from fomenting revolution, "actually opposed the extension of the franchise to those who still remained outside the citadels of power. There was no reason for these lower middle-class voters to identify with the poor masses if they could just as well identify with the aristocracy and upper middle class".

This will not occur in South Africa because there is no chance that any significant number of Africans or 'coloureds' will overtly identify with the interests of whites.

"It is commonly expected that reform will produce a crop of moderate blacks who have a 'stake in the land' as a result of prosperity, education and increased political participation. Many whites, including the South African government, pin their hopes for the future of the country on some sort of accommodation with these moderate black leaders. This is an illusion as events in South Africa have already begun to demonstrate" (op. cit.).

Throughout the history of decolonisation in Africa, radical leaders have always triumphed at the expense of moderates, notes Arnheim.

This theme is echoed again and again by right-wing spokesmen. They generally use the example of Zimbabwe's moderate Muzorewa government which lasted a mere eight months before being ousted by Robert Mugabe's ZANU PF in the election that followed the Lancaster House agreement. Whites had accepted the Lancaster House agreement on the understanding that 'Marxists' would be kept out of power by a coalition of moderates. The right wing considers it inevitable and understandable that black leaders are pushed towards radicalism by the demands of their own constituencies. Those who remain moderate are inevitably ousted in favour of the most vocally radical leader on the political spectrum (SABRA, 1985: 9).

"Blacks aren't interested in sharing power with whites. This is the lesson that Africa has taught the whites of South Africa," says Booysen (1985a: 6).

The Right argues that the government is fuelling black expectations by failing to use sufficient force to quell township resistance:

"Rioting in the black townships has been allowed to continue, because the government fails to deploy the security forces it has available, and to exert sufficient force. The reason for this would appear to be its fear of international reaction should a significant number of rioters be killed in a single incident" (Treurnicht press statement, September 1985: 2).

'FOREIGN MEDDLING'

The right wing believes that South African whites must learn their political lessons from Africa rather than Europe or America, and bitterly resents 'foreign meddling' in South Africa's affairs. They believe that foreign intervention has nothing to do with 'moral outrage' against apartheid, but is blatant self-interest masquerading behind a moral mask. South Africa, with its strategic position and minerals, has become a pawn in the struggle between the two superpowers. Both are willing to sacrifice the whites of South Africa in an attempt to win the favour of those they regard as a potential future black government (Booysen, 1981: 3).

To the Right, it makes no difference whether white self-determination is threatened by the African states, the communist bloc, the United States or the 'West' in general:

"They all have a common goal, which is to break the ability of the whites to determine the political destiny of South Africa and of themselves" (Booysen, 1981: 3).

The right wing's major ideological battle is with 'communism', but they direct equal energy against 'the international forces of liberalism'. These forces have achieved unprecedented power, and are symbolised by the United States, a country that "threatens the fate and future of small nations across the world and that has, in our time, become the greatest single cause of the Afrikaner's crisis of culture and survival" (Boshoff, 1985b: 1).

Right-wingers are particularly angered by what they perceive to be international double standards:

"Other African states may apply strict influx control with a view to controlling squatting and slums, but in South Africa such actions are condemned as contemptible manifestations of apartheid. . . The world applies double standards when judging South Africa and other African states" (Booysen, 1985a: 18).

'FIRST WORLD/THIRD WORLD'

At the root of South Africa's problems, the Right believes, is the fact that first and third world nations are artificially locked within the boundaries of one country. The haphazard borders of southern Africa, in part a legacy of nineteenth century imperialism, are regarded as immutable by the international community, despite the fact that these lines on the map take no cognisance of ethnic or racial divisions.

The only solution to the subcontinent's problems lies in drawing more realistic borders in order to give each nation its own country. The only way whites will avoid continuing accusations of oppression and exploitation is by separating the first and third worlds territorially, as is the case in the rest of the world (Booysen, 1985a: 20). The differences in living standards would then be just as acceptable, argues the Right, as the vast discrepancies between the first world countries of Europe and America, and the third world African states.

Regarding regional policy, the Right believes that the government should take stronger action, both economic and military, against neighbouring countries harbouring ANC guerrillas. The Right is totally opposed to the South African government retaining transport and trade links with 'hostile neighbouring states' and considers this an indication of the government's unwillingness to 'win the war'. A prolonged war, the Right believes, is a convenient excuse for 'liberals' in government and the military to convince white South Africans that reform will bring peace, thus creating a climate for far-reaching changes to apartheid (Marais, 1983: 94). The right wing rejects the contention that the South African Defence Force is engaged in a civil conflict to crush resistance against an unjust system. It believes that the war is being waged against revolutionaries who are pawns of communists exploiting the local situation to spread their sphere of influence.

Right-wingers also believe that the majority of the security forces oppose the government's reform and regional strategies. They acknowledge that the government has drawn senior military personnel into political structures, particularly through the National Security Management System, to co-ordinate and implement a wide range of 'security-related' policies at local and regional level. However, they deny that this implies far-reaching support for the government within the ranks of the military. The right wing draws a distinction between the upper echelons of professional soldiery and the military rank and file, of whom 90 per cent are conscripts. Right-wingers believe that the deployment of troops in the townships has boosted right wing support. "Many conscripts move right when they experience the revolutionary climate in the townships," says Professor Barney Uys, a University of Pretoria academic who plays a leading role in monitoring electoral trends for the Conservative Party.

The right wing also claims strong support within the police force, particularly the security police, a point underscored by other political observers (for example, Adam, 1987b: 42). They point out that the police have never taken direct action against the AWB, despite its threats of violence, disruptions of meetings and illegal gatherings. Other than this, right-wingers generally rely on un-named 'personal contacts' and anecdotes to substantiate their claims of support, particularly within the ranks of the military.

"They (the government) may have some generals in their pockets, but we have the support of the vast majority of the security forces. We have had clear indications of this for a long time, which were confirmed during the election when soldiers and policemen quite openly went to Conservative Party booths at many polling stations" (interview, Derby-Lewis, June 1987).

Uys gives a specific example:

"I had a first-hand account of events at the polling booth where 240 troops voted in Vereeniging. Of these, two went to the PFP table, 16 went to the NP and the rest went to the CP. In my monitoring of the election patterns this seems to have been a trend throughout the country" (interview, June 1987).

Right-wingers also maintain that the influence of the military was a key factor in the government's decision to downplay the regional detente policy, promoted by the Department of Foreign Affairs in favour of direct support for rebel movements fighting against the MPLA government in Angola and the FRELIMO government in Mozambique.

But right-wingers discount the possibility of a right-wing military coup, and no grouping officially supports this option. They aim to win majority white support in an election which would give them legitimate control of the army. The AWB believes that con-servative groupings need only gain majority electoral support in the Transvaal and Orange Free State to give them legitimate con-trol over the army in those provinces as well – an important step in the secessionist strategy (interview, Terre'Blanche, June 1987).

ECONOMIC POLICY
While the Right supports a 'free market system', it condones 'strong state control' of the economy for the benefit of the nation.

82

This system is neither 'absolute capitalism nor absolute socialism' (Booysen, 1981: 3). State control would co-exist with private ownership in a racially exclusive social democracy which cares for the sick, poor and disabled – on condition that they are white.

In particular, the Right accuses the government of betraying the white worker – a potent political message at a time of growing economic insecurity and increasing white unemployment.

"Every nation in the world cares for its workers, protects their interests, and gives them preference and excludes workers of other nations by immigration and influx controls and by means of work permits. A sovereign Afrikaner nation will also do that in its own country" (*Afrikanerverbond*, 10 October 1985).

Right-wing organisations are divided on whether black workers should be employed within the 'white' economy. Officially, the Conservative Party perceives no contradiction between the doctrine that white South Africans constitute a separate nation entitled to political self-determination – and the fact that the economy to which they lay claim is largely dependent on black labour. They regard black workers as *Gastarbeiter* (guest labourers), comparable to Turks working in Germany. "Because we have enabled them to find employment and earn a living in our economy does not mean that we have to sacrifice our country to them" (interview, Derby-Lewis, May 1987). Other right-wingers, many of whom voted for the Conservative Party in the May election, believe that there is a fundamental contradiction between the claim of whites to their own country, and their willingness to employ black workers to do their hard and unskilled labour.

"If we are serious about having our own country, we must be prepared to do the work involved in running it. We must be prepared to clean the streets and work the factories, to wash our own dishes and care for our own children. There is no other way that is logically and morally consistent with our claim to national self-determination. That may mean a drop in our living standards, but it is a small price to pay for survival" (interview, Verwoerd, January 1986).

The BBB makes a similar point, rejecting "the lie that the South African economy is permanently dependent on non-white labour . . . Despite the fact that all other white national economies of the Western world flourish without non-white labour, or non-white purchasing power and in most cases without mineral wealth" (pamphlet, 1987).

The Right dismisses the contention that equal political rights in a common system will generate an economic revival and restore investor confidence. The withdrawal of foreign investment capital and the freezing of loans has nothing to do with revulsion against white rule. On the contrary, the Right believes foreign withdrawal is the consequence of the popular international perception that white rule is about to come to an end. Overseas investors do not object to oppression. They withdraw their funds when they perceive that the government is unable or unwilling to crush resistance and restore stability.

"Bankers don't worry about human rights, otherwise they wouldn't lend billions to countries like the Soviet Union. Our press . . . says the international community is pushing for reform. The Conservative Party's business contacts say the opposite – reform will precipitate revolution.

"We believe the international investment community is worried about the security of their investments, and they don't fancy the prospect of Nelson Mandela controlling their cash" (Treurnicht, press release, 4 September 1985: 1).

Apart from its vacillation and weakness in dealing with black resistance, the government has also contributed to the country's economic decline by creating what the Right calls 'a welfare state for blacks'. Far from oppressing blacks, they believe, whites have done more for them than any nation has done to help any other anywhere in the world. Apartheid has given them two countries – their own homelands as well as a 'common area' of South Africa while whites have no territory they can call their own. In addition, they believe that 'white taxes' have subsidised black administrations, education, housing, transport and pensions.

Although right-wing organisations recognise the need for foreign investment in South Africa, they believe that it must be carefully monitored and controlled. They are opposed to what they describe as the machinations of multinational capital which they refer to as the *geldmag* (literally 'money power'). The prevailing view holds that multinational capital is a powerful force which wields its influence across the globe, spurred on only by the profit motive, and willing to wipe out anything that stands in its way. Its victims are usually small national groups trying to preserve their own culture, traditions and identity. Multinational capital is the vanguard of a uniform internationalism, willing to manipulate the political destinies of small nations to ensure conditions that will maximise profits and entrench sympathetic governments (Boshoff, 1985b; Marais, 1983: 84).

Constitutional versus other methods of opposition

Right-wing political parties are officially committed to using constitutional methods to achieve their objectives. Their stated policy is to win power by gaining the majority support of the white electorate, after which they say they will implement radical partition.

In the round of interviews following the May election, right-wing leaders who had previously expressed scepticism regarding the efficacy of parliamentary opposition conceded that parliamentary politics had regained an important role – albeit as part of a broader mobilisation strategy (interview, Boshoff, May 1987; interview, Terre'Blanche, June 1987). This discernible change in attitude was clearly prompted by the fact that the Conservative Party had managed to become the official opposition. Right-wing organisations had not anticipated this development in the weeks preceding the election, despite their extremely accurate prediction of the number of winnable seats. A week before the election, the CP's chief election statistician, Professor Barney Uys, predicted in a telephone interview that the party would win 22 seats, but would fail in its bid to become the official opposition.

Right-wing analysts agreed that the CP's new status (and the election outcome in general) would have several important consequences.

It would sound a death knell for the Herstigte Nasionale Party (which contested 83 seats but failed to win any and only retained four deposits). Most HNP voters would probably support the Conservative Party, effectively ending the crippling division between right-wing parties.

The Conservative Party had achieved a 'critical mass' of support, breaking an important psychological barrier and gaining the image of a party capable of winning seats. At the same time, it would provide a boost for right-wing extra-parliamentary organisations (most of whom had voted for the CP), proving that they could achieve results by political organisation and mobilisation.

Most significantly, the election results would increase the tension and conflict within the National Party and would result in the government's political paralysis. Although the election had indicated a marked voter shift to the right, right-wing analysts believe that the National Party will face increasing reformist pressure from various quarters. The primary pressure would come from the reformist bloc within its own caucus, which was strengthened by the election outcome. Several right-wing Nationalists were not returned to parliament, either because they had retired or had been replaced in nomination contests. A significant number of Nationalist right-wingers had been defeated by Conservative Party candidates. Reformist Nationalists, on the other hand, had taken several seats previously held by the Progressive Federal Party and the New Republic Party. According to the CP's calculations, reformist Nationalists now hold a solid block of 60 seats (20 of these belonging to the *ultra-verligte* 'New Nats') in the NP's 133-member caucus (interview, Derby-Lewis, August 1987).[12]

In addition the NP would face increasing pressure for reform from abroad, from the local business community and from the escalating tide of black resistance.

On the other hand, the NP would face enormous pressure to put a brake on reform:

"The government got a bigger fright in this election than most people realise. According to my calculations the National Party no longer represents the majority of Afrikaners. The most optimistic calculation for the government on the basis of the May election is that it still has the support of about 47,3 per cent of Afrikaners. This is almost exactly the same as the 47 per cent of Afrikaners who supported the Right. This is a very serious development for the government because it knows that Afrikaners are its only reliable support base. The English are fickle voters, who change allegiance very easily. The NP cannot afford to allow the erosion of its Afrikaner support to continue and this will be a very major priority. The right wing is a much more immediate threat to the government than the ANC" (interview, Uys, August 1987).[13]

The NP also knows that the CP could take a minimum of 19 additional marginal seats – and possibly as many as 43 – if the reformist drift continues.[14] Some prominent CP officials believe that this process will snowball and that their party will stand a good chance of winning the next election:

"If we could become the official opposition within five years, we can take the government at the next election. The number of seats we won in May (1987) is not a good indication of our relative strength. It is more important to look at the number of votes and the shift in support this represents. If our support had been proportionately reflected in terms of seats, we would have had 43 seats. In the Orange Free State, the Right won more than 42 per cent of the vote but not a single seat. The CP merely needs 12 000 additional votes to have majority support in that province and that should be achievable by the next election if our record of the past five years is anything to go by. The Conservative Party is the fastest-growing political movement in South Africa's history" (interview, Derby-Lewis, May 1987).

Most other right-wingers are not prepared to predict a CP election victory.

Uys, the CP's official election statistician, is far more cautious.

He estimates that under foreseeable circumstances the CP can hope at best for 50 seats at the next election.

"Most people who are still in the National Party have been conditioned to accept change. Those who were not prepared to accept reform are already in the Conservative Party. The party has not yet reached its ceiling, but its growth will slow down in the years ahead unless something very dramatic happens that precipitates another right-wing split from the National Party or generates a massive swing of voters. This can only happen if P.W. Botha does something drastic like releasing Nelson Mandela and unbanning the ANC. If something like this occurs, then it is possible the CP could take power. Nor will the senior police and military people take that lying down. That is why it will not happen. The government knows it cannot change its policy on the ANC and keep the military on its side" (interview, June 1987).

According to Uys's statistical projections, the CP should be able to take power in a general election by 1997, but he is wary of a firm prediction.

"I think we will see reform slow down dramatically as the NP tries to stop the erosion of its Afrikaner support and possibly regain some. Whether the CP can take power by 1997 or not will depend on how successful the NP is in doing this" (interview, August 1987).

However, Uys believes that the CP will be able to take control of the majority of municipal councils in the Transvaal and at least one-third in the Orange Free State in the municipal elections scheduled for October 1988. This, he says, will put the party in a particularly powerful position. Municipal government would provide a good platform to resist the reform policy at local level, enabling the CP to "promote its image as the protector of local communities against the government's reform and integrationist policies, particularly any deviations from the Group Areas Act". Strategic use of this platform could gain the CP significantly increased support before the next general election (interview, Uys, August 1987).

On this basis, many right-wingers believe that it will at least be possible to capture the majority of parliamentary seats in the Transvaal and Orange Free State by the next election. This perception has given strong impetus to proponents of alternative partition models who plan to establish a *Boerevolkstaat* somewhere within the geographic area of the northern provinces.

This perception has encouraged the AWB to assert its position strongly within the CP, believing that as soon as the party has captured the majority of seats, these provinces will be able to declare their independence and re-establish Paul Kruger's Boer Republics.

"If the Right wins the majority of seats in the Transvaal and Orange Free State, we will be in effective control of the economy, the army and the police which are centred in these provinces. We will be in a very strong position to declare our independence. That is the solution and things are moving in that direction" (interview, Terre'-Blanche, June 1987).

Other secessionist organisations, such as the Oranjewerkers who support a different model of partition, propose a different strategy to achieve it. While they acknowledge that a sympathetic political authority would facilitate the attainment of their objective, they say that they cannot place all their faith in the CP wresting power from the government in an election. Indeed, they perceive only a minimal role for parliamentary politics in the secessionist strategy.

A growing number, exemplified by Professor Carel Boshoff, believe that the time has come to withdraw from parliament and enter 'the next, more effective phase of resistance' (interview, November 1986). The correct strategic time for such action would occur when the government attempted to draw Africans into a common system of government. Once this threshold had been crossed, it would become impossible for whites to reverse the tide by winning a House of Assembly election, because they would soon become a dominated minority.

"Even if the government brings blacks in by using a token gesture, such as appointing a black cabinet minister, the eventual outcome of black majority rule will be unavoidable. You see neither the moderate nor the radical blacks will accept a token gesture. They all want a transfer of power and control over the major institutions – the army, education, the reserve bank. So anything less will be totally unacceptable to them and the government will have to continue making concessions to try to satisfy their political demands without ever being able to do so until there is majority rule" (interview, Boshoff, November 1986).

The 'next phase of resistance' would involve the "calling of a national gathering (*volksvergadering*) or a congress in which Afrikaners would be urged to withdraw from parliamentary politics and take direct action towards claiming a geographic territory of their own".

"We must make the occupation of that land area the greatest priority of our people. That can either happen peacefully or it can happen with violence" (interview, November 1986).

Whatever their policies, most other right-wingers agree that a 'new phase of resistance' may be imminent. Even Dr Andries Treurnicht, the cautious leader of the Conservative Party, has warned that he will prepare a 'resistance movement' among his own people if blacks are brought into the tricameral system (*Cape Times*, 11 October 1986).

All those interviewed said that they would prefer a peaceful transition to partition, but were prepared to resort to force and violence if necessary to defend their right to rule themselves. If reform and the escalating demands it unleashes prove a threat to Afrikaner self-determination, right-wing groups make it clear that they will fight back. "We must show the world we are prepared to struggle and fight for our survival as a separate nation," says Booysen (1981: 10).

SABRA expresses it like this:

"People can temporarily be deceived and robbed of their power and belongings, but there are many nations throughout history that fought a bitter struggle lasting centuries to win back their freedom. When constitutional development in South Africa is discussed one must discount the possibility that the Afrikaner nation will allow itself to be written off or will surrender its country and traditions and character . . . Sooner or later disadvantaged groups find out that they have been cheated and revolt . . . Throughout East and West Europe and the whole of the third world, minorities in unitary states are struggling to achieve territorial rights so that they can maintain themselves" (SABRA, 1985: 10-11).

Such statements are based on a presumption that people are willing to fight for the cause. But the Right does not take this for granted. They all consider apathy – born of comfort, materialism and a lack of awareness of the dimensions of the current crisis – as the major obstacle to the political progress of the Right and particularly to potential support for a resistance struggle.

"I think this option (violent resistance) is an illusion because the Afrikaner has never rebelled on any significant scale. Look at the rebellion of 1914. This was only twelve years after thousands of women and children had been murdered by the British. Then the Afrikaners went and fought with those people and only a few hundred, two or three hundred, resisted! Look at the Second World War. The resistance was very weak. I don't think for a moment there will be mass Afrikaner resistance. The Afrikaner has become a middle-class person with a nice Mercedes and a nice house. He is really more worried about whether his Kreepy-Krauly is working than what is happening in politics" (interview, Z. B. du Toit, November 1986).

Most right-wingers agree that the resistance struggle will only be engaged by the committed hard core, but like the militias in Lebanon and the death squads in South America, which are very small, these groups could cause enough disruption to destroy social stability. "It is possible to turn a country upside down with 5 000 people, and in the case of South Africa it is possible to do so with 500 strategically placed people," says Uys. The price of ignoring their demand for a separate state would become so high that no majority government would be able to ignore them in the long term.

Uys believes that approximately 2 per cent of adult Afrikaners (approximately 70 000 people) will eventually be prepared to engage in or actively support an armed resistance struggle to defend their right to self-determination. This, he estimates, will occur within 15 years. This hard core will be able to engage in successful resistance, he predicts, for which neither conventional arms nor many soldiers are required. "We could do it without any help at all from outside."

"You get hold of cyanide and you throw it in Soweto's water supply and you kill 50 000 people at a go. Very cruel, very nasty. But if you were robbed of your freedom in a way you thought was unfair, you would do something like that even knowing full well they could catch you. But you would have got your quota. This is not my personal opinion, I want to emphasise that, but I am telling you what the mood is here . . . Look at a power station. A technical guy who knows what he is doing can blow up a power station within half an hour without a single gram of explosives . . . We are not talking about a bush war where you need to re-supply guns. But anyway, given the different international interests, you will always find someone who is prepared to finance an Afrikaner Resistance Movement" (interview, Uys, November 1986).

Right-wingers do not consider this outcome inevitable. They believe that the government has no intention of being overwhelmed by majority rule and that it has the power to prevent it. As whites began to realise that no formulae for reform could defuse escalating resistance, they would move to the right and attempt to entrench their position.

"There will be a checkmate situation. What P. W. Botha and the NP are prepared to offer will never win the co-operation of any credible black leader. Politics are far too radicalised for reform to succeed. The whole model of multi-ethnic consociation will fail because it won't have any credible black participants. You have the mass of blacks that support the ANC on the one hand and the whites who are getting more and more frightened about the possibility of a black government and are moving right, and P. W. Botha will fall between them and nothing will happen. You will have control by force for a long time . . . You see, I think whites are going to be able to control the revolution. I think blacks are relatively impotent politically . . . There is no black revolution coming in the foreseeable future that can challenge white power. But whites must use this time to make sure that they safeguard themselves politically: they must safeguard their space. We must do so economically and territorially. We must do so without relying on neat ideological schemes. This is the only way that we can show we will not be defeated and that we will always be a serious and powerful political factor. There is then a chance that we could reach a long-term solution that will respect the right of the Afrikaner nation to rule itself" (interview, Z. B. du Toit, November 1986).

As the government's policies increasingly fail, it will become clearer to whites that there is no 'middle ground' between partition and majority rule. Because most whites would not accept majority rule under any circumstances, they would move to the Right in search of a feasible formula for partition.

Postscript

Perhaps the most commonly asked question about the Right is: "Are they serious?" Certainly, right-wingers are as serious about their policies and objectives as any other political movement. But it is impossible to say, with any accuracy, whether they will ever attempt to act on their threats – or even implement some of their less conventional strategies.

There are, however, some potential future pointers that may make a more accurate assessment possible.

If the CP wins a majority of seats in the Transvaal and the Orange Free State, for example, it will be possible to judge the seriousness of the AWB's secessionist strategy and the extent of its support. If reform proceeds to the point that Africans are brought into a common system of government, it will be easier to judge the Oranjewerkers' determination to occupy their proposed *volksland* – and how many people will follow them. Only when white power is directly threatened will it be possible to attempt an accurate assessment of the right wing's capacity for violent resistance.

The extent of the right wing's future growth will depend to a considerable extent on factors outside itself, such as the pace and direction of government policy and the state of the economy, which will determine the level of economic insecurity experienced by whites.

Despite the difficulties of precise predictions, one thing at least seems clear: the right wing is a serious obstacle in the way of South Africa's transition to a society beyond apartheid. Its strength is unlikely to wane. The Right is no paper tiger.

3 Exile and resistance: the African National Congress, the South African Communist Party and the Pan Africanist Congress[1]

HERIBERT ADAM

The reason for the increased presence of the African National Congress in South Africa lies in its legal absence. The more the Pretoria government criminalises the Congress movement, the more its symbolic appeal spreads. The meagre military impact of the ANC's 'armed propaganda' and fledgeling 'people's war' stands in sharp contrast to its political clout. "In a free election in South Africa," speculates Tom Karis, a long-time American analyst of resistance politics, "the now-outlawed African National Congress could possibly win three-fourths of the black vote as well as some white votes" (Karis, 1986: 267-287). Even if one considers such a prediction an overestimate in the light of political restrictions and unreliable survey evidence about preferred leaders, there is no doubt that the ANC remains the dominant, though by no means the monopolistic force in the opposition to apartheid. Even in the 1987 white elections, the illegal organisation participated like a silenced phantom after the National Party elevated the ANC to a position of main foe in the campaign. 'Patriotism' was measured by the apartheid state in the distance political parties maintained from the ANC – which the government sees simultaneously as a lurking danger and a spent force.

Since the renewed internal protest in 1984, the ANC has achieved its most spectacular success so far in the diplomatic arena in winning the battle for being seen as representative of the bulk of South Africans in most Western countries. In the United States in particular, the ANC is supported among such establishment pillars as the Democratic Party, most churches, the media and the universities, the major foundations and the Black Caucus. Only the right wing of the Republican Party and lobbies like the Heritage Foundation and the *Washington Times* remain hostile, while even the

State Department officially cultivates relationships with a movement which is openly allied to a Moscow-oriented Communist Party. Western Europe is likely to follow the American and Scandinavian lead in lending material and political support. From a shadowy exile existence, the ANC has become elevated to a government-in-waiting. In this process it has acquired substantial veto power over domestic and foreign policy issues, despite its doubtful ability to control major events in the townships. The rise of the movement clearly came in response to domestic developments inside South Africa, which the ANC has inspired rather than directly instigated.

How did the organisation avoid the pitfalls of exile to which its rival, the Pan Africanist Congress (to be discussed later), largely succumbed? This account will not be concerned with the history of the seventy-five year old movement, with its alliances, failures, splits and achievements, or with its changing strategies after fifty years of moral persuasion and nonviolence to symbolic sabotage in 1961, when the ANC was outlawed, went underground and established its headquarters in exile. Instead, the focus will be on more recent and current operations of the ANC, and on the ideology and tactics of an organisation which is either demonised or romanticised, but seldom scrutinised analytically.

The ANC comprises a large bureaucracy with an approximate budget of $100 million in 1983 and a total personnel of close to 10 000 people.[2] It caters for an army, refugees, bureaucrats and diplomats with permanent facilities in Zambia, Angola and Tanzania and small offices in various world capitals. In Mazimba, Morogoro in southern Tanzania, the ANC operates a self-sufficient educational complex with a crèche, hospital, maternity home and small furniture and clothing factories on 800 hectares of farmland. The community of 1 500 students, teachers, children and administrative staff includes a secondary school, the Solomon Mahlangu Freedom College (SOMAFCO).

Organisationally, the ANC can be divided into four distinct groups. Firstly, about 300 ANC people work at its modest headquarters in various parts of Lusaka, including a supporting cattle farm nearby. Together with permanent or roving ANC representatives abroad, the Lusaka contingent could be called the ANC's 'bureaucrats'and 'diplomats'. Secondly, five ANC camps in Angola provide military training for between 5 000 and 7 000 soldiers of the separate Umkhonto we Sizwe (MK). Thirdly, the membership of the South African Communist Party (SACP) is kept secret, but is comparatively small, since the SACP considers itself an elitist, vanguard group. Whilst probably all SACP members are also members of the ANC, the converse is of course not the case. Fourthly, the exiled South African Council of Trade Unions (SACTU) also operates with overlapping membership, particularly with the SACP, but has recently been overshadowed by the rise of independent South African trade unions. Given the desired warm relationship of the ANC with internal unions, especially COSATU, the continued existence of an exile union makes little sense, except for providing the SACP with union legitimation. (SACTU will not be analysed in this chapter.)

The four separate but allied organisations (the ANC, Umkhonto, SACP and SACTU) with their own leadership and constitutions are co-ordinated and guided by a thirty-person National Executive Committee (NEC) which determines policy. It was last elected and enlarged by 250 delegates at the 1985 Kabwe Consultative Conference. At that time, it was also decided to admit whites to the NEC, who before then were only entitled to ANC membership.

The military versus the political option

In military terms, Umkhonto has not even begun to dent the formidable armed machinery of the South African state. With a loyal ethnic bureaucracy and police, several hundred incidents of ANC guerrilla activity during the last ten years have led to a more consolidated and strengthened state force instead of doing much to advance Umkhonto's 'seizure of power'. As a result of the Kabwe decision to move from 'armed propaganda' to 'people's war', armed clashes, however, have increased considerably. Until 1984, the reported incidents remained under one hundred per year, but increased from 44 in 1984, to 136 in 1985, 251 in 1986 and about the same number in 1987.

The ANC stated at Kabwe that its organised underground needs to be developed. It admitted that a strong underground ANC presence as well as a large contingent of units of Umkhonto we Sizwe is missing. It considers the widespread rebellions as having 'steeled' thousands of activists to become organised contingents of the revolutionary vanguard movement. In addition to area committees, 'ANC core groups' are envisaged as being active in all the 'democratic mass organisations'. It is recommended that full-time organisers should be increasingly deployed. For the first time, urgent and special attention is urged for the infiltration of the SADF, the Bantustan armies and the police force. The SAP have already admitted to several cases of individuals, including a major, working for the ANC. However, the penetration of the ANC by informers for Pretoria seems far more widespread and efficient.

The South African press quoted a Colonel Jack Buchner, described as 'a top South African police expert on the ANC', who stated that the ANC had "no infrastructure here. They have some 3 000 people outside, of whom roughly 30 are active at any time in South Africa" (Temko, 1987). This estimate definitely seems too low, and contradicts other assessments of several hundred (400) foreign trained insurgents operating inside South Africa in 1987, including rapid response units. The contingent of MK inside the country has substantially increased with the new strategy 'to train trainers' who would be able to teach basic weapons handling and guerrilla tactics in the townships and the countryside without the new recruits ever having to leave the country. The ANC considers its outside trainees as its officer corps, the core of the future people's army. MK also wanted to avoid losing its best men by deploying them forever as combat units, arguing that no army in the world fights with combat units composed of officers. At the beginning of 1987 the South African police reported that in the past ten years "a total of 507 trained terrorists have been neutralised in South Africa; 379 of them have been arrested and 128 killed" (SABC Comment, 21 April 1987).

The ranks of the ANC-trained cadres inside the country were also swollen by the MK decision to infiltrate camp trainees after a shorter training period. The local population has shown a growing readiness to assist and shelter 'cadres on mission'. In 1981 when the question was posed in a representative survey of blacks in KwaZulu-Natal: "If the ANC were to come in secretly, asking people to help it and work with it, which of the following would happen?" 48 per cent of respondents replied that 'most' or 'many' people would help the ANC (Buthelezi Commission Report, 1982: 214). At that time even 44 per cent of Inkatha members fell into this category. The subsequent politicisation and mobilisation of street committees has undoubtedly expanded the potential for a rudimentary insurgent infrastructure. With time and experience, the military resistance will become ever more professional.

With the conflict in South Africa assuming the moral dimensions that the Spanish Civil War did for a previous generation of the international Left, it can also be expected that the military involvement of committed whites and foreigners will increase, accompanied by growing international recognition and financial assistance of the ANC. Whilst the ANC has not yet been approached about enlisting foreign brigades, individual white volunteers, such as Marion Sparg and the Dutch national Klaas de Jonge, have been operating in growing numbers, together with Cuban and East European advisors in the camps. There is a possibility that the Commonwealth offer of military assistance to the frontline states could in future be extended to the ANC, if for no other reason than to wean the movement away from the Soviet orbit and influence it through Western military supplies.

In April 1987, the South African police claimed that in the past year they had discovered more than 3 000 hand grenades and 150 limpet mines, 31 RPG-7 rocket launchers and 378 AK rifles. This indicated a quantitative increase in weapons inflow. However, due to the crash-course nature of local training, Brigadier Herman Stadtler asserted in a telephone interview that the quality of application of these weapons had declined. While grenade attacks were on the increase, incidents of car bombs and the use of land mines had recently decreased. The policeman admitted that "our intelligence is a bit cut off" in the townships, due to "intimidation and the partial success of establishing so-called free zones". Nevertheless, the police believed that the local population co-operated on the whole with the authorities, illustrated by various anecdotes of assistance to injured policemen.

There seems to be an unshaken self-confidence on the part of the security establishment that they can handle any situation. Little recognition is extended to the new daring acts of combat or the suicidal identification of growing numbers of youth with the slogan 'freedom or death'. "All that is different is that some have learned to throw a few hand grenades like youngsters throw stones," explained another brigadier. The police do not show any appreciation of the fact that the absence of terror (the bombing of cinemas, schools or sports stadia) is not a question of capacity by the resistance movement but of political will. Inasmuch as this self-restraint remains unacknowledged and politically unrewarded, it is likely to be watered down.

Within the ANC, as within the youth opposition inside South Africa, two principal attitudes towards the armed struggle vie for recognition. Neither of these doubt the need for armed intervention, but debate only its size, targets, ultimate cost and impact. The more uncompromising stance does not wish to count the cost, as it believes that the ultimate settlement in South Africa is based on military might and that there is no alternative to armed struggle as the decisive factor in the seizure of power. "The talking is over. Get on with it," a prominent ANC leader said. Johnny Makatini, a polished, soft-spoken diplomat and longtime ANC representative at the UN, dismisses the inhibiting costs of death and concedes that a prediction of three or four million killed may be a correct assessment for South Africa. In this chilling view, even the elimination of most of South Africa's inhabitants would be worth the prize of freedom. The view is held that if there were only four million left after the revolution, that would be better than the present situation (Neuhaus, 1986: 287).

However, the dominant view quietly maintains that a military victory is not on the cards and that armed resistance is mainly necessary for self-defence, that it increases the costs for the opponent and reinforces the leadership of the movement both domestically and externally. This strategy wants to bomb Pretoria to the negotiating table. For the adherents of this position, including the SACP, the South African conflict essentially represents a shifting, dynamic stalemate whose ultimate settlement must be a political one. Indiscriminate attacks would be counterproductive as they would alienate the majority (both white and black) from the liberation movement, and confirm the South African propagandistic labelling of the ANC as terrorists. The tension concerning these strategies partly overlaps with generational differences. Older activists, particularly among the UDF and the SACP leadership, increasingly warn against being used as cannon fodder. With a new realism after the declaration of the State of Emergency in 1985, they counsel a 'long march' rather than making the movement vulnerable to state retaliations. Sections of AZAPO have always held this more pragmatic attitude, stressing organisation rather than mobilisation for the sake of protest politics.[3]

Official ANC statements must be decoded as a scarcely concealed compromise between these competing strategies. Strident rhetoric encourages impatient young militants. A statement by the NEC early in 1987 exhorts members to take the war to "the enemy" and increase the number of casualties among "the enemy's" armed forces. It talks of "the final stages of mortal combat", of certain victory when "the enemy" will no longer have the possibility to withstand the assault by the "shock troops of the revolution". When Umkhonto we Sizwe fighters are addressed the language of the leaders is particularly martial. It praises the "majesty" of fighting to the last bullet by combatants who are prepared to welcome death in order that the people should be victorious in the end.

The "brilliant" attacks on Sasol, the military headquarters at Voortrekkerhoogte, the nuclear power station at Koeberg and the bomb blast outside the headquarters in Pretoria of the "racist South African Air Force" (in which many civilians were killed) are celebrated. A long list of fallen heroes have created

MK's own mythology. The Luthuli detachment of the Wankie Campaign – when in 1967 ANC guerrillas crossed the Zambezi and briefly joined ZAPU in Rhodesia "in order to hack a path home" – features prominently in the boosting of "the uncompromising warrior pledge – Victory or Death". As can be expected from military postures anywhere, negotiations are not even mentioned as part of the "seizure of power" by the "majority of the people".

But a NEC statement simultaneously also speaks of conflicting values and strategies. The leadership is obviously concerned about the excesses of the slogan 'Make the country ungovernable'. It urges discipline: no elements from the ANC should impose their views on others. A warning is sound against 'revolutionary arrogance and individualism', and unity against factionalism is praised. Reliance should be placed on "political work" to organise and mobilise the masses. The youth is reminded of existing guidelines that govern people's courts and education. Any actions should be arrived at democratically, ensuring unity of students, teachers and parents, and counselling the return to school as a 'revolutionary act'. The ANC underground is ascribed 'vanguard functions' in leading the masses, while at the same time impatient activists are reminded that there must never be actions apparently in conflict with the understanding of what the masses of the people see as their interests. The ANC clearly sees itself as fighting for a people's government, elected by, and accountable to the people, envisaging a pluralist multiparty state rather than the so-called democratic centralism of its one-party socialist allies, or the Marxist dictatorship ascribed to the ANC by Pretoria.[4]

Official ANC strategy, as recently as 1987, explicitly stresses its refusal to act against civilians both black and white, making allowances only for civilian casualties in crossfire after due care has been taken to avoid harming noncombatants. An exception is border farmers who are considered legitimate targets as part of the defence link-up system. However, there is clearly ambiguity and even disunity among the leaders on the issue of necklacing. While some executive members, including Tambo, have condemned the necklace, others have praised it or condoned it, at least by implication. Typical of the latter group, then army commissar Chris Hani expressed understanding of the necklace in rendering the townships ungovernable when he said that he refused to condemn people who mete out their own traditional forms of justice to collaborators. The Amanzimtoti bombing by an MK commander was also explained as the "very angry and emotionally disturbed" response to a situation of which the ANC is not the author and in which "the so-called civilians (*sic*) are caught in the process". Hani reiterates that the ANC is not a terrorist but a revolutionary movement. The ANC has signed the Geneva Convention about rules of warfare. Pretoria, however, refuses to do so, or to grant MK members the protection of legitimate combatants, but treats them as criminals instead. It is not known whether Umkhonto has ever instituted any disciplinary action against cadres acting on their own against orders. At the Dakar meeting, an MK commander replied: "How can I reprimand a cadre who not only is on death row, but acted in justifiable anger?" Here, the very success of Pretoria in cutting the links between MK soldiers in South Africa and their command stations abroad may backfire by granting local units greater autonomy.

The ANC finds itself in a dilemma with regard to the extension of the people's war. This strategy would seem to contradict the goal to "pay the greatest possible attention to the mobilisation and activisation of the white population". With every bomb or mine which explodes in white areas, the National Party gains new voters. The party propaganda deliberately exaggerated and manufactured 'ANC terrorist threats' in the 1987 white election, which paid off handsomely. The white electorate on the whole moved to the left on apartheid laws, but to the right on security issues. With 'traditional' apartheid certainty falling into wider disrepute, law and order issues came even more to the fore. If the ANC prediction should come true that the government is "set to lose its political control over the white population" as it has lost it over the black masses, the resistance has yet to facilitate this trend instead of allowing the military establishment to exploit security anxieties. Such a strategy of security assurances would entail paying much closer attention to intra-white political cleavages, which the ANC statements generally ignore.

Furthermore, the ANC will have to watch carefully how its nonracial message is communicated. Instead of defining the implementation of democracy as "a transfer of power from a white minority to a black majority", nondiscriminatory individual rights and securities need to be stressed. A truly nonracial democracy, by definition, should not be equated with racial majority rule. Similarly, 'fascism, racism and ethnicity' should not be lumped together. Ethnicity without racism remains a worthy feature to preserve, as implied in the concept of national groups in the Freedom Charter. Even the internationalist SACP rightly recognises that the new South Africa could "be enriched by all that is healthy in the cultural and linguistic heritage of the different groups, including that part of the Afrikaner's heritage which is not rooted in racism". The ANC has yet to consider constitutional safeguards, for example proportional representation, which would give meaning to such legitimate claims. Its equation of all proposals for federalism with 'manoeuvres' to perpetuate Bantustans under new guises ignores regional cultural differences as well as democratic theory, which remains perfectly compatible with various degrees of regional autonomy within an undivided, unitary state, provided that the federal units are not based on race.

Negotiations

On the crucial question of negotiations the ANC is pragmatically ambiguous. It treats negotiations as a question of tactics rather than principle, covering itself against possible criticism from hardliners as well as accommodating the pressure for entering into a dialogue with the opponent. This explains two contradictory statements in the same document: "No negotiations are possible until all those concerned accept the need to create and build a democratic South Africa." Should these be interpreted as negotiations for the transfer of power only, it is also emphasised more open-endedly three paragraphs later: "We reiterate our commitment to seize any opportunity that may arise, to participate in a negotiated resolution of the conflict in our country". Indeed, the ANC put the onus for negotiations on Pretoria, which has so far refused to recognise the ANC or to free its detained and exiled leaders as the crucial party to any deal. However, if there were the prospect of the South African government changing into a political formation that has abandoned the doomed concept and practices of white minority domination, "in all its guises", this would constitute a grouping with whom it would be possible, and indeed necessary, to negotiate. Contrary to Pretoria's propaganda, it is the SACP which is more realistic about the protracted conflict. The SACP, far from exhorting violence as a cathartic exercise, constrains the tendency to indiscriminate attacks on civilians through its influence on MK. It is not the communists who radicalise the townships, but the youth who radicalise the communists and the ANC. Because the SACP as a small, elitist group is relatively insulated from the township sentiment, it can afford to be far more consistent and dogmatic than the ANC which is constantly torn by the need to be on the same wavelength as its amorphous constituency at home. The focus on resistance from those in exile can easily distort this crucial symbiotic relationship between Lusaka and 'home'. Observers of the Kabwe conference reported the deep impact which the uncompromising militancy of newly arrived comrades had on the old guard of long-time exiles. Even on the question of negotiation, the alleged fanaticism of the SACP members turns out to be more accommodating, forthright and politically shrewd than the party is given credit for. For example: "If a real possibility emerges of moving towards the total abolition of apartheid, without escalating violence, there is no sector of our liberation alliance which would reject such a path or refuse to talk to people of goodwill about how to get there". At the same time Tambo warned that the ANC rejects negotiations in bad faith, which Pretoria would enter into as a ploy in order to extend the lease on its life.

If the ANC were to accept Pretoria's precondition for legalisation – the rejection of violence – it would commit political suicide.

Given the militancy and politicisation in the townships, any ANC leader entering into a dialogue under such a condition would be branded a traitor and lose his following. A controversial settlement under these circumstances would not be worth the paper on which it was written. The ANC also believes with some justification that their people had only been taken seriously, whether in Pretoria, London, Washington or Bonn, because of their armed activity. For a military organisation with units operating with great autonomy, it would be difficult to resume suspended activity should negotiations fail. Combat enthusiasm cannot be switched off and on at will. Indeed, the halt of violence cannot be made a precondition of negotiations as long as this is the very goal of talks. Historically, a truce has seldom preceded a settlement but is usually its outcome. The successful Lancaster House talks about Zimbabwe's independence as well as the United States' negotiations with North Vietnam took place during an ongoing full-scale war.

Suspension of armed struggle while negotiations got under way was therefore the most the ANC would reluctantly agree to when pressed by the Commonwealth 'Eminent Persons Group' (EPG). Pretoria explicitly rejected this face-saving formula for both sides since, as Pik Botha argued, no self-respecting government would negotiate with a gun pointing at its head. Pretoria and the ANC, however, came close to formal talks when members of the EPG were given South Africa's 'bottom line' conditions. These were accepted by the ANC. However, the planned meeting was sabotaged by the surprise raids into Zimbabwe, Zambia and Botswana which led to the collapse of the EPG exercise in 1986. Analysts now speculate whether the South African government "was dumbfounded by the unexpected ANC acceptance and desperately launched the raids to extricate itself from the situation" (*Southern Africa Report*, 6 February 1987). What seems more likely is that some cabinet moderates (Pik Botha, Gerrit Viljoen, Barend du Plessis, Kobie Coetsee) had agreed to the ANC meeting but were undermined by the military and by fellow hardliners who launched the raids to sabotage the proposed talks. Furthermore, Pretoria did not have any negotiating plans, or an agreed-upon constitutional blueprint to accommodate a legalised ANC and a released Mandela. The split within the government was also confirmed by the early warning of the impending raids, which the targets received through Zimbabwe intelligence on a tip-off from their South African counterparts.

The failure of the EPG mission simply reflects the fact that no shared perception of stalemate exists at present. Contrary to the ANC assumption of a panicking 'enemy that took fright', Pretoria felt that it was in the ascendency with relatively effective new repressive measures and it saw no need to accommodate an ever-growing alienation. It also underestimated the strength of its opponent and the committed rage of those "who know how to die for their future".

In surveys among whites, a majority felt that the government should negotiate with black leaders immediately, and less than 10 per cent of respondents were completely opposed to negotiations (Rhoodie et al., 1986: 19). However, 39 per cent of those favouring negotiations had Buthelezi in mind, 10 per cent were prepared to include every black leader, and only 4 per cent mentioned the ANC or Mandela. This clearly reflects the success of the official appellation of the ANC as terrorists beyond the pale.

Political education, religion and women

POLITICAL EDUCATION IN THE ANC

Contrary to the image it has of a fanatical group indoctrinated by political commissars, the exiled ANC has grossly neglected the political education of its cadres. Its Department of Information and Propaganda (DIP) has always been more concerned with its external impact than with its members' political literacy, which was taken for granted. However, more recently it has become aware of this shortcoming, and the 1985 Kabwe conference deplored self-critically "that there is no authority responsible for political education". A new Department of Political Education is supposed to rectify the deficiencies of the new recruits in revolutionary theory and South African history. This theoretical deficit, however, seems not only confined to new members. In the ANC literature as a whole, intellectual discourse frequently succumbs to sloganeering, exhortation replaces strategy and passion substitutes for analysis. In invoking an inevitable unfolding of a predetermined history, the literature has lost sight of an open-ended alternative to apartheid which political debate could shape. As there is little comprehension of past mistakes beyond the practice of hero worship, there is even less theoretical exploration of the future. With a few exceptions, such as the 1986 York conference or the 1987 Dakar meeting, the ANC until recently has shied away from participating in the numerous academic conferences about South Africa, as if it wanted to avoid being tainted or drawn into embarrassing controversies. Nine out of ten times ANC representatives appear on platforms from which they preach to the converted. Expectations of revolutionary militancy then reinforce a rhetoric which deludes both speaker and audience. Sober strategic debate is stifled by the need to display unwavering commitment. It is always astonishing to see how normally critical individuals surrender their faculties of autonomous judgement whenever a professional revolutionary enters the room. By playing on the guilt of inactive sympathisers, particularly among pampered audiences without a worthy cause in the West, the activist from the frontline can sell almost any policy, regardless of its implications.

ANC representatives generally show an extraordinary and almost nostalgic interest in news 'from home'. It is also now realised that "our movement pays insufficient attention to analysing the content of the different ideological trends in our country". (This would explain the exaggerated importance which ANC executive members often attribute to political trends at Stellenbosch.) Since the ANC plans to set up regional libraries abroad and is particularly interested in 'literature from the home front', it would be a worthy endeavour to extend as many free subscriptions of South African newspapers, journals and academic research papers as possible to the various ANC branches. In this way a more accurate assessment by the ANC of domestic trends could be ensured.

In its self-understanding the ANC is not an elitist, secret organisation with selected members, but is consciously mass-based. 'People's power', it is stressed, cannot be won without active mobilisation of 'the masses', in 'whatever formation they live'. The leadership distinguishes between reactionary and progressive mass organisations. Activists are asked to work in both, strengthening the latter, and exposing in the former the conservative leadership and radicalise such groups as Inkatha.

The new emphasis on internal contradictions has also revealed tensions regarding the cultural isolation of South Africa, particularly in the case of the academic boycott. The calls for academic boycotts were based on the strategy of isolating South Africa totally after Pretoria banned its major opposition in the 1960s. All state-supported institutions, including universities, were then considered part of the apartheid system which they perpetuated, albeit unwillingly. White academics living in South Africa became, by definition, guilty of participating in racial privilege, however reluctantly. Tacitly, the exiles held up their departure from the scene of the crime as the morally superior stance. Anything South African became tainted. With the resurgence of political alienation and resistance in the eighties this absolutist isolation strategy raised serious problems among whites also. As a South African academic depicted the dilemma: "Progressive academics cannot be asked to ally themselves with forces opposing apartheid, while internationally they are attacked as upholders of apartheid" (Morris, 1987). Selective boycotts became *en vogue*, but little consensus has emerged about the criteria of selection, or about who does the selecting. To a greater extent in the ANC than in the international support groups, moralistic universal condemnation has given way to a strategic reasoning that aims at exploiting contradictions, eroding state support, and expanding organisational advances. Instead of isolating South Africa, the strategy has shifted towards isolating the government. While the ANC nominally supports the total cultural and academic boycott of South Africans abroad, it makes exceptions when consulted. ANC representatives themselves participate in conferences with South Africans away from home. But international support groups, particularly the British Anti-apartheid Movement, have displayed a far more rigid stance.[5]

The official ANC criterion for any legitimate cultural exchange – "approval from the mass national democratic structures within South Africa and/or solidarity groups abroad" – lends itself to a reversed censorship. It easily leads to confusion of artistic or academic excellence with political commitment of an approved kind. Thus it has been suggested (*Weekly Mail*, 50, 1987) that the cultural boycott of South African artists abroad tends to develop into a reward for UDF/ANC supporters and excludes apartheid opponents with Black Consciousness, Inkatha or liberal sympathies.

RELIGION AND THE ANC

One of the more significant fault lines in the ANC divides atheists and agnostics from religious adherents. The latent tension arises from the simple fact that the majority of South Africans are churchgoers, while the overwhelming majority of ANC cadres are not. "None of this religious crap in schools and public life will be tolerated when we get into power," explained an ANC executive, who probably represented the one extreme. Oliver Tambo, on the other hand, is known to be a self-confessed Christian.

As is well known, many early black political activists received their first education at mission stations, or benefited from church-sponsored scholarships. Customs, ceremonies and the moral and political conduct of the South African population as a whole is deeply permeated by religious prescriptions. Even the national anthem of the excluded – *Nkosi Sikelel'i Afrika* (God Save Africa) – reflects this tradition. Church-state conflicts did not arise only with the arrival of liberation theology. Individual members of the church hierarchy have clashed with the apartheid regime since its inception. They were joined more recently by committed anti-apartheid groups of other religions. It probably could only happen in South Africa that the pro-Israeli 'Jews for Justice' share a public platform with the equally militant 'Call of Islam'. Such is the hold of Islam over its 400 000 adherents in South Africa that even Y. M. Dadoo, chairman of the SACP, requested a Muslim burial. Young

Muslims of Indonesian descent in the Western Cape in particular (who reject the label 'Cape Malays') have emerged as a militant force, some of them looking to Libya and the PAC for assistance. The image of the conservative, anti-African Muslim trader of Gandhi's time has also gradually changed.

The ANC has belatedly recognised the importance of what is known in ANC parlance as 'the religious front'. The organisation has a special Religious Department. Even an official SACP publication now warns members to be sensitive and tactful in dealings with religious people and their institutions. Gone are the days of the 1930s when political pilgrims to Moscow denounced all church ministers as tools of imperialism, and praised the 'New Jerusalem' in the Soviet Union. Nevertheless, the same publication reprimanded Desmond Tutu in 1986 for what were called anti-communist sentiments which are seen as splitting the ANC/SACP unity and playing to the Reagan/Thatcher "gallery".

The ANC policy recommends infiltration of the churches, "to create ANC units both within the established churches and the independent churches". Some 30 per cent of all Africans belong to independent churches, but as far as the leadership of these hierarchies is concerned the ANC so far seems to have been singularly unsuccessful with its aim of giving political content and direction. Much more has been achieved with other goals, such as to make some churches "important platforms to expose the regime's atrocities internally and externally".

However, there are definite limits on the extent to which churches can be converted 'into centres of resistance and struggle'. One internal ANC document rightly points out that "most of the resolutions taken against the state are not interpreted and filtered down to the grassroots for implementation by the church followers". As hierarchical organisations, many denominations, particularly the ecclesiastical Anglicans and Catholics, do not practise the rules of democracy, but rely on ill-understood or resented guidance from above. Given a conservative flock in the mainstream white congregations, the churches make an ambivalent ally of the ANC, despite their rhetorical militancy. Although the churches possess what is probably the widest domestic and international social network of all organisations in South Africa, the resolutions of the South African Council of Churches, for example, are often not backed by solid compliance and support. This would also explain the surprising absence of civil disobedience among the South African clergy of all denominations. Even the morally conscious clergy, with few exceptions, do not challenge immoral race laws head-on.

However, the radical redemptive politics of some clergy may also contradict the political strategies of the resistance movements. For example, the Kairos document defines the South African conflict between oppressor and oppressed as 'irreconcilable'. This is the perspective of a holy war between good and evil, regardless of costs and likely outcomes. Under these auspices negotiations become meaningless, since the conflict can only be resolved by the total defeat and eradication of the oppressor. It is doubtful whether the more politically minded ANC members adhere to this absolutist stance and reject negotiations for nonracialism and democratic alternatives. Under this redemptive perspective politics cease, since conflicting interests are not able to be bargained for or compromised with until the utopian state of the elimination of all oppression is reached. Such a perspective negates the pragmatism for which the Congress alliance has always been praised.

WOMEN AND THE ANC

The ANC recognises the 'triple oppression of women'. It is aware that political liberation is incomplete while discrimination against women continues. It also rhetorically ascribes the task of rectifying women's unequal position to women and men alike. The ANC statements, however, either idolise 'the womenfolk' as 'giants' and 'the titans of our struggle' or women are inferiorised by being described as 'underdeveloped'. Neither attitude accords women equality. Thus the Kabwe resolutions diagnose the 'backwardness of women', for which traditional patriarchal relations are blamed.

The proposals recommend a 'conscious development programme' to be undertaken by the movement together with 'positive discrimination' in favour of women. However, separatist male language and practice often contradict the high-sounding intention that the "progressiveness and success of our movement will largely depend on the participation of the womenfolk". Only three out of thirty ANC executive members are female. What is referred to as 'the women's question', has been left largely to a token 'women's section' to resolve. Above all, they, and not their male counterparts, are supposed to be in need of emancipation. This is implied by the chauvinist language, though it is undoubtedly not the intent: "Our policy is to liberate *them* from legal, economic and social disabilities." Like handicapped people, they deserve special treatment and have special capacities to be utilised: "A concerted effort should be made to develop and exploit the creative abilities and talents of our women cadres." With this attitude the ANC in exile remains as wedded to traditional female subordination as the youthful township activists who also mostly *use* 'girls' rather than incorporating them as equals in the struggle. Had the dominant male faction shed its traditional role stereotypes, it would not be necessary to recommend that a study commission be sent "to such countries as Vietnam, Cuba and Nicaragua to learn how they are solving the women's question". Besides, Cuba and Vietnam can hardly serve as models for South Africa. If the ANC is to reap 'one of the greatest prizes of the democratic revolution' in the 'unshackling of women', the organisation clearly has to move beyond such stereotypes as 'mothers of the nation'.

The post-apartheid economy and socialism

In its drive to isolate South Africa and have mandatory sanctions imposed, the ANC rejects the argument that a wounded economy would be an obstacle to peaceful reform of the system. The ANC claims that the booming South African economy between 1967 and 1976 coincided with a period of mounting repression, when some of the worst features of apartheid were implemented. Conversely, it reasons that the government felt constrained to move away from some apartheid measures during the most severe recession since 1976. However, correlation does not establish causation. It could well be argued that it was the earlier boom period that enabled blacks to force the government to make some concessions. Without the emergence of unions in strategic positions of power and the rapid expansion of higher education which created rising expectations, the subsequent organised resistance would have been inconceivable. In contrast to internal union leaders who are more ambiguous on disinvestment, the exiled ANC hardly takes into account how mounting unemployment weakens resistance and union militancy. People who have to worry about their daily survival can rarely afford to take political risks. It is precisely the unconstrained youth, the better-off students and professionals, and some segments of the unionised workers, who are in the forefront of protest.

The labels 'workerist' and 'populist' do not altogether capture the strategic difference between those who advocate trade union independence and socialism now (termed 'workerists'), and the two-stage theorists of the SACP (known as 'populists'). In its understanding of South Africa as colonialism of a special type, the SACP aims, as is well known, first at national democratic liberation and then at socialism. In this process, it sees itself as the sole representative of the working class *as a whole*; a true political vanguard, which is a claim that the trade union movement cannot make. For the SACP, unions represent merely another important pressure group; the shop floor is another arena of class struggle which needs the overall co-ordination and guidance of the vanguard political party.

In contrast, the ANC views itself as an all-class coalition, not a classless alliance (populism). Like a church, anyone who agrees with its creed ('abolition of apartheid') is invited to join and is welcomed. In ANC speeches, the working class is categorised as 'the backbone', or *a* leading but not *the* leading force, as in this 1986 statement: "We want the working class to be involved in this struggle as a leading force, while we also seek to ensure that the capitalists, as well, act against the apartheid regime of national oppression." Therefore, the ANC as an organisation has no firm commitment to socialism. It is left to the SACP as an independent part of the Congress alliance "to assert and jealously safeguard" the dominant role of the class whose aspirations they represent. The ANC's publicity secretary stated explicitly that the ANC is not a socialist party, has never pretended to be one, has never said it was, and is not trying to be. The SACP agrees with this division of representation without claiming the dominant role in the ANC front of disparate forces.

On the crucial economic post-apartheid order, the SACP concedes that there will be a mixed economy within the framework envisaged by the non-socialist Freedom Charter. What is left undecided, it is suggested in a conciliatory tone, "could well be settled in debate rather than on the streets". The "disastrous Pol Pot philosophy", which "can project a pole vault into socialism and communism the day after the overthrow of the white rule" is rejected by the SACP. However, it has never been clarified how long the first stage of the mixed economy should last, and it is unclear whether the alliance with nonracial capitalism amounts to short-term expediency or long-term necessity. The latter possibility is suggested by a NEC statement that the new democratic state must also "ensure that the wealth of the country increases significantly and continuously". In the SACP perspective the two-phase strategy remains absolutely vital because "the immediate struggle" cannot be "effectively fuelled by the slogan of a socialist republic".

Increasingly, academic supporters of the liberation movement also warn against 'premature nationalisation'. Socialism is no longer seen as dependent "on an immediate far-reaching change in the property relations" (Davies, 1987: 85-106). Cadres, it is argued, should not be absorbed in taking over the day to day management of hundreds of enterprises, but instead merely control 'the major macro-decision' which affects the vast bulk of capitalist production (Davies, 1987: 85-106). Paradoxically, existing monopoly control would facilitate such a policy because of its built-in centralisation. However, this assessment may well underestimate the degree of managerial autonomy of each sector in the Anglo American empire, for example, which does not lend itself easily to regimentation from a single centre of control.

Similarly, central bank action is considered necessary to counter harmful anti-socialist capital movements. However, the rate of capital outflow during a socialist transition could hardly be checked by the nationalisation of banks, since this would have been more or less completed long before such a transition. The problem for a post-apartheid society would seem to be the opposite: how to attract massive new foreign investment for creating employment in a growing urban population. In order to fulfil the heightened expectations of a liberated constituency, an ANC-controlled government could not afford the mistakes made by Mozambique and Angola by not retaining its skilled human capital. After all, the potential wealth of South Africa lies in its fragile social relations above ground, and not merely in its minerals underground. Nigeria or Zaïre are as rich in scarce minerals as South Africa, and yet they count among the less developed states. Even more so than in Zimbabwe after the 1980 ZANU takeover, a nominally socialist Azania would have to safeguard the conditions under which private sector initiatives could flourish.[6] This applies even more to the developed economy of South Africa, from which the popular analogies with the rest of the colonised and abused African continent distract.

A 'socialist' South Africa would still have to trade mainly with its traditional markets in the capitalist West. Subject to terms of trade and dependency, any drastic structural change which increases the 'brain drain', dries up capital, harms investor confidence, destroys productive labour relations and undermines stability and predictability generally, would therefore have to be severely constrained. The accumulated historical advantages in education and expertise among whites ensure that a secure future would exist for most members of the formerly privileged, on whose skills the new regime would have to rely, regardless of its ideological predilections. This is illustrated by the Zimbabwean experience.

The ANC has expressed concern over the high white emigration rate in the wake of the 1984 rebellion and subsequent emergency. For the first time in 1987, UDF affiliates have called on politically conscious whites to stay and contribute to the transformation towards a nonracial democracy. This stance is in marked contrast to the attitude in the 1960s and 1970s when many black activists and white liberals thought it best to leave a racist polity behind by emigrating.

The ANC vagueness concerning the post-apartheid economic

order is very much tied to its strategy of an all-class alliance and the SACP's two-stage revolution. It has to be ambiguous in order to reconcile business as well as working-class interests. If the movement were to spell out a socialist programme it would inevitably alienate substantial NAFCOC and some big business support for a nationalist alternative.

The predicament of an amorphous political alliance, therefore, leaves the unions with a much clearer socialist thrust. The unions, and not the SACP, can give content to the socialist demand. However, for the unions too, 'socialism' often amounts to an untheorised slogan of anger against 'the bosses' in bed with Pretoria. When pressed, the socialism of COSATU leaders boils down to the social-democratic Swedish or British Labour Party model. Potentially, however, the unions could become more radical than the Congress movement. In this latent tension, COSATU has toed the Congress line up until now by not explicitly espousing an immediate transition to socialism. Since the ANC has acquired a new constituency in the form of Western public opinion and governments who are suspicious of supporting anti-capitalist programmes, the potential cleavage between independent socialist 'workerists' and the strategic 'populists' of ANC diplomacy could well deepen.

As is well known, there are many challenges to this two-stage theory, inspired by different socialist traditions.[7] 'Workerists' consider the unions capable of achieving liberation without the compromising alliance with principally antagonistic forces. Trotskyites distrust the Moscow-oriented Stalinist elitism of the SACP. Black Consciousness adherents fear a betrayal of their revolutionary militancy in negotiations. The National Forum (AZAPO, Unity Movement) despises the ethnic branches of the Congress and envies its comparative diplomatic success, compared with the self-destructing PAC. All anti-Charterists claim that Congress is in danger of being hijacked by the petty bourgeoisie, with racial capitalism being replaced by an equally exploitative system in which the socialist promise is reduced to rhetoric and unnecessarily postponed. In 1985 the conflict with what the ANC calls 'ultra-leftists' led to the formal expulsion of a group of white Marxists (Legassick, Hemson, Ensor, Petersen) who continue to push for socialist vigilance in their quarterly *Inqaba Ya Basebenzi* (Journal of the Marxist Worker Tendency of the ANC).[8] Seven years earlier eight 'Africanists' were expelled for taking the very different position of 'chauvinistic ghetto nationalism', which criticised the multiracial character of the organisation.

When a handful of progressive South African businessmen meet ANC representatives informally in London or New York, both groups are usually surprised about the ease, or even warmth, with which personal relationships are established on the basis of a common South African background. Notwithstanding different political strategies and ultimate goals, the common aversion to National Party rule and anachronistic apartheid laws provides a backdrop of understanding and even solidarity in some instances. However, these tentative personal alliances quickly fall apart when their mutual expectations are spelt out.

In the ANC strategy, progressive businessmen serve the twofold purpose of splitting the enemy and adding power to the broad antiapartheid forces. ANC stategists are under no illusion that South African capital as a whole is prepared to throw its weight behind the organised resistance. The two crucial indicators mentioned in interviews with ANC personnel are the 'Key Points Act' and wage payments for conscripts. In the first instance, business is seen as having established a voluntary security alliance with the military establishment to defend vital installations and train its own auxiliary forces to supplement the state. In the second case, the ANC finds it significant that employers willingly pay the wages of army draftees, thereby raising a voluntary war tax and encouraging conscription rather than working against the perpetuation of a simmering civil war. ANC spokesmen also emphasise the difference between potentially more sympathetic multinationals who are concerned about markets abroad and domestic capital, which is dependent on government patronage for tender or protective tariffs.

In the view of progresssive businessmen, the tentative alliances with the political alternative come to nothing when ANC spokesmen exhort carrying the war into the white areas shortly after they have talked about finding solutions to violent escalation. The businessmen feel compromised and manipulated as 'useful idiots'. One of them explained that "my solidarity ends when it comes to having my factory blown up and my employees killed". Others argue that they could not afford to meet with 'these guys' again, as long as 'they throw bombs around'. The ANC military strategy as well as its calls for sanctions therefore puts South African capital effectively into the government camp, and counteracts the strategy to split the opponent. On the other hand, it could be said that without the militancy of organised resistance, South African business would have pursued its complacent course and not even contemplated the ANC alternative in the first place.

After the Chris Ball investigation, Pretoria has for the time being successfully intimidated corporate heads to avoid their being labelled 'friends of the enemy'. Business, on the other hand, has largely failed to educate its own organisations for nonracial alternatives, and for negotiation outside government parameters. A conservative in-house constituency, a fear of government action and a political timidity born of prosperity constrain even the handful of far-sighted entrepreneurs who seek to come to terms with the revolutionary forces.

The Communist Party

It has been argued "that focusing on the role of communism or the Communist Party risks misunderstanding the nature of the ANC" (Karis, 1986: 267). The preceding analysis would strongly support this view without being complacent about Soviet imperialism. The ANC represents too amorphous and broad-based an alliance to be used as a front organisation for the SACP. The ANC has never made a secret of its historical alliance with South African communists, among whom were the first whites to support the liberation cause without reserve. Most of these joined the Communist Party for domestic reasons rather than support for Stalinism or external Soviet Policy. Similarly, the ANC's close alliance with Eastern-bloc countries grew more out of the necessity to find diplomatic and military support for an exile movement, whose requests for assistance were initially turned down by Western states. It would seem unrealistic to expect the ANC to break those ties and split because of belated Western recognition.

Nevertheless, the role of the Soviet Union, as of the United States, in furthering its interests in the region needs to be recognised. The SACP categorically denies any such collusion and has said officially: "The SACP does not take orders from Moscow, nor does Moscow give them. Neither does the SACP direct the affairs of the ANC." Given their overlapping membership and their close working relationship, the statement rings true that members of the SACP who are members of the ANC are subject to ANC discipline and carry out their duties in accordance with ANC directives, just like any other members. Interviewed NEC members ridicule the speculative head count when they are themselves not aware of the irrelevant distinction. It may indeed be wishful thinking on the part of Pretoria to rely on fictitious competition and conflict between so-called ANC nationalists and communists in order to split the movement. As has been argued, such a weakening of the SACP would not even be in Pretoria's interest, because the SACP tends to restrain potential terrorism and has a much more pragmatic policy concerning negotiations and the post-apartheid economy than other forces in the alliance.

There is also mounting evidence that current Soviet policy on South Africa is low-key, cautious, realistic and conservative, counselling a negotiated settlement rather than escalation, which Moscow could not control anyway.[9] Victor Goncharov, deputy director of the Institute of African Studies in the USSR Academy of Sciences, has indicated that "the Soviet Union would like to see more flexibility and objectivity from the ANC and less use of dogmatic formulations" (*Work in Progress*, 48: 7). He cautioned those who advocate the socialist revolution before the problems of national liberation are settled, and compared this stance to a 'disease', equivalent to Lenin's 'infantile disorder'. In the view of informed Soviet analysts, an ANC victory will take years: "Maybe ten years, I say not less than ten years. Yes, I believe that in the end South Africa will become socialist, maybe not in 25 years, but in a century . . . I am an optimist."[10] Such long-range vague hopes indicate that South Africa ranks low in Moscow's international concerns. The Soviet Union's current priorities are to normalise East-West relations and improve its domestic economy rather than to get involved in another confrontation with the West over South Africa.

However, in the view of Pretoria and the U.S. administration, the Soviet Union, through the SACP, aims at escalating armed conflict in South Africa. The October 1986 report by the American State Department to Congress on 'Communist Influence in South Africa' reasons that through increased emphasis "on armed struggle, the ANC will most likely become still more dependent on Soviet-bloc (military) assistance". With limited inside influence, particularly among the unions, the SACP is portrayed as relying increasingly on military pressure rather than negotiations to achieve its 'ultimate goal of a Marxist-Leninist State'. Therefore, communist interests are said to be served by "isolation of the ANC from contacts with Western governments". However, there is no evidence that the SACP feels threatened by the growing recognition of the ANC in the West; on the contrary, this is hailed as a substantial breakthrough for the movement for which the SACP also takes credit.

Finally, there remains the widespread suspicion that, as in Vietnam and Nicaragua, communists would only use the democratic forces and then suppress their former allies once the revolution were achieved. However, such a design would be very difficult to implement, given the independent democratic union movement as well as the predominantly religious and Western outlook of the majority in South Africa.

If the image of Soviet tutelage of the ANC and the SACP persists nevertheless, the organisations have only themselves to blame. From the platform of a false solidarity, the ANC monthly *Sechaba* and the SACP's *African Communist* support Soviet policy to the hilt; from the excuse of Chernobyl to the vindication of Bulgaria in the shooting of the Pope.[11] There has not been a single public criticism of an ally, who, therefore, appears to be a mentor. On the Soviet role in Afghanistan and on the Polish government's action against Solidarity, ANC praise for the Soviet stance is clearly not in line with dominant black thinking within the borders of South

Africa. In David Hirschmann's interviews with 45 black opinion-leaders, "nearly all . . . were critical" and opposed Soviet imperialism in Afghanistan (Hirschmann, 1987: 22). On the other hand, Afghanistan is of little interest to black South Africans, while the role of the United States looms larger in black consciousness because of the Pretoria-Washington ties. It is the apparent Western support of apartheid, and Pretoria's policies, which foster sympathies for the communist alternative.

Besides the misplaced ideological affinity of some ANC members, there is another pragmatic reason for the organisation's uncritical silence on Soviet policy. A senior ANC executive explained these practical constraints bluntly: "We have to choose between guns and what we may like to say. They (Moscow) simply do not tolerate critique." Being able to carry on the 'armed struggle' had to have unquestioned priority in this predicament, according to the respondent. Asked whether this choice did not imply compromising ANC independence and integrity, the answer was: "No, they leave us alone as long as we are not interfering with their policy."

Competing exile forces – the Pan Africanist Congress

Compared with the relatively cohesive Congress alliance in exile, the PAC has been plagued by consecutive leadership crises and internal fratricide. After the PAC founder Robert Sobukwe had died, and credible leaders like Zephania Mothopeng were imprisoned in 1979, Sobukwe's successor, Potlako Leballo, had his rivals detained in Botswana and Swaziland. After the forced resignation of Leballo, his successor, David Sibeko, was assassinated by a squad from the PAC military wing, and Sibeko was followed by John Pokela who died in 1985. The present chairman, Johnson Mlambo, has also faced various resignations from the central committee. A recent analysis of the PAC concludes: "Whether these disputes are over power, ideological or pragmatic differences or car theft and Mandrax smuggling, is not obvious to outside observers" (Moss, 1987: 16). From interviews with the PAC London representatives it could be established that the organisation embraces 'scientific socialism' without being too clear about its meaning. The PAC is recognised by the OAU and receives some limited support from Zimbabwe and Tanzania where it has 'external headquarters'. It publishes an official journal, *Azania News*, with much livelier and more eclectic commentary on the South African scene than its counterpart *Sechaba*. There is also trial evidence of renewed but limited PAC guerrilla activity in South Africa. There remains residual support for the PAC among some black trade unions. When the new federation of the Council of Unions of South Africa (CUSA) and the Azanian Confederation of Trade Unions (AZACTU) was launched in October 1986, the flag of the PAC was raised and fraternal greetings exchanged, "although it is unclear what significance should be attributed to this" (*Africa Confidential*, 28, 1987).

Frequent rumours of merger talks between the ANC and PAC, arranged by the Organisation of African Unity (OAU), were denied by both movements. According to a senior PAC official, the organisation is prepared to have "a principled united front" with all organisations and forces "opposed to the racist regime". The emphasis on *principled* unity, however, precludes the goal as long as the Congress opponents of the PAC and Black Consciousness groupings charge the ANC with *unprincipled* compromises. The mutual denigration in the movement's publications, in which the PAC excels more than the ANC, (which usually ignores the PAC) has so far not prepared followers for any potential merger. The frequent violent clashes between AZAPO and UDF activists inside South Africa during 1985-1987 have also left a legacy of bitterness and suspicion. However, on two contentious issues – socialism and the role of whites – the PAC seems to have moved closer to the ANC position. According to the PAC leadership, the "organisation is socialist in a pragmatic way"; it is also prepared to accept whites as "individual members of the struggle".

From the ANC perspective, the PAC is a 'nuisance factor today' because of "its virtual nonexistence at home and its inactivity internationally". The ANC fears that the PAC will be "used in future as a centre for counter-revolution". The ANC resents the fact that "the PAC is being mentioned side by side with the ANC and is being put forward as a participant in possible negotiations in the future".

For AZAPO and PAC adherents on the other hand, the dismissive attitude of the ANC merely confirms the undemocratic nature of the ANC. Its refusal to share a platform with other liberation groups is seen as an indicator of petty-bourgeoisie authoritarianism. Given the historical following which the Black Consciousness/AZAPO tendency has acquired, especially among black academics, the ANC is depriving itself of a substantial pool of talent by dismissing it as 'Trotskyite childishness' or 'ghetto chauvinism'.

Effective government repression of black resistance and the criminalisation of the ANC and the PAC have both helped and weakened the nonracial movements. While government action has unintentionally granted the Charter forces wide symbolic appeal, it has given the ANC a radical image and bestowed revolutionary expectations on it which will be hard to meet. That makes it vulnerable to a 'left wing' Africanism, which would shed nonracialism in the name of raw, indigenous counter-racialism. When coupled with notions of redemptive violence and the cathartic exorcising of colonial humiliation, the rational insistence by the ANC on 'colour-blind', democratic alternatives will appear comparatively modest. It must be remembered that the PAC was in the vanguard of radicalism throughout the 1960s, after it split from the ANC over the alleged influence of white and Indian Marxists in 1959. The newly acquired socialist tinge of the PAC and Black Consciousness tendency in the 1980s would seem a poor guarantee against a renewed lapse into a populist creed of black supremacy and unrestrained warfare. A guerrilla organisation, such as the PAC-inspired Poqo in the 1960s, could easily re-emerge if the relatively moderate ANC fails to deliver its promised liberation. The appearance of a black Terre'Blanche is only a matter of time.

The choice the South African government faces is to either negotiate now, with a still much restrained and highly professional ANC leadership of a widely acclaimed resistance tradition, or face the atomised products of Bantu Education in the townships later.

4 The politics of internal resistance groupings

PAULUS ZULU

On 6 May 1987 South Africa held a 'whites only' general election. The governing National Party won the election on a ticket of security and reform. The security threat, according to the Nationalists, came from two concerted fronts: internally from the resistance movement in the townships and the factories, and externally from the African National Congress. The internal crisis, according to State President Botha, has made it difficult to carry on with the state's reform programme. The logical question to ask is, what precipitated the internal crisis? This question has two possible answers which are interrelated. These are the subjects of analysis in this chapter:

– The powerlessness, discontent and consequent anger felt by the majority of South Africa's black population.
– The failure of the state's strategy of containment, including the reform programme.

This chapter will focus on the crisis in South Africa and the internal resistance movement.[1]

The internal resistance in context

Generally, resistance is attributed to conservative anti-change forces that strive to maintain the status quo. In the South African context the opposite applies. Here, the state actively suppresses and contains those forces that seek change through the transformation of the existing power relations. Resistance in South Africa therefore implies a refusal to comply with the state's programme to facilitate social and economic domination, by the minority white population, of the black majority through legislation and practice which exclude blacks from participation in the decision-making machinery. By resisting the agents and institutions that facilitate this domination, certain organisations and movements have become resistance groups.

A THEORETICAL OVERVIEW

The resistance movement is best seen as a representation of social forces. In this sense "political structures can be reduced to socio-economic forces in which the state is nothing but an arena in which conflicts over basic social and economic interests are fought out" (Skocpol, 1979: 25). Within this model, contrary to liberal pluralist theory, the state is not an arena of legitimate authority supported by consensus and majority preference, where groups freely compete and members are socialised into a commitment to common values. Instead, the state resolves conflict through domination by classes or groups which depend neither upon value consensus nor popular contentment. The actors engaged in resistance therefore see the state as organised coercion. Resistance which might entail the use of violence is therefore a strategy or an attempt to bargain with the state in order to redress inequities.

In South Africa, resistance manifests itself in a collective mobilisation of grievances which operate at two interrelated levels. The first concerns deteriorating material conditions such as housing, education, transport and employment. At this level resistance is typically localised, or specific to particular communities or groupings. The second concerns broader politically based issues including the town council system, the tricameral parliament, the role of security forces in the townships and the state's repression of localised resistance. In short, resistance is protest against objective material inequalities and the state's strategy of managing the crisis which stems from these inequalities.

AN HISTORICAL OVERVIEW

Black resistance to domination and exploitation has a long history. The history of South Africa is strewn with interracial wars, rebellions and fragile 'treaties', such as the Frontier wars and the Bambada rebellion. Leatt, Kneifel and Nürnberger trace the first manifestations of organised resistance to the formation of Imbumba Yama Afrika (the Union of Africans) in 1882, the Natal Indian Congress in 1894 and the African People's Organisation in 1902. The central grievances behind the formation of these bodies were the disadvantages experienced by people of colour as a result of their deliberate exclusion from the centres of political and economic power. Exclusion from direct parliamentary representation at the formation of Union in 1910 led to the founding of the African National Congress (ANC) in 1912.

Throughout its history the ANC has undergone a metamorphosis in terms of its policy and practice. This metamorphosis was largely a response to the changing political and moral environment. The early founders of the movement were products of the Christian missionary tradition, and this accounted for the ANC's strategy of attempting to effect change by means of petitions. However, this strategy was futile as the petitions fell on deaf ears. The change from this stance to one of challenge came with the formation of the ANC Youth League in 1944. The Hertzog government had introduced two acts which confirmed that the petition strategy had failed. These were the Native Trust and Land Act and the Representation of the Natives in Parliament Act of 1936. The former reinforced the 14 per cent land ratio whilst the latter dashed any hopes of African political participation by removing them from the Cape voters' roll.

The Youth League introduced a new philosophy and a new strategy into the politics of resistance. It defined the African person as a union of body, mind and spirit – a wholeness derived from his historical striving for complete self-realisation. This rejection of a materialist conception of man found its economic expression in socialism. Its political component was democracy, which was partly an expression of traditional liberal values and partly an existential negation of the oppressed situation in which Africans found themselves. This democratic view found an ally in Christian morality which emphasised the brotherhood of man. Accordingly, the Youth League rejected participation in the Native Representatives Council – a body formed by the government as a substitute for direct political participation – as collaboration with the oppressor. This marked a practical turning point in ANC policy and practice from reactive politics to a pro-active strategy which became the forerunner of the present strategies by extra-parliamentary organisations. The beginning of the pro-active strategy was marked by the Programme of Action. This was partly an outcome of the pressure exerted by the Youth League on the organisation and partly a response to the open racist policies of the Nationalist government which came to power in 1948.

The 1950s were to witness not only mass action but also a close co-operation among the opposition forces. First the ANC organised the Defiance Campaign against unjust laws (1951-1952) and secondly, the historic Freedom Charter was drawn up by the leading resistance organisations in 1955. Among the drafters were the ANC, the Natal Indian Congress, the South African Congress of Trade Unions, the African People's Organisation also known as 'The South African People's Organisation' and the Congress of Democrats. To this date, the Freedom Charter is regarded as the spiritual manifesto for a democratic South Africa by the extra-parliamentary organisations.

The Defiance Campaign and the Freedom Charter temporarily settled strategy issues for the ANC. The breakaway of the Pan Africanist Congress (PAC) from the ANC in 1959 helped to define some basic issues. The ANC had stood by the original definitions: South Africa was a nonracial society and in the struggle for democracy the organisation welcomed all democratic forces. The PAC accepted this nonracial destiny, but argued that it could only come about through a complete overhaul of the existing system, brought about by a black majority government. Africans, according to PAC thinking, were the most oppressed and therefore the ones most interested in the transformation of the existing system. The PAC, drawing from the earlier programme of action, intensified protests against the unjust laws and in 1960 led protest marches in Sharpeville and Langa. In both instances the state's response drew the wrath of the international community. In 1961 the government banned both the ANC and the PAC, thus not only driving them into exile or underground, but also forcing them to engage in an armed struggle. The ANC formed Umkhonto we Sizwe, the underground military wing, whilst the PAC formed Poqo. Both were to become notable guerrilla organisations operating from outside South Africa's borders. Currently the ANC has a significant internal operation, as numerous security court cases have demonstrated.

The 1960s marked the longest lull in the politics of resistance, but were to be punctuated by the emergence of the Black Consciousness Movement at the close of the decade. Black Consciousness had its origins in both the Pan Africanist and the black American political philosophies. However, Black Consciousness went beyond the demands of both black Americans and the earlier ANC. It sought the dismantling of the South African political system instead of inclusion in it. The main purpose of the Black Consciousness Movement was to instil a sense of being and pride in the black man, who was perceived not as a negation of the white norm but as a complete entity with human dignity and worth. Black Consciousness filled the void created by the banning of the ANC and the PAC. It not only provided the resistance movement with continuity with the past, but also formed a link with the future. Without the intervention of Black Consciousness, the present popular resistance organisations and groupings would have taken a different form.

THE PRESENT ENVIRONMENT

The beginning of the seventies witnessed the consolidation of the Black Consciousness Movement as a factor evident in the protests which began in Soweto in July 1976. This resulted in three major developments:

- The schools became the focal point of the struggle.
- The exodus by a number of young people from the country increased the military and ideological power of the African National Congress.
- White South Africans, especially in the private sector and to a lesser extent in the government, came to realise that change was inevitable. The reform process was born out of this realisation.

The eighties were, therefore, to witness a large-scale dialectic between resistance and reform. Spurred on by the successes in the fields of labour (trade unions were legally recognised in 1979, and by 1980 the government had conceded the principle of equal pay for equal work among professionals; the private sector had since 1974 embarked upon a programme of 'black advancement' in industry) and to a lesser extent in education, the 'progressive' opposition groups intensified their campaign for social transformation.

By the early eighties the stage was set for large-scale confrontation. While black people were gaining confidence, the state was involved in a series of 'blunders':

– On the labour front, union strength was increasing at a rapid pace.
– The African National Congress had resurfaced towards the end of the seventies and was making its presence felt in the townships.
– Local government in the African townships was faced with a fiscal crisis and the alienation of the majority of the township residents.
– The establishment of the tricameral parliament convinced Africans that they were to be left permanently in the cold.

The effects of these developments increased both relative deprivation and collective consciousness, especially among African people. The rent crisis in the townships precipitated intensive organisation among the residents, who strongly resisted the proposed rent increases, especially in the face of an economic recession with consequent unemployment. Given the deteriorating situation in the schools, the forces of resistance could join hands against a common enemy. It was, therefore, a combination of predisposing and precipitating factors that created a specific conjuncture which facilitated the 'revolt' in the townships. However, the fact that the conflict spread unevenly and took a long time to manifest itself in other areas needs further explanation. This explanation is to be found in the differences in political culture across the regions.

The South African government has adopted two strategies for containing challenges to inequalities and powerlessness: co-optive and repressive. Within the co-optive strategy, reform and the talk about reform have dominated political and economic statements in the eighties.

By definition, reform is a unilateral response to a dialectical process, or an attempt by those in power to contain challenges to the existing power relations. Conflict arises when there is a dispute over the definition of the status quo. In the South African context, the disadvantaged groups seek a redefinition of the power relations and, inevitably, the settlement needs to be negotiated and cannot be unilaterally imposed. The South African state made two fundamental blunders: by unilaterally defining what constitutes conflict and reform; and by consciously co-opting government sympathisers and redefining them as the leaders of the people.

In this case reform is no more than either an imposition or a mobilisation of bias in favour of the existing social and, therefore, power relations. Following upon the historic strikes of 1973 and the student protest which originated in Soweto 1976, the state concentrated its reform programme on three areas which concerned the African sector of the black disadvantaged. These were labour, education and local government. To accommodate the coloured and Indian sections, two houses of parliament, each responsible for its 'own affairs', were created and located in Cape Town to give them a semblance of efficacy. In spite of the state's wishes, it was these reforms that precipitated a crisis in government, a crisis which both started and sustained the current wave of resistance.

Reforms in local government further deepened the legitimacy crisis which had engulfed African local administration for decades. The removal of control over urban Africans from the Development Boards to newly created local authorities precipitated a fiscal crisis. The new bodies had no independent source of revenue, but were entrusted with the correction of a situation that had been deliberately ignored for too long. They thus resorted to over-taxation in the form of rents and service charges.

Reforms in the sphere of labour resulted in the legal recognition of African trade unions, but the state warned against any 'political involvement' by the unions. In a situation where the politics of production and reproduction are inseparable, this was a clumsy provision which could not withstand the test of reality. The unions soon redefined the power relations.

The schools have been the terrain of the struggle since 1976, and any reforms in education have always fallen far too short of demands. Reforms such as parity in the salaries of 'qualified teachers', pronouncements of free and compulsory education and the upgrading of school facilities have neither eradicated the inequalities in redistribution nor addressed the question of separate and unequal education.

Mapping out the forces of resistance

The analysis that follows focuses mainly on township-based resistance. It excludes the labour movement except where its activities overlap with those of civic and youth organisations. In many instances the coincidence between the politics of production and reproduction makes the overlap inevitable.

In South Africa, the state has created objective material inequalities between black and white, and in turn redefined social relations in terms of these inequalities. It is these social relations which have resulted in the dialectic between resistance and containment. In the eyes of the state, containment entails concessions in the form of co-optation and reform, and in overt repression where resistance is seen to 'threaten law and order'.

To the subordinated people of the townships the existence of objective material inequalities has brought about increased social awareness and an anti-state ideology. Therefore it is the deterioration of material conditions at the local level as well as the pervasive nature of apartheid which precipitated mobilisation.

SOCIAL COMPOSITION AND STRUCTURE

Specific issues in black politics affect both the composition and at times the nature of the resistance movement. For instance, rent issues have been specific to townships controlled by development boards, while education is a common denominator in all townships, including coloured areas. A hike in transport costs, however, could affect a specific region. These specific issues then draw the contours and determine the terrain of resistance in each situation. Besides these ad hoc groupings, issues such as local government in African areas, education and labour have a relative permanence which has greatly affected the nature and duration of organisations that seek transformation within these areas. Given this explanation, resistance groupings therefore fall into a number of broad categories:

1 Youth organisations which are mainly located in educational institutions but which include a significant section of the unemployed youth and some of the youth affiliated to the unions.
2 Civic and community organisations with a cross-cutting membership which may include church, women's, and even youth organisations. Most of the ad hoc groups such as rent, transport and anti-removal organisations fall within this category.
3 Worker and labour organisations mainly located on the factory floor but which are also involved in civic and community issues.
4 Professional and occupational groups sympathetic to and co-operating with civic and national organisations.
5 Institutional groups such as the churches.

In one way or another these organisations are affiliated to or work in a close relationship with regional and national umbrella bodies. The United Democratic Front is a loose conglomerate consisting of various civic, community, youth and labour organisations. The National Forum has the same composition as the United Democratic Front.

In addition, professional and occupational organisations have in many instances co-operated with or supported civic or national extra-parliamentary organisations by organising or acting outside the state-created institutions. Some professional bodies have even directly affiliated to the national umbrella bodies such as the National Forum or the United Democratic Front.

Perhaps not unexpectedly, the youth has occupied the centre of the struggle for political influence. The socio-political nature of black education is largely responsible for this. The post-1976 conjuncture in youth politics has its roots in the philosophy of Black Consciousness. The schools became the focal points because Black Consciousness was active in the educational sphere. Education had come under close scrutiny as the central means by the state of producing servants of apartheid. The fact that Black Consciousness had developed more as a philosophy than a set of political structures, and that it was more active in educational institutions, made the schools an appropriate medium for its transfer. Since Bantu Education was a symbol of oppression and therefore an object of attack, this facilitated mobilisation around the schools.

Colin Bundy advances the following reasons why the schools play an active role in resistance:

"The glaring defects of black education; the very substantial expansion of black schooling over the past couple of decades; the issue of unemployment among black school leavers; and the way in which organisational capacity and experience have transformed consciousness" (cited by Leatt, 1987: 3).

Nzimande and Zulu confirm Bundy's views:

"The late sixties to the early seventies were the years of economic boom in South Africa. Economic growth had demonstrated the need for more skills at an increasing scale. This necessitated an investment in education, particularly in African education. Ironically the increase in numbers in African schools further revealed the contradictions in a racist society. When the recession of the late seventies set in, the Lumpenproletariat was young, better schooled and more politicised. Conservative provisions of the sixties could not contain the consolidated fury of the mid to late seventies" (Nzimande and Zulu, 1987: 2).

The United Democratic Front (UDF) came into being in 1983 mainly in opposition to the government's tricameral plan. This plan accepted coloureds and Indians as junior partners in parliament (the 4:2:1 ratio guaranteed the white majority party in parliament supremacy in decision-making). Moreover, it came into being in opposition to the Koornhof bills which meant further entrenchment of the influx control system.

While these two major developments were crucial in defining the organisational focus of the UDF, the Front further consolidated its work by taking on civic, student, professional, worker and community organisations as affiliates. It therefore situated itself well within local and national politics by defining these within the context and domain of national politics. To this end, the Front has a two-fold strategy organised around immediate local issues; and taking local issues to the national body in order to challenge the state.

In its composition the UDF is both nonracial and has a multiclass character. By the beginning of 1987 there were well over 600 organisations affiliated to the UDF. In terms of geographical distribution, there is a broad representation across the four provinces of the Republic. The Front proposes a two-stage strategy for the transformation of the South African society: national liberation; and socialist transformation.

Both stages are linked to the Freedom Charter which forms the canonical text rather than the constitutional blueprint for the Front. Hence there are varying interpretations of both 'national liberation' and 'socialist transformation'. At best, national liberation can be equated with 'one man, one vote' in a unitary South Africa, whilst the socialist transformation approximates the 'mixed economy' model with an emphasis on equitable distribution. To the popular movements, socialism is more than merely a mode of production. It is an existential state, a way of life and a negation of the oppressive state in which the subordinate groups find themselves. Both the heterodox and multiclass nature of the UDF facilitates these two ideological positions.

The policy of the UDF is to isolate the state from civil constituencies at both the local and national levels. To achieve this, it appeals for national unity among both black and white South Africans on the basis of the Freedom Charter. The main strategy of the UDF is mass conscientisation and mobilisation, especially against the government-created co-optive institutions, both at the national and local levels. The Front has devised strategies for setting up alternative structures such as street committees for the upholding of order in the townships, as well as alternative educational structures in consultation with the National Education Crisis Committee.

Tactically the UDF acts on a broad consultative basis, although in some instances affiliates make local decisions as the situations demand. However, these decisions have to fall within the broad organisational philosophy, policy and strategy of the UDF. While this facilitates the flexibility of the Front in responding to local demands, it at times negates the principle of accountability so that organisationally it may encounter problems of discipline. There are times when affiliates take decisions contrary to the stand of the leadership, or go beyond the limits expected of them. However, in spite of this major shortcoming, especially given the hostility of the state towards extra-parliamentary opposition groupings, the consultative principle has worked at times in very testing situations. The call for pupils to go back to school at the beginning of 1986 is a case in point. Here the UDF in consultation with the National Education Crisis Committee together with other Charterist organisations and individuals took the decision that 'the struggle for a free education' had to be waged on school premises. Further, co-operation between the UDF, the youth and the Congress of South African Trade Unions (COSATU) has resulted in significant stayaways by workers on a national scale at least twice, as well as in a number of well-supported local stayaways. Local and regional consumer boycott campaigns have been organised along the same lines.

While the UDF symbolises the relative success of Congress politics, tactical and at times ideological differences with the National Forum, another popular organisation, have resulted in a partial polarisation within the opposition groupings. At the strategic level, the UDF emphasises the mobilisation of mass action. The National Forum, on the other hand, believes that this strategy is premature. What the Forum advocates is conscientisation before mass action, a stand which is negated by mass activity at the street level. To the Forum, Black Consciousness constitutes a stage of conscientisation. Contrary to the Forum's stand, the UDF believes in a 'broad coalition of progressive forces', hence the adoption of the Freedom Charter as its canonical guideline. In spite of these differences, however, in the eyes of the masses there is a very thin dividing line between the two organisations. In many instances there has been co-operation at the operational level without any consideration of differences in ideology.

THE NATIONAL FORUM AND AZAPO

Black Consciousness organisations are best represented by the National Forum (NF), the main component of which is the Azanian People's Organisation (AZAPO), at least in terms of numbers. Maphai contends that "AZAPO regards itself as both a liberation movement and a political party, and . . . insists on its right of existence, including that of being a potential member of a post-apartheid government" (Maphai, 1987: 1).

The hostility of the state towards extra-parliamentary opposition movements makes it difficult to estimate their true membership. Notwithstanding this, AZAPO, according to Maphai, "claims membership of 98 branches differing in size and spread throughout the country". Further, the organisation ". . . tends to attract only militant people, who are prepared to carry the consequences of being card-carrying members of a political organisation" (Maphai, 1987: 1). Differences between AZAPO and the UDF on the question of future visions for South Africa are subtle. Both subscribe to the two-stage theory of the struggle in which the first stage consists of the fight against apartheid and the second constitutes the struggle against capitalist exploitation. Where AZAPO differs is on its accentuation of the socialist alternative.

A second area of difference lies in attitudes to race. AZAPO believes in the 'unity of the oppressed'. The oppressed are the blacks in South Africa, but 'black' is more of a political than an ethnic connotation. Hence, even though the unity of the oppressed is limited to those who, in the South African political definition, do not vote, it can transcend racial boundaries. AZAPO contends that not all black-skinned people are 'black', but only those who subscribe to the basic principles of ". . . anti-racism, anti-imperialism, anti-sexism and anti-collaboration with the ruling class and all its allies and political instruments" (Maphai, 1987: 6).

Avoiding dependence on white leadership is a medium-term strategy designed to enable blacks to develop self-awareness and pride in their being black. Psychological liberation is a precondition for political liberation. Psychological liberation is essential, particularly because of the dangers posed by white liberalism. White liberals want to dominate the thinking and strategy in the struggle in order to wrest control and use it for their own purposes. The argument here is that white liberals want to benefit from both worlds, that of the oppressor and that of the post-liberation era.

While Black Consciousness castigates white liberals, it equally condemns 'collaborating' blacks and refers to them as 'non whites'. These include the homeland leaders, community councillors, police informers and a wide spectrum of participants in government-created political institutions.

THE CHURCHES

The late seventies have brought changes in the politics of the church. Leatt lists the following reasons for these changes:

- The emergence of mass movements in politics (the UDF and NF), labour (COSATU) and education (the Congress of South African Students (COSAS) and the NECC); as well as the intensity of mass-based struggle on an unprecedented scale.
- The radicalisation of the analysis of the South African problem, using class rather than race.
- The pressure from prophetic agents, individuals and organisations to mobilise the church. Here one thinks of individuals like Tutu, Boesak and Naudé, of ecumenical agencies like the South

African Council of Churches and para-church organs like the Institute for Contextual Theology.

– The development of a liberation theology which has provided the discourse of resistance, both at a sophisticated and a popular level. Here names like Albert Nolan, Buti Thagale and Itumuleng Mosala come to mind (Leatt, 1987: 26).

Leatt traces the changing contours of the church in resistance further and indicates the following important events:

1 The banning of the Christian Institute (CI) marked the end of a phase of resistance in which the dominant paradigm was liberal. Human rights, race relations and non-violence were hallmarks of this phase.

2 In 1978 the World Lutheran Federation declared a 'status confessionis' on apartheid which was later taken up by the Alliance of Black Reformed Churches (ABRECSA) when it declared apartheid a 'sin' and a 'heresy'. This was endorsed by the World Alliance of Reformed Churches in 1982 which suspended the NGK and NHK, marking a decisive theological and ethical rejection of apartheid and a clear call for it to be challenged politically.

3 Ministers and lay people found a vehicle for political expression in the formation of the UDF in 1983. Many leadership positions were filled by clergy, and Boesak and Naudé were made patrons. Other clergy and lay leaders became active in non-UDF resistance movements broadly affiliated with the National Forum. Protest action and political resistance have often been spearheaded by clergy and ecumenical para-church groups. The state's response has hardened over the decade, so that today church leaders such as the Reverend Francois Bill and Father S. Mkhatshwa have spent long periods in detention without trial.

4 On 16 June 1985, 'the call to prayer for an end to unjust rule', more popularly known as the 'call to prayer for the downfall of the government', was published. This document aroused controversy but it also sharpened focus on the unjust regime in a way with which many blacks could identify.

5 The closest thing to a charter for the church in resistance was the

publication of the Kairos Document (KD) in 1986, widely criticised but with widespread support in South African black townships. Its critical question is 'whose side is the church on?' Its analysis criticises the church and state theologies: the church for using 'reconciliation' and 'justice' as an excuse to remain uninvolved and therefore to maintain the status quo, the state for using religion to legitimise a repressive national security state. The KD uses a class analysis (oppressed/oppressor) and urges the church to recognise that divide in itself. The church must come down on the side of the poor and oppressed and oppose the tyranny of the apartheid regime in order to give hope for liberation.

6 The Harare declaration of late 1985 spelt out the implications of the KD for the world church. It called for sanctions, for 16 June to be an international day of prayer for the downfall of the apartheid state, and for solidarity with the victims of apartheid.

7 In May 1987 the Lusaka declaration, sponsored by the World Council of Churches, spelt out the logic of the KD when, for the first time, delegates 'endorsed the right of the oppressed people to take up armed struggle as one of the tactics for ending repression' in South Africa.

8 For years there has been a call for a 'confessing church', modelled on the one that arose in Nazi Germany. Many reasons have been advanced for the fact that there is no such church in South Africa. However, the question has been reopened by the Kairos Document. There is now a move to give confessional and practical unity in resistance some institutional form. This could take the form of a voluntary convenanting synod/assembly of congregations, para-church organisations and groups within churches. It would function parallel to existing institutional structures rather than replace them, and would be grass roots rather than denominational. It could be the most significant development yet in church resistance (Leatt, 1987: 27-28).

Finally, Leatt looks at the different church configurations, from institutional to independent churches, and concludes that institutional churches have problems in this regard.

"From the resistance perspective the role of institutional churches is limited. Their history as a social force shows that they represent too many constituencies, rely too heavily on white support, and carry too many overheads. They cannot clearly side with the poor and oppressed without sacrificing their financial base. It is doubtful whether this tension can be resolved. This is why groups relatively free of institutional baggage will emerge at the cutting edge of the church in resistance. This is not to deny what the main-line 'English language' churches have done and can do at regional synod and national assembly levels" (Leatt, 1987: 28).

However, there have been positive developments at institutional level, for instance ". . . the black Dutch Reformed Churches have challenged the dominant white Afrikaans-language DRC from within the reformed tradition but from a liberation perspective", and "the South African Council of Churches is formally a creature of the institutional churches". On the other hand he states that, although independent churches are viewed as apolitical if not reactionary, they may be a form of resistance as 'churches of the working class' and therefore may be regarded as part of political resistance (Leatt, 1987: 5).

BLACK PROFESSIONAL AND BUSINESS GROUPINGS

Two factors account for the emergence of black professional and business groups:

– The dominance of the state's ideology in traditional professional and business groups. For instance, the role played by the Medical Association in the Biko affair, and the practice of medicine, law and social work outside their political context have prompted the formation of 'alternative concepts' in these professions.
– The fact that the young professionals are products of the Black Consciousness era. Black Consciousness had encouraged black community programmes which located community problems within the political context of South African society.

With the formation of black professional and business associations, the 'alternative concept' has become both an ideological and a practical slogan. Associations which operate within the alternative concept aim at empowering communities to develop their own problem-solving capacities. To achieve this, communities first need to know what the causes of their specific problems are, and secondly the status and role of professional practice need to be demystified. Ordinary people have the capacity to diagnose and work out solutions to their problems provided they operate within a democratic environment and are enabled to work out the alternatives for themselves. This process encompasses not only the imparting of skills but also conscientising consumers of the programmes to their social lot; the nearest approximation is Frere's pedagogy of the oppressed.

At an organisational level, the National Medical and Dental Association (NAMDA), the South African Black Social Workers' Association (SABSWA), the National Association of Democratic Lawyers (NADEL) and the National Educational Union of South Africa (NEUSA), to name a few, fall within this category. They operate within the fields of health, community and welfare, law and education respectively.

Alternative associations operate on the premise that one cannot engage in professional practice or provide services without taking into account the social situation of the consumers or clients. In this context, 'professional neutrality' is equated with rationalising for the maintenance of the status quo which, in many instances, has disadvantaged members of the subordinate groups. For instance, a sound community health practice is impracticable within the contexts of relocations and migratory labour, while a welfare policy which disregards structural unemployment negates the very basis of human dignity. It is, indeed, through the activities of bodies like NAMDA that the lot of children in detention and the consequent repercussions on their health have become topical issues. On the legal side, bodies such as the Legal Resources Centre reflect the thinking that crystallised in the formation of NADEL.

Business groups have entered the resistance scene belatedly and from a different perspective. At first, business groups such as the

National African Federated Chambers of Commerce (NAF-COC), the Black Management Forum (BMF) and the Personnel Practitioners' Association (PPA) started as protective interest groups. Capital viewed these bodies as possible allies and helped practically to finance some of their activities. This was especially the case with NAFCOC and the BMF. However, the pervasive nature of apartheid drives black groups into the resistance camp. The problem with co-optive politics at any level is that co-optation does not remove the basic material disadvantages. Outside the national and regional conferences, black businessmen and professionals are first and foremost defined as non-citizens or as citizens of some disadvantaged homeland. As Kuper states: "Apartheid constitutes political baptism to the African" (Kuper, 1965). Hence NAFCOC, despite its heterogeneous political composition, can still take a stand not to participate in the Nationalist government's proposed Statutory Council, and both the BMF and the PPA seek closer identification with the communities and the independent trade union movement rather than with the capitalist establishment.

TACTICAL ALLIANCES

Despite their heterodox nature, individual resistance organisations share a common anti-state and a relatively anti-racial, anti-capitalist ideology. This common theme facilitates the formation of tactical alliances as issues arise. Thus it is not uncommon for an alliance of convenience between the socialist-oriented youth, workers and small businessmen who constitute the aspirant petty bourgeoisie to be established.

The formation of alliances has been functional to the resistance movement. Such alliances radicalise what otherwise would have remained conservative strata of the community. For instance, the taxi operators in the townships provided alternative transport when commuters boycotted the big transport monopolies. Police reaction to this has been to harass taximen by invoking the various transport codes. This has broadened the base of resistance. The list of 'victims' increases, and with it 'comrades in the struggle' find more common cause for opposition to the status quo.

Such alliances make it difficult for the state to 'smash' the resistance movement as a unit. While it is relatively easy to deal with a single organisation by isolating it, it is more difficult to isolate areas of confluence for purposes of legislating against them. The cross-cutting membership facilitates continuity of operation even in the face of the banning and detention of the leadership in the various groupings.

The formation of tactical alliances has, however, not been without problems. That the various formations within the resistance movement share a common base does not imply a monolithic ideology. There are differences between the exclusive Black Consciousness Movement as represented by AZAPO's 'unity of the oppressed' and the broad coalition of 'progressive anti-apartheid forces' espoused by the United Democratic Front (Maphai, 1987: 5). Such ideological differences have, at times, resulted in outbreaks of violence between the various groupings, despite their anti-state solidarity.

The nature of resistance

While this chapter does not purport to offer any conclusive explanations of the specific regional conflicts, it provides a critical exploration of intricate issues behind the conflict at the national level and offers tentative analysis for further debate.

A critical analysis of actors entails subjecting both their utterances and their activities to a predetermined set of criteria. This set is both subjective and normative since its origins lie within a specific sociology of knowledge and a specific value judgement. In the evaluation of actors within the resistance movement, two important observations need to be made.

Firstly, resistance is by nature a normative exercise against the legal. That is, actors engaged in the resistance movement do so out of a feeling of injustice meted out by a legally constituted system. Thus resistance implies a lack of legitimacy in the legal system and the actors engaged in resistance flourish through this illegitimacy rather than through the approval of the legal system.

By definition, therefore, they cannot be held responsible for long-term strategic plans because resistance is, in the eyes of the ruling system, illegal. This limits the resistance movement's strategic flexibility and in a sense reduces their effort to a struggle to diminish 'atrocities'. Action takes the form of numerous tactical manoeuvres, some of which may be entirely contradictory.

Secondly, the resistance movement is by circumstance a loose coalition of actors caught in a specific existential situation. Unlike a formal party or association, the programme of action developed by the resistance movement is often anticipatory and vague since its main intentions are to mobilise broad support. Having said this, however, one must recognise that individual organisations within the larger movement do have specific 'programmes of action'. In some cases these are rigidly adhered to, even to the extent of limiting tactical flexibility.

In spite of these constraints, the actors are united by, or organised around, a common set of values. These are a philosophical base, policy, strategy and techniques which require a measure of compatibility with the actors' basic values and with one another. A critique of resistance actors within this framework becomes a useful analytical tool.

Philosophical assumptions

Resistance groups assume that the problem in South Africa lies in the oppression and exploitation of black people by whites. They see these two problems as so closely interlinked that they are inseparable. Therefore, to effect changes in one while the other remains intact is to offer palliative rather than effective treatment. Their belief in equality and democracy is probably more a vehicle for protest and self-assertiveness – a negation of their existential experiences under apartheid. More than any other attribute, material inequalities have shaped and moulded the value base of activists. Hence, while they perceive racial domination in state structures they also see racial exploitation in the largely capitalist economic institutions. Resistance's reference to all anti-state and anti-capitalist organisations as 'progressive' has its origins in these perceptions.

To the victims of domination and exploitation, politics and economics are not merely theoretical constructs but have material impact for voteless workers and the unemployed. Notwithstanding their predicament, resistance actors have nonetheless articulated definite visions of the future. These are discussed in turn below. At this point it must be emphasised that these visions are by no means concrete, but are fluid in both content and time. In other words, the resistance movement stresses that the future structure of South African society remains open to negotiation with contributions invited from all sectors of the population. Further, it is agreed that the pace of transformation can only be decided by the people who are part of the struggle, and that this in turn is dependent upon the rate at which people are conscientised and mobilised.

Political visions of the future

If the present offers votelessness, poverty and powerlessness, then the future offers their alternatives. This is demonstrated in the usual retort made by parents when voicing ambitions concerning their children's future: "My child should not be what I am." However, this is the most elementary statement from the least articulate. Resistant groupings offer more sophisticated versions of this fundamental truism. They envisage a 'free, democratic nonracial South Africa' where skin colour is not an issue. If, as the reformists would argue, this is idealistic and difficult to attain, it reflects the extent to which the existential anguish under apartheid creates and nourishes 'illusions' within the subordinate sector of the population. It is, however, an 'illusion' with a reality calculated in terms of human lives and suffering. The number of people who cross the country's borders, get detained and imprisoned and risk their lives in street encounters with the police bear testimony to the seriousness of the 'illusion'.

Nor are the 'philosophers' without a cognitive map of the path to the 'luminary vision'. They feel that the government should:

"Renounce all violence against the people" by removing the army and the "political police" from the townships.

Free all political prisoners, release detainees, allow exiles to return and remove restrictions on freedom so as to facilitate a free political process to enable canvassing of political opinions. This will constitute the first stage to full political participation by the people.

"Call a national convention of the representatives of the people to draw up a programme and establish the mode for the transfer of power to the people" (extracts from group discussions with Youth and Worker Groupings).

To most resistance actors the state faces a legitimacy crisis in which ". . . the minority rules through brutal coercion on the pretext of legality". But this 'legality' does not reflect 'the wishes of the people'. Rather it rests on power relations as represented by the might of the state. The alternative future is best represented in the Freedom Charter – 'a people's document' which places sovereignty with the individual and not with the group.

Contrary to 'bourgeois liberal values', most actors in the resistance movement are not impressed by such documents as a Bill of Rights. Objections to such a Bill of Rights focus on two counts:

"The emphasis on the group rather than on the individual."

Suspicion and mistrust. As one actor observed: "For centuries we have been oppressed, exploited and downtrodden both as individuals and as a people. Now that whites fear the day of reckoning we hear all this moralistic nonsense. It's another attempt to maintain power" (group discussions, op. cit.).

It could well be that most groups have not thought through the future in detail. Most of them refute this allegation, though, and retort: "Let the people decide what is best for them." Their stand is that they are only catalysts – "The struggle is mainly facilitative, the people shall decide" (ibid.).

Economic visions of the future

These visions can best be summed up by the adage that "the grass is always greener on the other side". The existential reality under apartheid and capitalism compels its victims to denounce the system that relegates them to perpetual minority status. Resistance organisations perceive the world as a place for all to inhabit; hence the land and all material extractions from it belong to all the people. Individual accumulation is thus both exploitative and undesirable. This immediately discredits the free enterprise system, especially the version practised in South Africa which many see as 'an uneven race'. In this regard the Freedom Charter has become both a spiritual inspiration and a political programme.

Experiences of inequality have discredited capitalism and it is largely on this variable that socialism has found its best promoter. However, the socialist option, like its political corollary, democracy, is not fully articulated. Details for its implementation will be sorted out by 'the people'. In spite of this, the actors have expressed strong support for:

- Nationalisation of the major industries or a significant portion of them.
- Equality of opportunity in access to training and work as well as to rewards.
- A more equitable redistribution of the country's resources, i.e. land and profits.
- Free access by all to the state's social security systems including medical services and social welfare.

A significant number of the professionals and the older people within the resistance movements favour a mixed economy, particularly one on the Scandinavian model. When confronted by the shortcomings of socialism, such as the stifling of production and its lack of success elsewhere in Africa, they challenge the basis of these assertions. In the first instance, they argue that what constitutes productivity is a subjective and ideological concept. In spite of the high productivity in oil and gold, only a few of the Arab emirs and the South African 'Oppenheimers' have benefited. There are instances where a fall or drop in standards should be encouraged if this will benefit the majority of the people. The 'poor track record' of socialism in Africa fails to enlist sympathy for capitalism, given the glaring inequalities within the workplace as well as the structural inequalities in the living space. Further, most actors blame international and particularly American imperialism for impoverishing the so-called 'third world' countries:

- Colonialists did not train the indigenous people; when they suddenly left they created a skills vacuum.
- The continuing exploitation of resources by the Western capitalist countries is keeping Africa in a state of dependency and perpetual debt.
- State socialism as practised in some African countries is not socialism. It only benefits a few at the top.
- South Africa has plenty of resources and boasts of having the most developed black sector in the whole continent. Drawing parallels with the rest of Africa is therefore a political exercise (group discussions, op. cit.).

Educational visions of the future

The resistance movement believes that education should reflect the existential situation of the people. In this sense black pupils and students have begun to evaluate critically their current and future roles in society and the manner in which the education system is preparing them to fulfil those roles. While the Bantu Education Act of 1953 was designed to reinforce passive acceptance among blacks of perpetual servitude in a racist capitalist society, it was the deteriorating material conditions including education in the townships that produced generations of increasingly radicalised pupils and students. It was the youth who not only redefined their own role in society but articulated new visions of a post-apartheid society, that is an equal and nonracial democratic society. As Lulu Johnson, president of the now banned Congress of South African

Students (COSAS), reminds us, the education system is inextricably intertwined with the process of "preparing ourselves and building a future South Africa where representation will be genuine and democratic" (Leatt, 1987: 5). The current crisis in education is thus not about resistance to enlightenment, literacy or information but resistance to the underlying philosophy of a politically planned education system, and at the crux of the crisis is the political economy of South Africa.

In terms of future visions, 'people's education' and its corollary, 'people's power', have emerged. They emphasise full participation in all social structures. Implicit in this is the belief that education cannot be isolated from the broader struggle for liberation. Thus during 1985, for example, COSAS appealed to pupils to "organise and unite . . . and to link our struggles around education with the struggle of the workers, women, community and youth so as to make a positive contribution to the people's struggle for a national liberation and genuine democracy in South Africa" (Leatt, 1987: 22).

In practical terms 'people's education' currently functions at two levels; that is, the building of democratic organs of people's power; and the development of an alternative infrastructure. The first has been partially successful through the establishment of pupil, teacher and parent committees at individual schools in some regions and the formation of regional committees and the National Education Crisis Committee (NECC) as a national representative organisation at the helm of this democratic structure. This latter body has been instrumental in co-ordinating meetings and conventions and initiating negotiations with the government. At a second level the NECC has enlisted the aid of different parties, such as employer groups, trade unions and universities, to develop an alternative curriculum. State repression has hindered progress at this level however, and black educationists concede that a new education system demands the implementation of a long-term strategy.

Black education has become for both the state and the people a scene of reform and resistance. The strategic logic of the reformists seeks the creation of black institutions capable of producing a black

150

'buffer' class. However, while the government is busy creating the illusion of a nonracial meritocracy through education by, for example, increasing the budget allocations to black education, increasing black pupil enrolment, raising the school-leaving age and improving teacher qualifications, its fundamental policy remains separate and racial under white domination.

While the resistance movement has painted a broad picture of an ideal South African society, the real essence of their vision is participation in the structures that will actually mould that society. Thus, both implicit and explicit in their pronouncements are the concepts of negotiation, flexibility and moderation in attaining these goals. Particularly noteworthy is the fact that radical strategies for transformation, including confrontation, do not receive prominence. Instead, the future vision is seen as being based on consensus negotiation. For example, although the free enterprise system is widely condemned, this is not to say that the nationalisation of industry is advocated dogmatically. In fact it is freely acknowledged that the lack of skills shared by blacks would make a mockery of attempts to nationalise industry. Pragmatism is further illustrated by the fact that resistance movements uphold the sanctity of property at an individual level – complete abolition of private property is rejected. Further pragmatism is displayed in the implementation of 'people's education' and in a consideration of its practical limitations.

For its part the state is trying to weave a path through the crisis. It remains, however, one step behind the demands of the resistance movement. For example, the state's attempts at addressing the deteriorating material conditions in the townships fail to take cognisance of the demands for meaningful political participation.

Policy, strategy and tactics

Given the fact that black resistance is supported by a philosophy of equality in the face of oppression and exploitation, the pertinent question to ask at this point is how, or more specifically by what methods, does the resistance movement envisage achieving their

151

vision of equality? In this context an analysis of the policies, strategies and tactics of the resistance movement is pertinent. Such an analysis must establish whether or not these methods are consistent with the resistance movement's vision of the future. However, any analysis based on these attributes should take into account the 'process' nature of resistance. This entails not only a shift in strategies and tactics but also a constant evaluation of the basic premises themselves. The resistance movement defines the social situation as the terrain on which the battle for control and resistance is waged.

All resistance groups share one cardinal attribute on policy: non-co-operation with the government and therefore, nonparticipation in government-created institutions. This principle is so central that it has led to the 'necklacing' of collaborators and the so-called 'black on black violence', that is, violence directed against those who operate in government structures on the pretext that they are the people's elected leaders. It should be emphasised that 'necklacing' was in the first place a reaction to the violence unleashed by the state against the people, and that 'collaborators' were seen as representatives of the state. This is particularly true of the post-1976 context.

Throughout the country the resistance movement has employed a wide range of 'non-co-operation' strategies including commuter, consumer, rent, community council election and education boycotts, and work-stayaways and strikes. These strategies are mainly tools for bargaining and have been conceptualised as part of an 'unfolding process' whereby people are conscientised and mobilised and simply made aware of the fact that they have control over their own lives, or that they have been used to force the state or an aspect of the state to the negotiating table.

Consumer boycotts have been instrumental, for example, in forcing chambers of commerce to apply pressure on the government. While the politicisation of nearly every aspect of society has been inherent in this process, interestingly so too has the healthy promotion of debate and discussion about the future vision of society. Most importantly, these tendencies have resulted in co-operation between a wide range of disparate groups and have led to an

152

on-going critical evaluation and clarification of strategic objectives.

Nowhere is this more obvious than in the case of education where pupil and student groups, trade unions, parents' associations, and various national organisations such as the UDF, AZAPO and CO-SATU have repeatedly worked together to steer a path through the evolving crisis, and where strategic shifts have been based on self-analysis and realistic assessments of state power. With regard to this latter point one need only be reminded that the Soweto Parents' Crisis Committee (SPCC) was instrumental in negotiating a return to school under the banner 'Education for Liberation' at a time when pupils were willing to forego their education and were advocating 'Liberation Now, Education Later'.

The resistance movement taken as a whole should not be viewed as working towards a predetermined model of society within a specific time frame. Detailed and specific agendas are regarded as 'premature' when many people remain to be conscientised and mobilised. For example, Father Mkhatshwa, during his address to the National Consultative Conference on the Crisis in Education conference, stressed that a national democratic society needs to be organised. This, he added, means consciousness-raising, mobilising people and organising or consolidating these forces (Mkhatshwa, 1985: 7). Thus in evaluating the strategic logic of the resistance movement, careful attention must be given to the success of the resistance organisations with regard to these three closely interrelated elements.

The formation of the UDF provides an excellent opportunity to evaluate the overall success of the process of conscientising, mobilising and consolidating resistance forces. The formation of the UDF can be traced to the spirit of resistance revived by the Black Consciousness Movement in the early 1970s. Essentially, Black Consciousness was concerned with fostering self-pride in black people and encouraging them to reject the notions of second-class status imposed on them. In many respects Black Consciousness was an educational process which made black people aware of the conditions that oppressed them and the means by which these could be overcome. Most importantly, however, Black Consciousness instilled the necessary confidence to tackle state oppression. Consequently, when 17 Black Consciousness affiliates were banned in October 1977 national activists went 'underground' and began to address local community issues such as rent, housing and transport. Within 18 months of the bannings civic organisations were forming throughout the country. For the communities themselves the most important gain from mobilisation was political conscientisation. Specifically, this meant an understanding that local issues are inextricably linked to the wider structures of society. With this fresh insight these community organisations soon coalesced into a purposive mass-based movement under the auspices of the UDF. The impetus for the formation of the UDF was the government's constitutional plan to draw coloureds and Indians into an alliance with whites, compounded by the introduction of the three 'Koornhof bills' (Piet Koornhof was then minister for Co-operation and Development) to strengthen controls over the process of African urbanisation. The UDF emerged in response as a heterogeneous umbrella body of affiliates, each retaining its identity under a single banner but co-operating with other groups on common interests. The UDF's strategy is characterised by the politics of refusal which tactically relies on protests, boycotts, civil disobedience, obstructionism, support for disinvestment and sanctions and limited political confrontation.

In the post-Black Consciousness era the most powerful strategy for conscientising and mobilising people has undoubtedly been the emergence of what might be termed 'micro-committees', for example pupil, parent and teacher committees at schools, street committees, and worker committees at factories. The influence of these 'micro-committees' should not be underestimated. Street committees, for example, offer alternatives to the township authorities imposed on people by the government and have been instrumental in introducing the concept of democracy. Further, they have enabled people to distinguish between 'right and wrong' as opposed to 'legal and illegal' and have been useful in eradicating petty crime in the poorly policed townships.

In the analysis of resistance strategies and policies, cognisance must be taken of the fact that these are by no means limited to

154

discriminated and exploited groups such as the youth and workers. On the contrary, both the black middle class and whites have been identified as potential allies in the struggle and singled out despite their having largely escaped the exploitation and discrimination under Nationalist rule. Economic sanctions, disinvestment and cultural and sporting boycotts have been deployed to motivate a wider cross section of participation in the struggle for change. While the resistance movement acknowledges that no section of society is immune to sanctions, it argues that whites will suffer disproportionately and be forced to align themselves with the oppressed. Any argument that blacks will suffer undue hardship is rejected as a non-issue in the face of existing material conditions of dire deprivation in which they already live.

Finally, strategy is determined by practical considerations. For example, 'people's education' was conceptualised within the existing infrastructure because an alternative infrastructure would be too costly. At this point in the analysis it is expedient to examine the various tactics employed by the resistance movement to assess their compatibility with the movement's future vision and strategies.

Tactics, while calculated to aid plans, are largely spontaneous. Consequently it is difficult to make evaluative pronouncements based on conventional logic. 'Moment actions' of the resistance movement are typically situated at street level. Nonetheless, for evaluative purposes resistance tactics can be classified into the following functional categories:

– Operationalising policies and strategies.
– Ensuring that strategies are effected as planned.
– Mobilising wider support.
– Expressing protest.

Essentially, tactics are dictated by policy and strategy. Where, for instance, the broad policy has been 'nonparticipation' in government-created institutions, resistance groupings have mobilised individuals into boycotting and coerced incumbents in official institutions into resignation. For example, community councillors in the Eastern Cape have either been forced to resign *en bloc* or leave their respective townships. Likewise, Soweto councillors spent the whole of 1986 living away from their homes.

Similarly, tactics ensure that the machinery of the resistance movement functions; that is, that plans are carried out. Occasionally tactics have assumed violent modus operandi to thwart dissent. For example, the slogan 'Liberation Now, Education Later' coincided with the destruction of schools in some townships. This was expedient in that the absence of school buildings would render futile any calls for a return to school by government 'collaborators'. Similar tactics have been applied in the cases of consumer boycotts, where people's purchases have been confiscated; work-stayaways, where buses ferrying commuters have been stoned; and transport boycotts, where public transport has been destroyed.

The boycott tactic is the principal means by which support is mobilised. For example, the 'sympathy strikes' in support of the Vaal Triangle, where pupils did not sit for the 1984 year-end examinations, mushroomed from community-based educational organisations to culminate in the formation of the NECC 15 months later. Likewise, labour organisations have used 'sympathy strikes' to forge alliances. Here consumers have boycotted the products of companies locked in disputes with unions, thus mobilising support for the labour movement.

Finally, it should be noted that tactics converge not only as expressions of protest, but also as attempts at reconstruction. In this role they emerge largely as reactions to specific fuse situations in the political system. Although tactics range from peaceful demonstrations to violent outbursts, the nature of each reaction hardly reflects the intensity of the fuse situation, nor would it necessarily be repeated under similar circumstances.

Critique

CONSCIENTISATION AND MOBILISATION

Developments inside the country demonstrate that the resistance movement has achieved a number of critical successes. This is evidenced not only by the proliferation of grass-roots organisations, but also by the quality of the debate which has developed under the auspices of these organisations about the structure of a future South African society. Thus conscientisation and mass mobilisation augurs well for providing the people with the experience and theoretical insights needed to cope with the momentous task of transforming the institutional structures of society.

Discussions and debate about the future have not been confined to the resistance movement. Business lobbies, religious groups and even white professional associations have begun to rethink their positions, as the pilgrimages across the Zambezi testify. The private sector has shifted its stance somewhat and has made positive shifts in addressing the material conditions in the townships (housing, education and general community welfare) under the rubric of corporate social responsibility.

PRECIPITATING A LEGITIMACY CRISIS IN GOVERNMENT

Faced with large-scale resistance, the government has embarked on a reform programme. It has expanded its alliances to include the coloured and Indian groups, has attempted to address the material conditions in the townships, and has eroded petty apartheid. Concomitantly, the National Party has reinforced its commitment to security with a range of draconian laws to crush dissent.

ISOLATING SOUTH AFRICA INTERNATIONALLY

The resistance movement has achieved more in eliciting international sympathy for the oppressed in South Africa than has been the case with the so-called 'forces of moderation', for example high-profile homeland leaders, multinational corporations and white political parties.

STRATEGIES AND TACTICS: A REVIEW

While acknowledging these successes, there are nonetheless a number of shortcomings in the strategies and tactics adopted by the resistance movement. These fall into two distinct categories: conceptual issues; and alienation problems. The former is located at the level of strategy and the latter at the level of tactics.

To what extent can the resistance movement rely on drawing both the white population and the black middle class into the struggle? The security platform on which the recent 'whites-only' election was fought, the high poll, and the subsequent results of the election suggest that few whites have been attracted to the struggle. While the government maintains control over the major socialisation institutions, that is the media and the schools, there appears little prospect of the resistance movement being able to conscientise the white sector. As regards the black middle class, Khoza (1987) concludes that the only difference between the economic and political visions of this class and the status quo is in the racial component of power and sharing.

Given that the resistance movement envisages that South Africa's future should be determined by negotiation, it is clear that the removal of apartheid is not equated with equality, because the removal of apartheid will not eradicate exploitation. This point is acknowledged by the actors themselves in such statements as: "The removal of apartheid will not change the ownership of the mines by Oppenheimer." But the abolition of apartheid does not require negotiation – the legislative vestiges are either removed or they are not. What the resistance movement appears to be arguing therefore, is that their future vision will be negotiated *after* the abolition of apartheid. However, the presence of a large upwardly mobile black middle class ushered in with the abolition of apartheid would certainly reduce the possibility of further social transformation to, say, socialism.

However, the black middle class is not that large in relation to the population as a whole, and the existence of the middle class does not necessarily equal anti-socialism. For instance, a large section of the middle class is located within the civil service, for example teachers, nurses and clerks. These segments have nothing to lose in the transformation to socialism.

A related issue, especially in considering the form of resistance beyond apartheid, is that the resistance movement is primarily a loose coalition at a specific conjuncture with often little more than anti-racism holding it together. Maphai (1987: 41) warns us: "As soon as ideological cleavages become marked the resistance movement will disintegrate." At this point it is also relevant to question whether the large informal settlements on the periphery of formal townships, particularly in the homelands, comprise a politically literate or illiterate force. If this group is unconscientised, then its susceptibility to co-optation by the state in return for material rewards poses a potential problem. Vigilante activity in the Durban region, for example, suggests that this problem has already arisen to some extent. The notion of 'disintegration' is, however, questionable since it is not only ideology that binds people together, but their material conditions as well.

To sum up, the resistance movement's visions are threatened on three fronts: by the presence of a black middle class; by the absence of ideological clarity; and by the presence of a large population which remains unconscientised and vulnerable to co-optation by the state.

Alienation problems

In the final analysis the success or failure of the resistance movement will ultimately depend upon its choice of tactics. In this regard the negative costs of the tactics deployed to date cannot lightly be dismissed. For the purpose of assessment these costs can be categorised into two divisions: political and social. While all the negative actions by the resistance movement will incur some degree of political cost in terms of alienation, the divisions used here are largely a function of scale. The former refer to actions that have prompted mobilisation against the resistance movement, while the latter refer to actions that invoke a loss of sympathy for the movement.

Political costs

In some instances the politics of co-optation and boycott have polarised communities into warring factions; for example, Inkatha and the UDF in Natal and the *witdoeke* and 'comrades' in the Eastern and Western Cape and Soweto. These are costs which have weighed heavily against the resistance movement. On the part of the state and the extension of the state apparatus in the form of co-optive politics, the determination to 'smash' resistance is inevitable. Where the resistance movement blundered was in its poor organisation as well as in its inability to anticipate the possible options that a determined state could take. For instance, poor organisation on the part of the resistance movement in some areas resulted in the adoption of coercive measures such as the stoning of buses to enforce a boycott or the confiscation of goods purchased from boycotted shops. The state had a ready force in the police and the vigilantes to deal with 'crime', and by criminalising all protest behaviour, the protester had been redefined as a criminal. It was thus relatively easy for the state to elicit a measure of sympathy, and to channel vigilante activity away from the prevention of crime to dealing with 'rioters' and 'destroyers' as the state-controlled media so readily referred to protest action.

At another level some have argued that nonparticipation in government-created institutions has enabled the less capable to occupy critical positions in public life. A good example here is the Natal Indian Congress's boycott of the House of Delegates. Similarly, noncollaboration effectively means that any common ground remains undefined, which thus restricts strategic options. Furthermore, tactics such as the cultural boycott limit the diffusion of ideas and options. Admittedly, the state refuses to negotiate with the leadership from outside its own institutions because of their sophistication and ability to see through its smoke screen. In reality the state does not intend to negotiate, since by defining what is negotiable it maintains its position of power.

A number of organisations within the resistance movement are committed to 'ideological purity', for example, AZAPO, the National Forum, the New Unity Movement and the Cape Action League. This commitment is, in some instances, at the expense of tactical flexibility. The state has not been slow in picking this up and in many instances has been able to cast the actors in a negative light. For example, AZAPO's picketing of United States Senator Kennedy was justified on the grounds that he is a representative of imperial power. However, the picketing damaged AZAPO's relationship with the South African Council of Churches (SACC) – Kennedy was Bishop Tutu's official guest – which is one of AZA-

PO's funders. The situation was well exploited by the government-controlled media and, particularly in the absence of police action against the demonstrators, AZAPO was to some extent discredited.

Other tactics have also played into the hands of the state, for example, rendering the townships 'ungovernable'. As Zwelakhe Sisulu has cautioned, there is an important distinction between 'ungovernability' and 'people's power'. In a situation of ungovernability there is a power vacuum which can only be filled by an organised and disciplined force. In this instance we should not confuse "coercion, the use of force against the community, with people's power, the collective strength of the people" (Sisulu, 1986). Likewise, the school boycott raised logistic and communications problems for pupils who were no longer afforded the cover of school buildings in which to conduct meetings and plan further strategies.

Social costs

The use of violence to thwart dissent, for example the stoning of buses ferrying commuters during work stayaways, has undoubtedly contributed to some loss of sympathy for the resistance movement. In the face of government and business intransigence, stayaways, labour strikes and consumer boycotts frequently precipitate further material hardships among the poor. The position of 'victor' and 'victim' becomes blurred when the tactics employed increase anguish and suffering. Workers forced to strike for no economic gains lose income; shoppers forced to boycott must alter their shopping habits and patterns at their own expense and inconvenience; and commuters denied access to public transport incur various costs such as longer periods away from home and increased transport costs where alternative transport does not have access to direct routes. Similarly, the destruction of public property by acts of political violence results in the loss of facilities, given the government's reluctance to rebuild damaged property in some townships.

The resistance movement appears to be conscious of the implications of its strategies and tactics and in the end it must make its own evaluation. Violence is, of course, the most contentious tactic and any evaluation of its use must consider the question of legitimacy.

While coercion can legitimately override people's autonomy where 'free riders' reap the benefits of collective action while avoiding the private costs, under these circumstances the problem then becomes one of striking a balance between the use of coercion and seeking a mandate for every decision. One thing is clear, however: the resistance movement is willing to make sacrifices in the name of the struggle, and this is a prime motive behind many of their 'moment actions'.

Conclusion

The normative base for resistance is the desire to transform society. By implication the new society should be free of the existing inequities. In the South African context this means a 'democratic, nonracial society' where resources will be 'equitably distributed' and people will have 'control over their own lives'. This forms the bottom line for the resistance groups.

An examination of the resistance movement in terms of the above three values will serve to show whether the normative goal is possible. This necessitates an evaluation of the groupings in terms of their pronouncements and actions.

PRONOUNCEMENTS

Resistance groupings are trapped in a predicament which often defines their values. In most instances their values reflect the opposite of their existential anguish and imply a negation of the state which they hold responsible for their plight. 'Democracy and non-racialism' thus become the opposite of 'racial oppression'; 'equitable redistribution' negates 'exploitation and poverty', and 'control over our own lives' implies that at present people are denied this control. In a way this reflects the existential helplessness in which resistance groupings find themselves, whilst their actions demonstrate their determination to escape from their situation.

If their pronouncements represent the idealistic aspect of the resistance groups, their actions reflect the pragmatic. Caught between massive state power and popular aspirations, their actions are 'moment actions' designed to achieve the possible. In most instances they engage in activities that the state either frowns upon or defines as 'illegal' at any moment. In this respect the element of secrecy in their actions is not compatible with democratic practice. Harassed by the state, by the vigilantes and by 'unknown' assailants, they lack room for manoeuvre.

In spite of this, certain of their actions merit consideration. Firstly, resistance groups mobilise around an issue rather than an ideology. This gives a measure of flexibility to the individual actors and in turn allows for decentralisation of the leadership. This heterodox formation promotes negotiation on common issues. However, the same formation can be a source of conflict, since subscribing to an issue and not an ideology entails the right to dissent on other issues. To achieve unity, activists resort to coercion on dissenting actors in spite of their alliances on other issues. Also, the practice of violence against opponents of the resistance movement does not augur well for democracy, although it must be admitted that the violence meted out by the state against the opposition has produced counter-violence.

A critical assessment of a constituency that enjoys a relative measure of unhindered operation will demonstrate the extent of democratisation within the resistance movement. Trade unions function with relative tolerance from the state. The accountability of the leadership to the membership, the practice of holding ballots to decide on strike action and the constant report-back meetings offer promise for the future. Further, the entry of unions into community issues will inject a measure of debating skills and will consequently democratise popular organisations. The negotiation over issues such as stayaways and boycotts has amply demonstrated that this possibility exists.

At a popular level, structures like the NECC have been saddled with the task not only of acting as protest vehicles, but also of drawing up an alternative curriculum. This takes protest action beyond rhetoric and introduces an element of reconstruction.

5 The incrementalists

ANN BERNSTEIN AND BOBBY GODSELL

Introduction: incrementalism –
a category of logic, not a collective actor

Conflict in South Africa is often conceptualised as a head-on collision between 'black' and 'white' political interests. Such a concept perpetuates the essential apartheid perceptions that political
interests are determined by race, and that these racially defined
interests are necessarily and inevitably in conflict with each other.
Alternatively, conflict in South Africa is presented as a dichot-
omous clash between a monolithic status quo and those who seek
change.

Both these views seriously distort the nature of conflict in South
Africa. South African society is clearly in a state of transition. The
issue is not change versus continuity but rather how change is to be
brought about. An earlier chapter has depicted a South African
government committed to what it would describe as 'controlled
reform'. The two chapters on resistance groups paint a picture of a
diversity of actors committed to a fundamental transformation of
South African society. These groups are pursuing strategies which
include armed struggle, popular mobilisation, protest and international pressure in the form of moral censure, boycotts, and especially the prevention of normal economic exchange between
South African and world markets.

This chapter will look at a further diversity of actors – Inkatha,
the Labour Party, the Progressive Federal Party and business.
These are four very different groups with positions in society
which differ widely and with potential constituencies which vary
greatly in size, class and composition. Nevertheless, they share a
number of common values, interpretations and attitudes to change
in South Africa. We would argue that they are all operating within
what can be called a common strategic logic, that of incrementalism.

All four of these actors share a common way of thinking about change in South Africa. Their values and their attitudes towards the status quo, to the process of transition, and to the nature of the future society coincide sufficiently to classify them (broadly) together. The four groups do not think alike on all matters, however. Nor do they have common policies. In practice they have only acted together, or in concert, on individual issues at disparate times. Open animosity exists between some of the groups, most notably between the Labour Party and Inkatha, but also at times between the Labour Party and the Progressive Federal Party.

What are the four groups' common values and attitudes?

Firstly, they reject the present apartheid policy, structured as it is on the basis of legislatively enshrined race discrimination concerning matters ranging from the franchise to social, economic and cultural affairs.

Secondly, they reject revolution as the best way of changing the present situation. On the one hand they argue that a successful armed struggle is not likely to succeed in South Africa, and that its costs in terms of human life and destruction of the existing social, physical and institutional infrastructure will be enormous. On the other hand they envisage that change brought about by violence will undermine the chances of a future society being prosperous, democratic, relatively peaceful and free of race discrimination. In essence these approaches reverse the dictum that the end justifies the means and argue that the means help to determine the end. In other words, the way in which South Africa changes away from apartheid will influence the nature of the future society.

The third belief that all four actors share concerns what has been called by Chief Buthelezi the 'multistrategy' approach to change. There is an explicit acknowledgement that change will not be brought about from one source alone. Change is already taking place in many arenas, and in many different ways. No claim is made that the particular chosen route of any of the South African actors is the only way in which change can be effected. On the contrary, there is a recognition of the need for many different actors and approaches to try to 'normalise' South Africa from whatever base they can.

The fourth shared attitude is the recognition of the enormous power of the existing state and the immense resources available to the South African government to maintain control by force, and to take punitive action against any or all of the groups that try to defy its dictates in one way or another.

The fifth point is that there is also a shared recognition that change in South Africa requires economic growth as one of the essential motors for increased deracialisation and the continuing development of the society. This, combined with their attitude to revolutionary change, leads to strong opposition to disinvestment from South Africa by foreign firms and to sanctions, although not to foreign pressure of other kinds.

The sixth shared viewpoint is that there is an explicit recognition that participation in state-created institutions or structures is a tactical question and not a principle applicable to all situations, and that this participation or engagement needs to be assessed for each particular situation, and thus reassessed at regular intervals.

The seventh point indicates that these actors do not see apartheid and capitalism as synonymous. They envisage a future society located somewhere on a wide spectrum ranging from a 'free market' approach to some form of social democracy, with or without a commitment to 'African socialism'.

The eighth common attitude is a commitment to the rights of the individual, the rule of law and civil rights, based essentially on liberal values. Across the board there is a belief that the best form of protecting and institutionalising these rights, besides the franchise, is a bill of rights to be enforced by an independent judiciary.

The ninth shared belief concerns a commitment to negotiation as the best means for resolving South Africa's conflict. All four of these actors are committed in one way or another to a negotiated settlement in the country, based on some form of democracy.

The tenth shared attitude can best be described as a common opposition to what could be called 'protest politics'. Protest politics use dramatic events and generally involve mass mobilisation instead of ongoing institutional or other activities to oppose a particular law or act.

Finally, all four share a common attitude to white people. They accept the responsibility and contribution, or potential contribution, of whites in the struggle for a nondiscriminatory society as well as their place and necessary role in that future society.

In a sense this group of incrementalists operates on the basis of a society in transition, with an outcome which is not inevitable or predetermined. They function from a base of consciously articulated strategies which perceive change as a sequential process and not a mechanical one. It is a pragmatic and cautious approach to social change, but one which is cognisant of human fallibility and ignorance. It proceeds in a step-by-step fashion in order to minimise the human costs of transition as much as possible.

There are other actors in South Africa working as democratically as they can, who are prepared to engage in negotiation with authorities about major issues and thus in effect are also working for incremental change in the country. These include many trade unions and bodies such as the National Education Crisis Committee and other civic and community organisations. These groups would see themselves fitting in more comfortably to what we have termed in this project the resistance groups. They would differentiate themselves from the incrementalists by arguing that they do not participate in state-created political institutions and that they support disinvestment because that is one of the few ways open to black South Africans and the outside world to put pressure on the South African government. They are often openly committed to a socialist political economy for the future or at least to a social-democratic system. They support 'protest politics' and mass mobilisation – often seemingly as an end in itself, and also sometimes regardless of the consequences that could follow from state reaction to that mass mobilisation. However, despite these differences, the fact remains that these actors are involved in the process of peaceful change in South Africa, based on a commitment and willingness to negotiate with the relevant authorities, which inevitably involves them in a process of incremental changes to the status quo.

We do not contend therefore that the four groups described in this chapter are the only incrementalists at work in South Africa. They are used here as examples of the kind of strategic logic and arguments for action which confront those engaging the system from what could be called an essentially incrementalist value base.

This chapter is divided into two sections. In the first we will describe the four actors, who they are, what their vision of the future is, and what strategies they have for getting there. In the second section we will raise and explore some strategic questions for incrementalists in general and for each actor individually.

The actors described

THE BUSINESS COMMUNITY

The nature of business

How can one accurately delineate 'business' in South Africa? 'The business community', 'capital', 'the private sector', 'free enterprise' are all descriptive terms which are either inadequate or misleading, or both. 'Business' is not a 'community' in any conventional use of that word. 'Capital' can describe only a part of business, unless a crude conspiratorial conception of the role of the boardroom in the total life of business is employed. 'The private sector' describes more than those who refer to 'business' usually intend (organised and unorganised labour, the 'informal sector', non-profit organisations, etc.). 'Free enterprise' denotes an economic philosophy rather than a set of social institutions.

For the purposes of this chapter it seems possible to talk about 'business' in at least three specific and useful ways: organised industry and commerce, private sector foundations and large corporations.

Industry and commerce in South Africa are both extensively organised and highly fragmented. Four national bodies exist:

- The Federated Chamber of Industries (FCI).
- Association of Chambers of Commerce and Industry (ASSOCOM).
- The Afrikaanse Handelsinstituut (AHI).
- The National African Chamber of Commerce and Industry (NAFCOC).

In addition, a multiplicity of industry-specific bodies exist, amongst the most significant of which are the Chamber of Mines (COM), the Steel and Engineering Industries Federation of South Africa (SEIFSA), the Building Industries Federation of South Africa (BIFSA) and the South African Agricultural Union (SAAU). Contact and co-operation between these national and industrial associations are sporadic and issue-specific.

There are a number of private sector foundations. The two major ones are the Urban Foundation, which was established by a coalition of business and community leaders in the wake of the 1976 Soweto unrest, and the older South Africa Foundation. The initial purpose of the Urban Foundation was to engage in project work to improve the urban environment of black South Africans. More recently it has redefined its mission. It now encompasses not only development projects to improve the quality of life in urban communities, but also engages in efforts to seek the transformation of structures and policies which promote discrimination in South African society. The South Africa Foundation was set up in 1960 in the wake of Sharpeville, in an attempt to combat international isolation and to improve South Africa's international relations. Again, in more recent times, the South Africa Foundation has become active in domestic lobbying, seeking a more rapid pace for change, as well as promoting a more objective understanding of South Africa abroad.

The South African economy is characterised by a considerable concentration of its private capital resources. The economy has seen the growth of a number of conglomerate groups, which the central importance of the mining industry has tended to promote.[1]

These conglomerates have acquired at least the appearance of considerable economic, social and political power, making their leadership important actors on the national stage.

Perhaps the unity of purpose which is most frequently attributed to business is that of its common economic interests. A good contemporary example of such attribution is found in Anthony Sampson's recent book *Black and Gold: Tycoons, Revolutionaries and Apartheid*. In this book Sampson (speaking for many) suggests, in the words of one reviewer, that "international capital" has sustained apartheid because it saw in it "a mechanism for securing cheap and compliant labour" (Simon Jenkins, *Times Literary Supplement*, 3 April 1987). Other commentators assume that a common set of political interests flows axiomatically from a shared profit motive, or from the more classically derived class interests of those who stand in an ownership relation to the means of production. What is common to such approaches is the premise that business has the power to end apartheid, but that it does not do so, because apartheid is really in the economic interests of business.

Merle Lipton (1985) has argued that this premise firstly fails to accommodate either conflicting interests within 'capital' (for example mining versus agriculture, mining versus manufacturing), or interests which change over a period of time; secondly that it acknowledges neither the manifest political opposition of large divisions of business (for example the Anglo American Corporation) to government policies over decades, nor the impotence of this opposition. David Yudelman (1983) has argued that capital/state relations in modern societies are essentially symbiotic, involving profoundly shared interests (production) and often significantly conflicting interests (legitimation). Whilst this debate cannot be pursued here, the questions it raises are important for assessing the strength of 'business', as well as for seeking to understand business visions and strategies.

The future vision of business

Whilst the business community lacks the organisational unity of a political movement, and therefore the capacity to spell out a future vision in a single document or speech, certain common themes characterise the necessarily more diverse perceptions of a post-apartheid society. Different members of the business community usually agree that South Africa must move towards a nonracial democracy, in which group identity would be based on voluntary association. The concept of democracy – most extensively described in the Federated Chamber of Industry's Charter of Social, Economic and Political Rights – is clearly liberal and pluralist. Predictably, business spokesmen envisage a market-oriented economic system, but there is widespread acceptance of the need for state intervention to redistribute wealth and address past deprivations.[2] There is general unanimity on the necessity for a process of negotiation to occur, but there are a diversity of opinions concerning what the preconditions for such negotiations are. Further diversity exists when consideration is given to the range of black leadership which it will be necessary to invite to the negotiation table, and the precise conditions of those negotiations.

Business strategies

A series of strategies pursued by the business community can be described.

Firstly, business has tried to change or influence government policies in a wide range of broadly political areas. The means of achieving these changes have most often been via 'behind the scenes' lobbying efforts. One example of an early success was the sudden scrapping of the Masters and Servants Act, apparently brought about at the urging of coal tycoon Graham Beck who convinced Prime Minister John Vorster of the dangers of United States union action in boycotting coal imports from South Africa. The repeal of job reservation and the extension of state-recognised union rights to blacks is another area where business attitudes and efforts promoted a highly significant change. The repeal of the influx control laws provides perhaps both the clearest and most significant example yet of successful business lobbying. Business involvement in the campaign to abolish the pass laws required a more comprehensive and co-ordinated strategy than had been used previously. This campaign included intensive research work, businessmen seminars, media briefings, visits to particular cities and informal settlements and extensive interaction with key politicians and officials. The activities centred on the Urban Foundation, which played a key leadership and co-ordination role.[3]

However, the track record of business as a lobby is replete with many defeats and stalemates. For example, repeated calls from business for the government to release political prisoners (especially Nelson Mandela), restore the rule of law, unban political organisations and to commence negotiations have fallen on deaf ears.

Secondly, business has itself been part of creating a post-apartheid society through the evolving labour relations process. Labour/management contact has had its share of conflict, nevertheless in important ways the factory, mine and office have emerged as beachheads of apartheid-free South Africa, where racism has been banished, power shared, and a new normative order and set of decision making processes and institutions have emerged. There is currently some indication that both the ambit and the agenda of the labour relations process is being extended to encompass the world beyond the factory gate. Some broader political issues such as the sanctions debate, the tensions which both gave rise to and are engendered by the current State of Emergency and pension fund investment are now being addressed.

Thirdly, through the economic resources which it can command, business has been able to participate directly in social change. Government attitudes towards urban housing policy (changes which were important preconditions for the scrapping of the pass laws) were very significantly influenced by the low-cost, self-help housing projects undertaken by the Urban Foundation. Equally important innovation in nonracial education has been significantly promoted by corporate grants and involvement.

A recent area of business activity concerns the establishment of the Private Sector Council on Urbanisation in November 1985. The Council comprises the six national employer organisations (FCI, ASSOCOM, SEIFSA, AHI, NAFCOC and the Chamber of Mines), the Urban Foundation and prominent individuals, both black and white. Its aims are twofold. The first is to establish coordinated private sector proposals for a new urbanisation strategy for South Africa. This work will encompass a reassessment of the full spectrum of policies that comprise the apartheid policy at present. Secondly, the Council is designed to forge an alliance for change with the business sector as the first and central buildingblock. It remains to be seen whether this Council can make good its stated goals.

Finally, another area of strategic initiative has been formed by the efforts of business organisations and individuals to facilitate the political process, and in particular to promote black/white negotiation. Examples of such initiatives include the joint statement issued by FCI, ASSOCOM, AHI, NAFCOC, SEIFSA and COM during Edward Kennedy's 1985 visit to South Africa, the FCI Business Charter and the visit of businessmen led by Gavin Relly to confer with the ANC in Zambia. Such initiatives have not had South African political actors as their only target, and South African business groups have played an active, if unsuccessful, part in the sanctions debate in the West. They have often mediated between South Africa and her black-governed neighbours.

It is too early to evaluate the efficacy of business in this last strategic role, i.e. the role of political facilitator. Certainly, in recent times, business forays into politics have increasingly produced angry responses from government,[4] whilst there is little evidence of business influence on black political groups, especially the ANC.[5] The outcome of the 1987 white election may also be seen as a rebuff to the call for faster reform or for the commencement of negotiations.

INKATHA

The nature of Inkatha

In 1975, Mangosuthu Buthelezi, who was head of the regional government, revived and reformed the Inkatha movement which was first created by Zulu king Solomon kaDinizulu in 1928. The name of the movement was changed to Inkatha Yenkululeko Ye Sizwe, and the organisation now characterises itself as a national liberation movement which seeks support from all black South Africans.

In 1987 the Inkatha movement claimed a mass membership of 1,3 million, organised in some 3 000 branches across the country. These branches comprise three 'wings' of the organisation: Inkatha itself (about 400 000 members), the Women's Brigade (about 405 000 members), and the Youth Brigade (about 500 000 members). The 3 000 branches are grouped into constituency and then regional formations. Supreme authority is vested in the Annual General Conference. The Conference consists of two delegates from each branch, the Central Committee, executive committees of the Women's and Youth Brigades, and representatives from other affiliated organisations. It elects Inkatha's president, and some members of the Central Committee, and it also determines the movement's basic policy direction. When the Conference is not in session, the movement is governed by the 101-member Central Committee. The Women's and Youth Brigades have an internal structure which essentially mirrors that of the movement itself.

Inkatha describes itself as a national liberation movement. But to what extent is it more than a Zulu movement? Inkatha membership records do not note the ethnic identity of members. The leadership believes that more than half its total membership is non-Zulu, but this is probably exaggerated.[6] Considerable efforts have been made to go beyond the boundaries of Zulu culture, with key speeches being regularly translated into Sotho as well as Zulu, and concepts such as *Ubuntu* (humaneness) being used in their Zulu/Sotho form (*Ubuntu/Botho*). However, a central Zulu character continues to be evident in the character of the national leadership, the close identity of the movement with the KwaZulu regional government, and the venue of national meetings, which is most often Ulundi, KwaZulu's capital town. Opinion poll evidence would also suggest a distinct regional and therefore ethnic character to Inkatha's support.[7]

The class base of Inkatha's membership is seen by the leaders as a combination of workers and peasants.[8] Inkatha's leaders have sought to make a virtue of this class base, contrasting it with the leadership of other black organisations, which is often criticised as elitist. Inkatha, in contrast, believes "in the wisdom of the ordinary black worker . . . in Inkatha . . . we believe that the ordinary black workers and peasants are kings as far as the struggle is concerned".[9] At times this contrasting class base appears to have been given a violent context, as in the clash between migrant workers and the more settled 'bourgeois' residents of the Lamontville township.

A further important characteristic is the movement's symbiotic relationship with the KwaZulu regional government. Though formally distinct, the extensive overlap of key leadership[10] has led to the perception of a very close relationship between the two. It has also given rise to accusations of coercive recruitment techniques in which civil service jobs and regional government controlled forms of patronage have, it is alleged, been used to force KwaZulu residents into membership. These allegations are forcefully denied by the movement itself.

Together with the allegations of coercive recruitment, Inkatha's opponents have accused it of brutal behaviour, linking the movement to vigilante violence against UDF supporters. The movement has vigorously rejected these charges, and litigation has ensued from both sides. Objective adjudication of one important incident – attacks on the delegates at the second National Education Crisis Committee – was obstructed when the Natal Bench of the Supreme Court ruled that a juristic person could not be defamed. While guilt or innocence cannot be established with any confidence, it is clear that both Inkatha supporters and Inkatha opponents have been victims of violence in recent times.

The most contested aspect of Inkatha is the degree of popular political support it enjoys amongst black South Africans. This too is a question currently incapable of definitive resolution: how is popular support to be assessed in the absence of democratic institutions to measure popular will? In the geographic domain of the KwaZulu regional government, Inkatha fought an election (in 1978) and won handsomely with a degree of electoral participation which indicates solid support in these areas. Apart from this election, Inkatha's support has been assessed by a diverse range of opinion polls. Yet measuring 'support' for political leaders and/or 'organisations' amongst people who have never had the opportunity to participate in the election of political representatives in national institutions is at best only roughly indicative, and at worst meaningless. Asking voters whom they intend voting for in a particular election is asking for the prediction of a concrete and known act. Asking nonvoters whom they 'support' out of a galaxy of prison martyrs, protest leaders, articulators of popular anger and politicians renders much less precise results. A careful analysis of competing polls over the last ten years reveals significant fluidity and important inconsistencies.[11] Outside of democratic institutions, support for policies and personalities do not have to be reconciled, and diverse and at times contradictory allegiances do not have to be put to the ultimate test. At the end of the day, all that can be said with confidence on this subject, paraphrasing the words of political analyst and Buthelezi critic Tom Lodge (1983: 352) is that Inkatha is (at least) an important regional participant which must play a role in South Africa's political development for the foreseeable future.[12]

Inkatha's future vision

Inkatha's vision for a future South Africa can be briefly stated as a united, nonracial, democratic society with a mixed-market economy.

The Inkatha movement has consistently made it clear that while it supports participation in KwaZulu, it views the homeland as a regional government within a united territory, contained within its historic boundaries (i.e. before balkanisation through the Bantustan policy). Inkatha's commitment to nonracialism allows for the role which group identity might play in the future political process, but only on the basis of voluntary association. This was made clear in its evidence to the Buthelezi Commission, and by the Inkatha position in the KwaNatal Indaba. Inkatha's concept of democracy is clearly that of a pluralist or liberal democracy.[13] The movement's economic policy is characterised by a qualified endorsement of capitalism. As Buthelezi has noted:

"There is a great deal in me which is formed by my deep affinity to African humanism – *Ubuntu/Botho* – and I find many aspects of Western industrialised societies offensive to my humanist tendencies. But I do seek that which works, and I do not believe that mankind has discovered anything more efficient than the free enterprise system with which to translate the very dirt of our soil into wealth" (Buthelezi, 1986c).

Inkatha's Statement of Belief contains clear references to wealth redistribution and state support for and protection of the poor, as well as the accommodation of private economic production.[14]

176

Inkatha's strategies

Inkatha has embraced a variety of strategies.

In the first instance, Inkatha has developed what might be described as beachheads or bases of institutional and membership resources. Thus the KwaZulu regional government has provided both resources and a measure of insulation from central government action. Buthelezi has advanced three reasons for his participation in homeland structures: firstly, people live in the homelands and require government and government services; secondly, by taking possession of this government-created structure Buthelezi claims that he has been able to frustrate government ideology by his refusal to accept independence; thirdly, KwaZulu gives Buthelezi a base from which to develop the politics of negotiation rather than merely engage in 'protest politics'. Co-option, Buthelezi seems to be arguing, can work both ways (Cadman and Godsell, 1987: 6-7).

Secondly, Buthelezi has often advocated the politics of mass mobilisation, using the power which blacks have in South African society through their economic muscle as workers and consumers. The strategic use of labour power has become complicated for Inkatha since the development of conflict between the labour federation, COSATU, and Inkatha. There has been only one instance of Inkatha's application of consumer power. This was by means of a boycott of brown bread in protest at a price hike. The boycott appeared to be successful as the price increase was withdrawn.

A third sphere of strategy can be described as alliance politics, or the politics of negotiation. Buthelezi has sought to build alliances within 'black' politics by means of the establishment of the South African Black Alliance (SABA), and more broadly, the Convention Alliance. SABA was severely damaged by the decision of the Labour Party to participate in the tricameral parliament, and the Convention Movement foundered on the rock of UDF/ANC opposition. Inkatha has been more successful in initiating instances of negotiation politics through the multiracial Buthelezi Commission, and the KwaZulu Indaba. Both provided nonracial alternatives to the policies of the present government.

Inkatha has rejected the strategy of armed conflict with the

South African state. The rejection is both principled and pragmatic:

"You cannot create a decent modern society through violence. Increased violence will result in increased polarisation and will reach such magnitudes that it will take generations to overcome its aftermath . . ." (Buthelezi, 1986a).

"I reject violence . . . because the logistics of succeeding are mindboggling" (Buthelezi, 1986b).

And, in acknowledging that the time for violence might arrive:

"You can be quite sure that I would never (commit you to violence) unless there was nothing else to do. You can be absolutely assured that I will not send you into the front line to be massacred in insane, harebrained tactics and strategies which must fail" (Buthelezi, 1985).

THE PROGRESSIVE FEDERAL PARTY

The nature of the PFP

The PFP had its origins in the decision of a group of United Party rebels to leave that party in 1959 to establish a liberal alternative opposition party to the National Party government. For the ensuing 15 years the PFP was engaged in a grim battle for survival – survival as an organisation, and the survival of liberal values in the South African political debate. During this period Helen Suzman alone was able to retain her seat in the white parliament. She became a liberal Joan of Arc, representing nonracial, liberal and democratic values on almost every issue of public contention. Her commitment to civil liberty led her to champion the rights of popular black nationalist leaders such as Nelson Mandela and Robert Sobukwe. This, and her consistent and forthright opposition to every detail of apartheid legislation, has won her widespread recognition from black South Africans.

From 1974, when five more Progressive Party candidates gained seats in parliament, to 1977 the party was engaged in a battle to destroy the United Party (UP) and to replace it as the major vehicle for white opposition to the government. During this period the Progressives merged twice with UP dissidents and so became the Progressive Federal Party. The party altered its political style more than its central values or policies in this process.[15]

In the 1977 election the PFP won 24 seats, becoming the largest single opposition party in the white parliament. In the 1981 election they increased their representation to 27. In the 1983 referendum on a new constitution which would give racially defined parliamentary representation to 'coloured' and Asian South Africans, but not blacks, and would give limited political rights within a racist framework, the party suffered a major setback when perhaps as much as two-thirds of its voter base ignored its call to vote 'no'. A further severe setback was suffered in the 1987 general election when the party saw its representation drop from 27 to 19, and its share of the popular vote from 17 to 14 per cent.

The political image of the PFP is that of an upper class English liberal party, despite the fact that two of the party's three national leaders have been Afrikaners, and that Afrikaans-speaking South Africans have significant representation in the PFP's parliamentary caucus. The voter base of the party, however, broadly supports this image. In the most recent election it was apparent that the party's stronghold continues to exist in upper-class and upper middle-class predominantly English areas. The PFP attempt to take over the role which the United Party played for decades as a vehicle for lower middle-class and working-class English-speaking South Africans has clearly failed, as is indicated in the results of the 6 May 1987 election.[16]

The PFP's future vision

The PFP's vision of a post-apartheid South Africa can, along with those of the incrementalists previously discussed, be summarised by the phrase 'nonracial democracy'. Party policy provides for universal suffrage within consociational institutions and a geographic federation achieved through a national convention involving all South African political groups. While race might continue to influence political allegiance, it would do so on the basis of voluntary association. Racial barriers to public life and public facilities would be prohibited. Finally the rights of individuals and groups would be protected by an extrenched Bill of Rights.

The economic policies of the PFP are vague, and resemble the social democracy of Britain's present day Liberal Party more than the market oriented policies of the liberal parties of Europe.

PFP strategies

PFP strategies have changed over a period of time. In the first 15 years its general strategy was simply its own survival and that of the liberal values it espoused. From the middle seventies the PFP was engaged in a battle to become the major white alternative to the National Party, but after the 1982 right-wing breakaway from the National Party, the PFP has sought to design a 'balance of power' role for itself. Since Colin Eglin's resumption of the PFP leadership in early 1986 the party has striven to develop what it terms 'alliance politics'. In the 1987 general election this took the form of an election pact with the New Republic Party (NRP) – the remainder of the United Party – and an informal agreement not to oppose or attack the three 'new Nationalist' independents who fought National Party seats in this election. The election results were a great setback to this strategy. NRP support moved almost entirely into the National Party camp. The PFP itself lost significantly to the National Party. On the right of the government the young Conservative Party emerged with twice the popular vote and slightly more seats than the PFP,[17] thus replacing it as the major white alternative to the NP. The three independent 'new Nationalists' did much better than the PFP, winning one of the three seats they contested, coming extremely close to winning a second seat (losing by only 39 votes), and doing well in a third. It is too early to see the full significance of the 1987 election results. The National Party fought the election under the slogan 'Reform Yes, Surrender No'. They attacked the PFP as being pro-ANC and soft on security. In a country in a State of Emergency, with landmine and bomb explosions occurring with increasing frequency, these attacks clearly paid off.

One way of interpreting the results is to say that on the scale of

'Less Reform', 'Reform At The Present Pace' and 'More Rapid Reform', three out of ten whites chose less reform or no reform, five chose reform at the present pace, and a little fewer than two out of ten opted for more rapid reform. However, perhaps a more accurate presentation would be to see white choices in terms of a reform/security equation with three out of ten wanting more security and less reform, a little more than five accepting the present balance, and a little fewer than two wanting more reform and less stress on security policies.

THE LABOUR PARTY

The nature of the Labour Party

The Labour Party was established in 1965 by a group of 'coloured' South Africans. These politicians rejected apartheid and the ethnic political compartmentalisation which was its inevitable consequence. However, in the previous year the National Party government had established a 'Coloured Persons Representative Council', and the Labour Party determined to prevent pro-government elements from gaining control of this council. Instead, they set out to win control themselves, something they were only able to do in 1975, despite winning 65 per cent of the elected seats in the council in 1969 (government appointees blocked control until the party won an outright majority of all council seats). The Labour Party used this council to protest apartheid policies by obstructing budgets and generating pressure for direct nonracial representation. When the 1983 constitution offered 'coloured' South Africans direct but racially structured representation, the Labour Party decided to participate in the new tricameral parliament. It won 76 of the 80 elected seats, and 74 per cent of the popular vote, thus becoming the 'governing' party in the coloured chamber. The party's leader, Allan Hendrickse, accepted a seat in the national cabinet as a minister without portfolio, which he has since resigned.

The Labour Party claims a paid-up membership of over 100 000.[18] Both its membership and its voter base (201 000 votes in the 1984 general election) are characterised as working class. The party is said to enjoy greater support in rural areas (Zille, 1986: 2).

Party membership is formally open to all races, but is over-whelmingly 'coloured'. Membership is organised into branches, which in turn are grouped into regions. The party's annual conference elects a national leader and sets policy. When the conference is not sitting, the party is governed by its National Executive Committee.

The Labour Party's future vision

The Labour Party's visions of a post-apartheid South Africa are non-racial in the sense that they clearly reject racial prescription in public life and support universal suffrage in nonracial political institutions. The Labour Party accepts that race may well influence a future political process, although on the basis of voluntary association:

"David Curry, the party's former national chairman, argues that it is a fact of South African politics that the majority of individuals define their political fears and aspirations on a 'race' or 'group' basis (despite popular rhetoric) and that 'all leaders, including politicians, use their particular race or group as bases from which to operate'" (Zille, 1986: 6).

The Labour Party envisages a democratic future in a liberal or pluralist tradition.[19]

The Labour Party's economic vision has changed significantly in recent years, from what could be described as a form of democratic socialism, with policy provision for the nationalisation of the mines, to a mild form of social democracy, or in its own terms a social market economy:

"That is, an economic system where government as well as the private sector respect the principles of a market economy but temper these with a properly balanced sense of social responsibility" (Hendrickse quoted in Zille, 1986: 11).

Labour Party strategies

The Labour Party's decision to enter the state-created and racially structured Coloured Persons Representative Council in 1969 may be compared with Buthelezi's decision to participate in the Kwa-Zulu Territorial Authority a year later. In one sense it was a defensive move to prevent National Party supporters from gaining control of the body. It also provided the Labour Party with at least a platform, if not a base. Eventually the Labour Party seemed to exhaust the possibilities of this platform, and was essentially responsible for its demise.

The party's decision to enter the tricameral parliament (inaugurated in 1984) created a major breach between itself and Inkatha, the two key members of the South African Black Alliance. It also strained relations between the Labour Party and the PFP. By becoming the governing party in the 'coloured' chamber, and even more so because of Hendrickse's cabinet membership, they have been accused of becoming 'junior partners in apartheid'. The party has defended its move as strategic in nature:

"We are determined not to repeat the mistakes and follies of the past,[20] a cardinal one among them being transforming the tactic of boycott into an iron principle that makes it impossible to act politically and therefore leads to a political death. Boycott is a strategy, not a principle. A good general does not put all his eggs in one basket. We are not politically strong enough to destroy the system by merely staying outside. We have to politicise our community not only by protest politics. It is we, the coloured people, who will make or break this new deal. If our going in will merely be used as come-into-my-parlour-said-the-spider-to-the-fly politics, then we shall take the necessary steps. The National Party is no longer that strong granite wall. From our political experience we have learned that political shrewdness is not the sole prerogative of white minds" (Curry quoted in Zille, 1986: 10).

What has been the experience of 'strategic participation' since 1984?

The party has claimed some victories, such as the repeal of the Mixed Marriages Act, the repeal of influx control, and the lifting of the coloured labour preference policy with regard to the Western Cape. In other areas, notably in the lifting of the Group Areas Act

183

and the inclusion of black leaders and organisations in a process of negotiation, the party has failed.

Would they have achieved more from the outside? The Party has certainly paid a price for its participation. Carter Ibrahim, for example, as the 'coloured' minister of Education, has found himself on the other side of youth protest, having to act as school policeman and apparently alienating large sections of the community by his actions. Allan Hendrickse, as a cabinet member, has been implicated in key security decisions, such as the South African Defence Force raids on Lusaka, Harare and Gaberone in May 1985, and the imposition of both the first and second States of Emergency.

The Labour Party has tried to combine protest and participation by 'sitting in' on the whites-only parliamentary dining room, and swimming on whites-only beaches. The latter act brought a harsh rebuke from P.W. Botha, followed by what some have viewed (though not necessarily fairly) as an 'abject' apology from Hendrickse. The dilemma has been how to combine a strategy which seeks to exercise influence over national policy 'from within' whilst holding a set of values significantly at odds with those of the national government. We shall return to this dilemma in the final section of this chapter.

The future course of Labour Party politics is uncertain. The National Party's desire to postpone the constitutionally required 1989 white election has been chosen by the Labour Party as its first definitive opportunity to block the National Party. Allan Hendrickse's attempt to use this power to 'horse trade' forced him out of the cabinet. This may produce more dynamic compromises within the tricameral system. Alternatively it could hasten its demise.

Some questions for the incrementalists

In evaluating the strategic logic of incrementalism, it is important to bear two things in mind. Firstly, most individuals and many organisations do not operate with a clearly developed strategic plan in front of them, as a rally driver follows his route map. Most of us

184

react more often than we act, and follow our instincts more often than we engage in a cost/benefit analysis, or often simply do what seems either possible or obvious.

This observation is not intended to devalue the process of strategic review, which is the very purpose of this exercise, but rather to suggest the need to combine this form of reflection with the exigencies of the real world.

The second observation is that South Africa is a land of distinctly limited strategic opportunity. A racial caste system has shaped the experience, fashioned the values, and informed the actions of generations of black and white South Africans. The single philosophy of one ruling group has prevailed for almost four decades. This has produced a political landscape which is barren in the strategic sense. It has also produced a political culture of powerlessness, in which it often seems that all that is available to those in opposition is moral purity and righteous anger.

Bearing these political restrictions in mind, how are the incrementalists to be viewed in the context of the realities of contemporary South Africa?

The overriding question facing the incrementalists as a group, and as individual actors, is: *How should South Africa be changed to move it away from apartheid and towards a nonracial democratic society?*

In rejecting the status quo and the dominant institutions of that status quo, political activists have two basic choices. The first is to advocate revolution and the various tactics whereby one encourages some form of revolutionary and thus (in the South African context) necessarily violent change. The second is to advocate peaceful change, which would encourage incremental but fundamental alteration to the present situation. In particular the extremely limited role for black involvement in the political process, particularly at national level, must be addressed.

The actors described in this chapter have all chosen the non-revolutionary route of change. Having made that basic choice, important questions must then follow. Strategic and tactical issues must be resolved, whether directly or implicitly. Within the framework of what we are describing as incrementalist strategic logic, one can try to assess effectiveness, or at least pose questions and raise issues that challenge the incrementalist actor from within his own paradigm.

In the next section we raise some broad thematic concerns which are relevant to those acting within the general framework of incrementalist strategic logic. Having done that, we pose what we think are critical questions for business and then for the three political parties.

GENERAL CONCERNS

Two themes are explored in the incrementalist approach to the process of change. The first theme concerns the method of change; the second concerns the elevation of tactics of change into principles.

METHOD OF CHANGE

If revolution is rejected, then it is important to define alternative avenues for change. Incrementalist actors need to couple their twin rejection of both the status quo and of armed struggle with vocal and thoughtful answers as to what other means of political change are available to both black and white actors. Additionally, restrictions on such alternative avenues need to be identified and opposed.

Incrementalists need to identify their reasons for rejecting the armed struggle or violence. Revolutionary change can be rejected in principle (as imposing too great a cost, or what is more, producing outcomes likely to be worse than the present), or for pragmatic reasons (because such tactics will not work). Whilst the actors can choose either or both of these reasons for being incrementalists, it is important that they be clear about their choice. A pragmatic rejection of change by means of armed struggle produces a different set of attitudes towards revolutionary violence than does the principled rejection of revolutionary change. Those operating between these positions run the risk of sending out unclear signals on choices which are vital in societies which are experiencing high levels of violent conflict. For example, government allegations that the PFP favoured an alliance with the ANC cost the PFP support and seats in the last election. An alliance with the ANC is not sought by the PFP, and would make no sense for as long as these two actors remain committed to fundamentally opposed strategic principles. The danger is always that of a false dichotomy. Because the ANC is committed to a strategy of revolutionary change by means of an armed struggle, and because incrementalists reject such a strategy, this does not mean that the ANC does not exist. Nor does it mean that the ANC should be denied access to the political process. Indeed it is just such a denial that is now used to justify violence as a last resort. A similar false dichotomy occurs in incrementalist attitudes towards state coercion. A distinction can be drawn between a rejection of the armed struggle, and an affirmation of mass political organisation. This seems essential if incrementalists are going to resist emotional solidarities with a coercive government or a revolutionary resistance.

For many people, opposition to revolution is based on considerations other than a simple resistance to violence. Revolution implies the sweeping aside of the old order and its replacement with a totally new kind of society. Incrementalists on the other hand, do not envision a comprehensive replacement of the status quo. In examining South Africa's existing social, economic and infrastructural base, they differentiate between positive and negative elements. For example, they would argue that there are certain institutions and practices in present-day South Africa which should be maintained and strengthened in the transition to a nonracial order. Here one could refer to South Africa's press, its independent judiciary and the trade union movement, all of which are severely constrained but are nonetheless comparatively freer and more independent than elsewhere in Africa and many other parts of the developing world. One of the problems in the selective categorisation of the status quo is that incrementalists can often be misunderstood. This misunderstanding arises in connection with precisely what they are rejecting in the status quo, and in what they are advocating for the future. Incrementalists will minimise misunderstanding by having and stating their concept of a nondiscriminatory future society which will build on South Africa's present strengths and help the country to deal with its enormous political and developmental challenges. This vision of a future society must contain political, economic and social aspects, and it must indicate how the envisaged market-based system will provide the best available mechanisms and opportunities for all South Africans to share in the economic wealth and development of a growing nation, *and* have the greatest chance of producing and ensuring a democracy.

The incrementalists' alternative approach to change is process oriented and based on a perception of South Africans negotiating their own futures. In this context, one can ask whether some of the actors examined now placed sufficient emphasis on the preconditions necessary for such a negotiation process to begin and to have some chance of success? One of the important prerequisites for such negotiation concerns the existence of organisations with strong leaders and mobilised constituencies, on whose behalf those leaders can effectively negotiate. In this area one has to ask whether business and the Labour Party with their sometimes implicitly supportive, sometimes ambivalent, attitudes towards the present State of Emergency, have thought through the consequences of arbitrary security action against black community leadership? Can such action be reconciled with a commitment to negotiation?

Incrementalists are committed to a multifaceted approach to the change process in South Africa. For some this is a tactic, because they can see no single actor working for change which is sufficiently powerful to be able to bring about such transformation on its own. For others, a commitment in line with Buthelezi's multistrategy approach, embodies a principle of social change. That principle is rooted in a view of the ends-means dichotomy, and it is argued that the nature of change in South Africa will fundamentally influence its future. Either way, the commitment to a multistrategy approach excludes the domination of any one actor or organisation in the struggle against apartheid, and this is an important point of difference between the incrementalists and the other actors. This commitment to a multistrategy approach raises three questions of interest.

The first is in fact a paradox. There can be little doubt that a unified black and white coalition of all the interest groups opposed to apartheid could hasten the demise of such a system if skilfully used. However, if change were to be brought about in this fashion – in a sense by a denial and postponement of all differences until apartheid is abolished – it is questionable whether the society that replaces the present one would have much tolerance for differences or for competing claims to articulate 'the people's voice'. The response to this paradox need not result in the encouragement of a multitude of relatively ineffectual independent participants with ensuing confusion of opposed voices. Incrementalists can work for tactical alliances on selected issues between otherwise autonomous and independent agencies. Alliances can be structured in such a way as to strengthen rather than undermine the participating organisations.

A second question is based on this reality of a great many diverse groups competing with and contributing to the process of transition in South Africa at present. This query concerns the suitability of certain types of action. Have incrementalists given sufficient consideration to the effects which their actions and political choices have on the other actors striving for nonviolent change? A relevant example concerns the unexpected support which many people in the business community gave to the introduction of the tricameral constitution, against the express wishes of Inkatha and the PFP.

A third related question concerns leadership. A multistrategy approach to change requires a complex and unusual kind of leadership which combines the courage to speak out in an often hostile environment with the strength to share that leadership role with others. How successfully have business, Inkatha, the Labour Party and the PFP met both aspects of this challenge?

PARTICIPATION

One of the defining characteristics of the incrementalist group has been their willingness to negotiate within the system and to participate in state-created political and other institutions. Other actors who have adopted a boycott position, which is essentially related to nonparticipation in any establishment-created political institution, initiative or group, have been attacked for this view by the incrementalists. It is argued that the boycott response has been elevated

189

into a principle rather than a strategy. However, this argument can be reversed and we would ask whether the incrementalists are not themselves susceptible to being caught in the same trap. Their tactic of participation has often been accorded the status of a principle and has not been treated as a strategic response which must be assessed and reassessed in the light of events, and particularly of the experience gained in the process of participating.

Participation often provides a means of mobilising a constituency more effectively than non-participation. It provides opportunities to influence events in strategic arenas of action. However, it can also become a trap, and organisations that decide to participate in order to change the status quo can be drawn into sustaining the present order rather than undermining it. The question of participation needs to be handled with considerable tactical skill. Some examples will illustrate the complexity of the terrain.

How does the KwaZulu government administer a pension system on the basis of financial allocations decided by the central government? These funds are hopelessly inadequate to meet the needs, and have been allocated on a racially discriminatory basis. The KwaZulu regional government is the author of neither poverty nor racial maldistribution, but as the dispenser of state pensions it appears to be the agent of both.

Opponents of racial domination can only use participation as an effective tool towards a nonracial society if they engage in the present system on the basis of clearly defined values with a political programme of their own. Participation without such an agenda for change, whether in the tricameral parliament, the Economic Advisory Committee or the Joint Management Committees, will be most likely to lead to collusion and co-option. Participation will always have costs and benefits. These need to be identified and carefully weighed before any particular act or process of engagement is embarked upon. The mere act of participating will have consequences, and these will in time affect the cost/benefit calculation. Therefore, an essential component of a strategy for change incorporating participation must include a regular and critical process of review.

The business sector is increasingly being called upon to play a political role in South Africa. This demand comes from many parts of society as well as from within the business commmunity itself. The calls range from government demands on the private sector for financial contributions to the socio-economic aspects of its reform programme to demands from black actors for business to take a stand and publicly identify with a nonracial future. The common error in many of these demands from both Right and Left is for both sides to see business as a unified category. The government tends to consider the private sector as an entity somehow akin to the public sector. Those to the left, whether international commentators or local activists, tend to regard business as being more akin to a political party. The fact of the matter is that business, unlike the other three actors which we have examined in this chapter, is not a political group, party or movement. That fact is a key element in assessing the potential political contribution of business to the South African conflict. The central strategic question for businessmen and business organisations is: How can the business sector continue to perform its essential function of 'business' of producing goods and services and yet simultaneously contribute significantly to the process of political change?

Often, business has seen its role in terms of a quiet, lobbying function. The success of such a strategy has depended on the prevailing political climate, on access to the government and on skills in performing this lobbying function. However, there are other ways in which business can contribute meaningfully to change. The business sector has access to significant resources, and this is what makes it a potentially critical actor in South Africa's process of transition. Has business used its human, financial and other resources to maximum effect?

An assessment of the way in which significant changes have occurred in South Africa (for example, the labour reforms and the abolition of influx control) reveals a common pattern which demonstrates that change has been brought about through the interaction of a number of forces. These include the economic, social and demographic realities of an increasingly urbanised and industrialised country; black organisation and opposition to existing laws and practices; the disintegration of the apartheid philosophy leaving room for other groups to influence government thinking on how to cope with the failures of the existing policy, and pressure from a variety of groups ranging from foreign governments to the local and international business community. No one factor has been sufficient to bring about change on its own. In this context, what kind of role can business play?

Business can use its resources in anticipation of events. Change occurs if a range of currents and pressures is combined to undermine the racially structured status quo. Business can actively use its resources on a large scale to hasten and strengthen that process. Examples include assisting nonracial residential settlement, financing black organisations committed to negotiation and constructive problem solving, and supporting urban informal settlements in their plans for physical and social upgrading. Business can also be proactive in putting forward proposals for the removal of racially discriminatory laws and policies, and in providing for their replacement by developmentally oriented alternatives. Not only can resources be used to define these laws and alternatives, but resources can go into sophisticated marketing programmes to change the public environment and ultimately influence decision-makers in their approach to these issues.

Business resources can also be used creatively. The government's strategy of socio-economic reform requires the active participation of private sector development organisations, financial institutions and key individuals in order to succeed. This gives the business sector some leverage. The leverage of participation and active involvement need not be given away unconditionally but can be used as a tool for opening up the system. Business has publicly committed itself to a future nonracial society and to a process of negotiation in order to facilitate movement from 'here' to 'there'. Individual businessmen, corporations and organisations must assess their actions against such a political programme.

Of the four incrementalist actors described in this chapter, three are political parties or movements. The specific strategic dilemmas they confront are different from those which business as a community or individual businessmen must face. We will deal with each separately.

In looking at Inkatha, the Progressive Federal Party and the Labour Party, there are two themes that run through the analysis. The first concerns power and influence – whether participation in the KwaZulu Legislative Assembly, the tricameral parliament or the white parliamentary chamber has increased the potential contribution of this actor to the transformation of South Africa or not. The second question revolves around the issue of ethnic mobilisation – the problem of using uniracial building blocks to create a nonracial society and polity.

Inkatha

The Inkatha movement has followed a strategy of what may be described as critical or selective participation in state-created structures. They have made use of the structures of regional government provided by the state in terms of its apartheid ideology. They have, however, refused the intended final stage of development of these structures: 'sovereign independence'. In respect of the structures of local government, the movement has adopted a pragmatic position: neither lending formal support nor preventing Inkatha members from participating. Some state structures have been rejected outright. Perhaps the central example is the tricameral parliament. Previously Inkatha had rejected the proposed Black Council. It has also rejected both the new structures of provincial government, as well as the regional services councils.

Such a selective policy is entirely consistent with the 'strategic logic' of incrementalism. Equally, it is subject to the problems of this logic. Participation provides an opportunity for building an institutional power base. It also offers the chance to achieve benefits for those whom the incrementalist actor is seeking to serve. However, the 'space' to build a power base, and the chance to deliver benefits, are achieved within the constraints of the existing order. The South African government has defined the KwaZulu government structures ethnically and not regionally. This has allowed Inkatha's critics, from both the right and the left, to brand the organisation as 'tribal'. Though the organisation has done much to challenge this label, its location in an ethnically defined regional structure will always pose it a dilemma. The dilemma is essentially the same as that faced by all South Africans who profess nonracialism but have chosen to work through racially defined or confined structures.

A second dilemma is that of any organisation which seeks and exercises governmental power: to assume responsibility for a system or subsystem of government and administration is inevitably to clash with those seeking total transformation. Clashes in the KwaZulu education system illustrate this. Such clashes cannot be avoided, but as is noted elsewhere, it is important that clashes result from a deliberate and conscious choice by the incrementalist to preserve a specific structure or promote a particular policy. Such actors will always have to be careful to avoid being cut up in the wake of a different conflict, i.e. that defined around national political structures.

A third dilemma faced by Inkatha is also shared by other incrementalist actors. This dilemma flows from the incrementalist conception of the way in which societies do and should change. As noted earlier, incrementalist conceptions of change are characterised by the plurality of change agents. A logical corollary of this conception is the strategy of building alliances. The dilemma is defined by the difficulty of building effective and principled alliances between organisations whose nature differs, and which operate in very different strategic environments. Two unsuccessful Inkatha alliances, the South African Black Alliance and the National Convention Alliance, well illustrate this point.

A final dilemma again refers to the difficulty of building a nonracial future with bricks baked in a racially defined furnace. The goal of greater black political unity has often been espoused by Inkatha and its leadership. In the context of the deeply divided black community this goal seems important. However, it can only be achieved (if at all) at the cost of avoiding or disguising ideological, analytic and strategic differences of the greatest importance.

194

Equally, the very pursuit of 'black unity' perpetuates an apartheid premise: i.e. that political interests are necessarily defined by race. No actor can ignore race. Yet all actors seeking a nonracial future must seek ways of transcending it.

The Progressive Federal Party

Traditionally the PFP's mission has centred on opposition to apartheid on the basis of fundamental liberal values, while expressing the predominant attitude of the unenfranchised black majority on key apartheid issues. More recently it has been trying to increase its white support and base of influence sufficiently to enable it to be an actor in the power politics of the white parliament. Is this traditional conception of the party appropriate to the South Africa of the 1980s?

The 1987 general election emphasised the hard truth that the PFP – a white political party advocating a nondiscriminatory South Africa – has little realistic chance of amassing sufficient electoral support to take over power or play a balance-of-power role in a whites-only parliament. However, one should not jump from this fact to the conclusion that there is no point to the party's existence. Participation in the parliamentary system has enabled the PFP to build and consolidate a base of support in the white community for the liberal values of human rights, and for a nonracial approach to society. This base consists of an established national organisational structure, a parliamentary foothold of 19 MPs, and a core of support from some 300 000 white voters. The educative role that the PFP leadership and organisation plays in the South African community as a whole should not be underestimated.

In the past, white liberal opponents of apartheid could see themselves speaking on behalf of, or siding with, some relatively uniform body called the black population. Whatever the validity of that strategy historically, it is no longer appropriate or possible today. The South African black population in 1987 is an increasingly heterogeneous, economically stratified and ideologically diverse group. There is no black point of view on many of the issues confronting the PFP.

In the past ten years, up to 1987, South Africa has witnessed a steady growth in the number of factors influencing the process of change, as well as in the speed of that process. In this period the nature of the white political debate has undergone a fundamental transformation. Throughout the 1960s and most of the 1970s, the PFP had to challenge white South Africa single-handedly on its reasons for opposing apartheid. The late 1970s saw the government acknowledge, however grudgingly, the need for a change in its approach to the future of urban black people. This change in official thinking and in the fundamental societal forces to which it was a response has irrevocably altered the scope of the white political debate. It is no longer sufficient to criticise the status quo and highlight its inadequacies, both moral and practical. Three sets of attitudes are now important. The first concerns opposition to apartheid and a clear definition of the intended meaning of that term in order to comprehend what one is opposing. The second revolves around an attitude to the process of change in South Africa. If citizens do not approve of the status quo, then how should South Africa be changed? Finally, the third concerns the nature of the post-apartheid, future society. These three issues, or clusters of issues, are the crux of the political debate.

The shift in political debate away from a defence of the status quo and towards competing alternatives for change in South Africa has important implications for the PFP, its strategy, role and purpose. In many areas of present-day government policy, it is PFP arguments and policies that have played an important part in paving the way to some of the positive changes that have been won. The party's core commitment and values have to be extended and applied in order to respond to changing circumstances. The basic liberal values that have informed its opposition to apartheid for so long must now be articulated, applied and advocated as a response to the new questions on the political agenda for achieving a post-apartheid social structure.

We are increasingly witnessing the emergence of divided opinions on how our future economy should be structured and our future society governed. These divisions have less to do with race and a great deal to do with ideology or a basic evaluation of methods for managing society.

The Labour Party has participated more extensively in the system in order to change it than any of the other actors which we have examined. This can be seen in their decision to enter the tricameral parliament, and later, through majority representation in the House of Representatives, their decision to accept membership in the National Party cabinet for a period. The experience of the party in this process of incorporation is enlightening.

Participation is a two-way process. The state requires other actors to become involved in their political institutions or initiatives. This means that those actors have a degree of leverage because the state has to gain their required involvement. Did the Labour Party take advantage of this 'moment of power' prior to entering the tricameral system? The same question can be asked concerning their decision to join the National Party cabinet – how did they use that moment of leverage? Did the Labour Party enter the tricameral system with a clear strategy by which to judge the government's programme of reform, and the costs and benefits of Labour's involvement in the status quo? Did the party think clearly through the question of how it would handle the other side of the government's reform strategy – namely the tight security and repressive measures?

The key question is whether the Labour Party's involvement in the tricameral system has strengthened it as an organisation working for the development of a nonracial society. There is no doubt that the Labour Party has won some gains. The problem revolves around two aspects of the nature of their participation. On the one hand the major breakthroughs that have occurred, such as the abolition of the coloured labour preference policy or the abolition of the pass laws, are issues that many other organisations and individuals have campaigned for. Thus, as one among very many change-actors, the Labour Party's role in bringing about these alterations – irrespective of the facts of the matter – is not perceived to be significant in the change process as a whole. How does one claim, and receive credit for changes, when one is not *the* major actor? And when the changes that occur stem from 'behind the scenes' intervention and not from public action? Also when there are many other actors, individuals and organisations, which are publicly indicating opposition to a certain law or policy?

On the other hand, the gains which the Labour Party has made and that can be directly attributed to their actions and influence have generally occurred in the arena of increased benefits for one group, namely the 'coloured community'. The Labour Party can most easily obtain benefits for coloured people and can be most influential with the government on political questions which affect that same community. The consequences of these two facts are that the Labour Party is unlikely to receive credit for the positive gains which it makes for the South African nation as a whole. It will also tend to concentrate more and more in the area in which it has already had, and is likely to continue having, success – material improvements for coloured people. The combination of these two tendencies could lead to increased alienation of the Labour Party from the broad nonracial movement for change in South Africa, and could start to distort their personal as well as their general commitment to a future nonracial society.

Concluding remarks

Actors who are working for incremental change are competing in a marketplace of ideas and strategies. The incrementalists promote a process which has far less symbolic and dramatic power than the armed force of the state, or the daring deeds of revolutionaries. The incremental actors are advocating a step-by-step process of negotiation, pragmatism and compromise, in the hope of small, quiet victories that minimise human cost but achieve change first by altering structures, and only later by changing symbols. Success for the incrementalists will therefore depend on great political skill and tactical agility. For these to be achieved they require a political base that includes a clear analysis of the problem at hand and an alternative approach to that problem. They also require courageous and sensible leadership, and the ability to 'get ahead of events'.

The four actors which we have examined all share the belief that one has to start from where one stands. In doing that, most of them (whilst being firmly committed to a nonracial future), have built predominantly uniracial launching pads to influence and claim their place in that future. The advantages in this strategy are the influence which they have in the present, and the opportunities and resources they possess which enable them to achieve an organised constituency. The disadvantages are their partial view of the South African reality, and the actors' concern with their particular base in the South African whole. In order to use their base constructively and not to allow it to become a negative feature of future conditions, these incrementalists need constantly to ensure that means relate to values, and that ends are consistent with stated objectives.

6 The economics of conflict and negotiation

PIETER LE ROUX

Man creates his own future,
but not under conditions of his choice,
nor with the consequences he intends.
GIDDENS, A. 1979[1]

Introduction

Many of South Africa's free marketeers and historical materialists have more in common than they would care to admit. Although Rostow called his stages of economic growth an anti-communist manifesto, he was guilty of the same economic determinism as those Marxists who claimed to have discovered the laws of motion. The different stages of economic growth through which South Africa ought to progress can be predicted with certainty according to the economic determinists of both the right and the left.[2]

This chapter is written in the conviction that the future is open. It is being determined not by inexorable laws, but by a combination of factors, including people's understanding of the present and their visions of the future. Perceptions of reality are considered to be of far greater importance than economic determinists and structuralists would care to admit.[3]

THREE SCENARIOS OF THE FUTURE

Broadly speaking, three different types of future scenarios are on the cards if one is to judge by the present actors' visions of the future. Firstly, there is the belief that the existing economic and political order can be preserved by a determined resistance to internal and international pressures. Secondly, there are some who put their faith in achieving a negotiated settlement. Thirdly, there are those who claim that true liberation will only be possible when the structures of economic and political domination have been destroyed. Each of these three scenarios contains a number of different visions of future economic and political systems.

The siege economy strategy is favoured by the ultraright-wing opposition to the government, who wish to re-establish a much greater degree of economic and political separation. It also seems to have the support of a strong conservative group in government circles, who, in order to preserve existing structures, intend to redistribute a limited degree of economic and political resources to sections of the black community; simultaneously resisting, with all the means at their disposal, internal and international pressures for a more radical transformation of South African society.

Very different visions of the second scenario, according to which the future economic system is to emerge from a process of negotiations, are held. One is that of the free marketeers, who wish to realise the libertarian vision of Hayek and his followers. Another is that of the democratic socialists, who hope to establish a democracy which will give the people full control of both the economic and the political spheres. And a third vision, which falls somewhere between these two, is that of occasionally reluctant social democrats who want to maintain the present structures of production and of the free market. These will be combined with a political democracy and a significant degree of redistribution of resources, often in the form of social investment financed by economic growth.

Those who believe that present structures have to be 'smashed' include traditional Marxist-Leninists in the ANC, members of the PAC, the radicalised youth in the streets and some of the African Socialists. This entire group can be distinguished from the others not by its support for violence as a strategy, but by its faith that, for reasons of either strategy or principle, liberation will only be possible if the struggle is carried on until both the economic and military power of the 'regime' have been destroyed. Many of those within the resistance groups who favour a negotiated settlement also believe that the South African regime will only seriously consider negotiations after a period of intensified armed conflict, whereas some of those who believe in a revolutionary transformation do not believe that the time is ripe for an armed conflict.

In this chapter the perceptions of each of the groups which support the different scenarios are presented and evaluated. These perceptions clearly did not emerge in a void, but each was conceived within a particular economic and political context. An ahistorical description of the various cognitive maps can thus not give one much of an insight into the South African situation. The nature of the struggles from which ideas emerged and the interests which they served cannot be ignored.

UNEXPECTED SIMILARITIES IN PERCEPTIONS AND THE POSSIBILITY OF NEGOTIATION

From interviews, discussions at conferences and a survey of positions adopted in the press and in academic journals and books, it is clear that a wide variety of cognitive maps regarding the nature of the future economic and political system are held by actors who are formally members of the same group. For example, within government circles there are marked differences regarding both the short-term economic strategies to be adopted and the desired nature of a post-apartheid economic system. Not surprisingly, the same is true for the ANC – for it is, after all, a movement and not a political party.

An analysis of the different perceptions reveals unexpected concord in visions concerning the type of economic system likely to emerge after a negotiated settlement between some of those in government and big business on the one side, and some UDF and ANC members, including some Communist Party members, on the other. In addition there are strong structural economic realities which favour some form of negotiated settlement. Particular attention is thus given to the possible nature of the economic system which is to emerge from negotiations.

This emphasis does not imply that a negotiated settlement is on the cards or even that it is likely. Although reason and economic rationality may favour such a settlement, the conflict itself has gained a momentum of its own which may prove to be irreversible. The question of whether a negotiated settlement is at all possible is considered in the final section of this chapter.

AN ECONOMIC FOCUS

Although the nature of the South Africa of the future is to be determined neither by the economic visions, nor by economic structures, but by an interplay of these and a number of other factors, the focus of this chapter is on economic issues. Economic questions are, after all, of far greater importance for a resolution of the escalating conflict in South Africa than is realised by those who play around with constitutional models.[4]

It is not always easy to discover what the economic perceptions within different groups are. Official documents are often compiled to cover up internal divisions or to impress one or another constituency. Except where stated otherwise, the points of view ascribed to different groups in this chapter are based on opinions expressed to the author in interviews and discussions, or put forward at conferences and seminars he attended. All of these took place during 1986 and the first half of 1987. Opinions are only attributed to specific people where they have publicly adopted similar positions to those expressed in the interviews. As fair a summary as possible of the different points of view has been attempted, even in those cases where the author finds the particular view offensive. In the critique of the different positions, the concern is with the economic and, where relevant, the political realism of the programmes. Moral issues, for example the strong ethical case for a negotiated settlement, are not considered here.

Towards a siege economy

The siege economy approach is a strategy for survival based on the assumption that white South Africa will have to 'go it alone'. It has been the approach demanded by ultraright-wing opponents of the Nationalist government for a number of years. During the past year or two the President himself seems to have been converted to it. However, contrary to what has often been argued, the goal he wishes to attain differs significantly from that of the ultraright-wing conservatives. Government thinking on this issue is ambiguous. The position of those who favour a siege economy can best be understood within the context of a specific explanation of the failure of the neo-conservative reform strategy to create stability.

Conventional wisdom would have it that P. W. Botha abandoned his political reform programme in order to counter the growth of the ultraright wing. This is not a correct picture. It may be that he stopped short of implementing some of his intended reforms, but in principle he still seems to be committed to the limited political reforms promised. What National Party spokesmen call 'unnecessary' apartheid has been or is in the process of being abandoned, and in the 1987 election campaign the government again committed itself to the principle that Africans need to be represented in central government – a position which is in direct conflict with traditional apartheid policy.

It is in the spheres of security, labour and economics, in particular international economic relations, that the Botha government has forsaken or may forsake the policies to which it was committed in the reformist years. The political reforms which were to give international legitimacy to the Botha government are now part of a strategy in which repression plays a crucial role. The hope for some legitimacy in the international community has not been totally abandoned, but far greater stress is now placed on internal stability, self-reliance and co-operation with regimes that are more reliable than the government of the United States, which is accused of constantly shifting its expectations and demanding more and more far-reaching reforms.

THE NEO-CONSERVATIVE REFORMS

In order to understand present thinking in government circles, and the right-wing criticism of government policies, some attention needs to be given to the neo-conservative strategy to which the Botha government was committed in its first years. Indeed, some neo-conservative reforms were already being implemented by the Vorster government. The scrapping of job reservation and the recognition of trade unions with black members were both steps of far greater immediate importance to the average black South African than was realised at the time. More recently the scrapping of the pass laws and, in the case of the Western Cape, of the coloured labour preference policy, together with steps to give greater freedom to black entrepreneurs, for example by legalising 'pirate' taxis, are some of the neo-conservative reforms of the Botha government which could, if effectively implemented, significantly improve the economic circumstances of some black South Africans.[5]

A combination of factors brought about this liberalisation in the government's economic policies. Amongst these were the strike actions by black workers and the revolts in black townships in the early and mid-seventies, and the subsequent demands by big business for reforms. However, a crucial catalyst in this process of transformation from an apartheid economy to a more market-oriented approach was the neo-conservative philosophy which was adapted to South African circumstances by some Pretoria economists.

The new vision was given its clearest formulation in a book[6] written in the mid-seventies by Professor Jan Lombard, head of the Department of Economics at the University of Pretoria at that time, and subsequently vice-president of the South African Reserve Bank. Given the Afrikaner tradition of thinking in terms of blueprints and ideologies, National Party politicians probably would not have discarded apartheid in the economic sphere so rapidly had it not been for this new ideology.

Lombard and the group of economists who supported him succeeded in converting Afrikaner nationalists to a version of the free market ideology. Conservative as this position was from an international perspective, it did imply fairly radical changes in the apartheid system. The alarm with which right-wing extremists viewed these neo-conservative reforms, which did away with old-style apartheid, found expression in the bombing of Lombard's offices.

In addition to the controversial political reforms discussed above, the neo-conservative strategy, enthusiastically supported by big business, led to a relaxation of controls in the foreign exchange markets, and in general to a reduction of direct controls over the banking sector.

The neo-conservative strategy was sold to reluctant political leaders with the argument that it would lead to a higher rate of economic growth. Peace, it was argued, would be bought on the labour front. The black communities which were being radicalised in the wake of the Soweto uprising would welcome the scrapping of petty-apartheid measures and particularly of discriminatory legislation in the economic field, and foreign firms would invest more readily in a South Africa rid of petty apartheid, in particular of discriminatory economic policies, and freed of exchange controls. Conservative governments in the West would find it much easier to support a South Africa which had scrapped its racist legislation.

In a long and bitter struggle the neo-conservatives out-manoeuvred the apartheid hardliners in the government. Their ideas became a potent force in the dismantling of Verwoerdian apartheid. But they had little appeal for the black proletariat and for black students. Neo-conservative reforms did not stem the rising tide of black resistance to government policies. Nor did international pressures on South Africa decrease in response to these reforms. Indeed, both the ultraright wing and conservatives within the government contend that pressures on the administration increased precisely because Botha seemed more willing to implement reforms than either Vorster or Verwoerd had been.

The ultraright-wing diagnosis of what has gone wrong is of some importance, as part of their analysis seems to have been accepted in certain circles in government.

THE RIGHT-WING CRITIQUE OF GOVERNMENT STRATEGY

From the outset the ultraright, then represented by the HNP (see Chapter 2), rejected the total package of proposals formulated by the neo-conservatives. Economic integration, they argued, would inevitably lead to political integration which would cause political instability, and hence to the withdrawal of foreign capital. Thus, they argued, the flight of foreign capital was triggered by the fear that the government was losing control and that South Africa was on the slippery road to a black government. South Africa was in an economic crisis not, as liberal critics had argued, because the pace of reform was too slow, but because it was too rapid.

Despite these criticisms, the government decided to stick to its political reform programme. However, if one is to judge by recent modifications in government policy, three of the points of criticism raised by the ultraright have clearly had an impact on government thinking.

The Conservative Party has long claimed that the easing of exchange control in 1983 was a grievous error. In an interview, the Conservative Party spokesman on economic affairs, Mr Jan van Zyl, argued that this facilitated a major process of disinvestment by South African companies, such as Anglo American and Rembrandt, which had a far more serious impact on the South African economy than the withdrawals by the United States. Furthermore, he argued, the onslaught on the rand would never have been as successful had the Reserve Bank not, under the influence of the free market ideology, paved the way for South Africa's enemies by making it easier to take funds out of the country.

Secondly, ultraright protagonists claim that the black uprising would not have been as sustained and as successful had the government not tied the hands of the security forces. Bowing to pressures exerted by the United States government under its constructive engagement policies, the government gave the revolutionaries free access to foreign correspondents who, by their very presence, fuelled black uprisings and, by selective reporting, created an image of a South Africa on the verge of collapse. Also because of pressures from the United States, it initially refused to give the security forces the powers needed to deal with the uprisings. Indeed, after the first big 'riot' in Uitenhage was quelled on Sharpeville Day in 1985, the government instituted a judicial enquiry which placed the security forces, and not the revolutionaries, in the dock.

The third point of criticism which many in government circles seem to be taking more and more seriously contends that the recognition of black trade unions enabled radicals to undermine the South African economy. During the seventies the trade unions, according to the Conservative Party version of events, pretended to be primarily concerned with workers' issues, but in recent years, with the founding of COSATU and the explicitly political demands made by the leadership of COSATU, the true intent of the trade unionists has become apparent.

REFORM, REPRESSION AND THE EMERGING SIEGE ECONOMY

The two States of Emergency and the detention of tens of thousands of people, including many children, as well as the limitations placed on the press in defiance of worldwide reaction, clearly indicate that the South African government had decided to use an iron fist to repress extra-parliamentary political dissent, regardless of international consequences. The government seems to have elected to face the threat of international sanctions rather than to acquiesce to the demands of the resistance movements. For the time being it has, if one is to judge by these actions, opted for a siege economy.

The dismissal just before the 1987 election of 18 000 workers of the South African Transport Services following an illegal strike, which, ironically, co-incided with the publication of an article by Professor Nicholas Wiehahn (chairman of the commission which initiated many of the labour reforms) in which he pleaded for the recognition of this union, indicates a greater reluctance by the government to tolerate black trade unions. The high political profile of the new president of COSATU, the UDF-affiliated trade union, has angered the government. It would seem as though there are moves afoot to act strongly against trade unions should they become more active on political than on worker issues. The subsequent reinstatement of all the dismissed workers and the recognition of the trade union shows, however, that the reformist element in the government may still be stronger than some of the repressive actions taken in defiance of international pressures would indicate.

Simultaneous with the stepping up of its repression, the government has decided to continue with its attempts to woo 'moderate' blacks. This 'reform' strategy entails further political amendments along the lines pursued in the past, and attempts to buy political stability by offering a variety of economic carrots. At the same time the government is considering steps to cut off foreign funding of extra-parliamentary groups. Subsequent developments suggest that the threat P.W. Botha made in this connection in his post-election speech may not be an idle one.

The 'redistribution for political stability' strategy, which is being implemented under the auspices of the Department of Constitutional Development, and is being planned in collaboration with the joint military committees, has as its objective the buying of political stability by the distribution of economic benefits. All sorts of infrastructural services, for example better roads, sport stadiums and housing, are being provided in areas where there has been political revolt, and employment is also being supplied, particularly in those areas where unemployment seems to have been a major factor contributing to political unrest. In addition, in collaboration with big business, funds are being put at the disposal of potential black businessmen, in order to create a petty-bourgeoisie class less susceptible to revolutionary slogans than the proletariat.

On a macrolevel, preparation for a siege has meant a re-introduction of foreign exchange controls and the implementation of steps to tighten import protection. These neo-protectionist measures have long been lobbied for by Fred du Plessis, chairman of Sanlam who as honorary professor in economics at Potchefstroom University delivered a series of lectures arguing that the South African economy would be badly hurt if liberalisation in the sphere of international trade and finance continues.[7] His contention that it was these policies and not Botha's Rubicon speech which caused the debt crisis is in direct conflict with the interpretations of people such as Tony Bloom, who was in personal contact with a number of international bankers when the crisis developed.[8] It is nevertheless true that in the absence of these policies the very rapid increases in short-term foreign debt which took place during the two years before the crisis would not have been possible.

Three arguments are usually mentioned in defence of a siege-economy approach. Firstly it is reasoned that, because order is being restored, and as a result of the restrictions on the press, South Africa will no longer remain in the international limelight. Sanctions are thus unlikely to continue to escalate. Secondly, sanctions could in fact be a stimulus for the development of South African industry as they were in the case of Rhodesia, and a period of high rates of growth rather than stagnation may therefore be experienced. Finally, referring to the experience with military equipment boycotts, confidence is expressed that 'sanctions-busting' will be effective, and that South Africa will be able to become more and more self-sufficient.

There are clearly important differences between the ultraright's and the government's versions of the siege economy. The government intends to continue with its political reforms with which it hopes to buy the acquiescence, if not the collaboration, of a significant proportion of the black community. In addition, the policy of redistribution for political stability is being undertaken on a very large scale indeed. The ultraright, as we have noted, condemns Botha's 'welfarism' as expensive and counterproductive, and proposes an even harsher policy of repression without any pretence of political reform.

There is no doubt that redistribution for political stability is economically inefficient. As we will show in the discussion of social democracy, it has been attacked as wasteful by economists within the government who would prefer to have economically rational social and infrastructural investments. A senior economist closely involved with the implementation of this programme accepted this criticism as valid. However, he argued that South Africa's present crisis is not economic but political in nature. Even though the expenditures undertaken may not be economically optimal, they would pay high economic dividends if they could bring about political stability.

The government's siege-economy strategy, with its combination of reform and repression, seems to be generally preferred in military quarters to the ultraright wing's strategy of harsh repression. It is believed that it is more likely to win the hearts and minds of the people inside the country, and that it will ensure South Africa's retention of significant support in conservative quarters outside. Hence the military, which can apparently demand virtually as much expenditure on arms as it may wish to, seems to favour the redistribution of a significant proportion of funds for purposes of political stability. However, it has been claimed that some senior police officers favour the ultraright approach of hammering the forces of resistance into submission. Because of the powers conferred on the police under the Emergency legislation, the latter strategy is at times the one which is in fact implemented.

It is difficult to predict the degree of success the type of siege economy which the government is implementing is likely to have. It seems that it will bring about somewhat more internal stability than the ultraright-wing tactics, and, because of its attempt to do away with some features of apartheid, it is certain to receive a more sympathetic hearing in conservative circles internationally than the ultraright-wing approach with its unrepentant commitment to apartheid. However, can this modified form of white domination last?

In addition to their concern about the economic irrationality of much of the distribution which is taking place for purposes of political stability, those within the government who oppose siege-economy tactics claim that in the end it will collapse. It is a strategy which is based on a self-fulfilling prophecy. Departing as it does from the assumption that rapidly increasing economic sanctions are inevitable, it attempts to diminish South Africa's dependence on international trade. Pushing local production at all costs will, however, make South Africa more vulnerable to outside pressures. As imports are progressively replaced by locally produced goods, South Africa will have to continue to import those goods which it cannot under any circumstances produce locally, or can produce locally only at a very high cost. This process will not only leave South Africa dependent on imports in the areas where it is most vulnerable, but will also increase the likelihood that sanctions will be imposed in these areas. After all, South Africa's major trading partners will be most upset by the attempt to promote local production in defiance of international trade agreements, and, as trade with South Africa declines, they will also have less self-interest in opposing full-scale sanctions. Furthermore, the costs of import substitution will become prohibitively high, as it is pushed further and further. The conclusions of these economists are that the neo-protectionist policies which are proposed in preparation for sanctions may serve the interests of local companies which are not tough enough to fight in an open market – hence the enthusiasm of some local industrialists for the neo-protectionist policies – but it is not in the interest of the long-term survival of the South African economy.

It is accepted by these critics from within the government that if mandatory international sanctions are implemented and South Africa moves irrevocably into a state of siege economy, there will be a period of a higher rate of growth similar to that which Rhodesia experienced in the post-UDI years. However, this prosperity will be illusory. In the end the South African economy will grind to a halt as it experiences increasing difficulty in replacing its capital infrastructure. Even during this initial period the growth rate would be much lower than that which would be possible if economically rational investment policies were pursued.

Critics within the government nevertheless believe that the siege economy may be relatively successful for at least ten years. Only then will serious economic problems arise, but even after that it may survive for many years. If, in addition to international pressures, one considers the impact of the increasing unemployment discussed below, it seems inevitable that the siege economy cannot prosper in the long run. How long it could survive cannot, however, be predicted at this stage.

In conclusion it must be pointed out that the South African government has not yet committed itself unambiguously to a siege economy. Even Dr Fred du Plessis, who is often seen as its major proponent, rejects this label and claims that he is in fact only arguing for neo-protectionism which he defends on economic grounds. The Department of Constitutional Development's policy of redistribution for political stability slots into a siege-economy strategy, but can be implemented independently. On the other hand, the redistribution-with-growth policy, which is favoured by influential economists such as Brand, Lombard and Dreyer, explicitly rejects the siege-economy type of model. It is, as we will note below, more in line with a conservative social-democratic approach.

In the debate in government circles regarding official economic policy it is, in fact, the redistribution with growth school which seems to be coming out on top. Although the inward industrialisation policy, which is contained in an important policy document of the Economic Advisory Council which was recently released, does make certain concessions to the neo-protectionist school, it is basically a victory for Brand and Lombard.[9] However, regardless of the position of its economic advisors, it is clear that the present government, rather than making any further concessions to international pressures, would opt for a state of siege. Although those who favour redistribution with growth might have won the academic debate, indications are that they will lose out when practical political decisions have to be taken in the face of international pressures.

Destroying the structures of domination

In South Africa it has become fashionable for all but the ultra-right to claim opposition to apartheid. The term 'apartheid', however, has very different connotations for different groups. When the government promises to move away from apartheid, it refers to the abolition of discriminatory practices which are unique to South Africa, and also to the inclusion of some blacks in the central government. To this all the groups to the left of the government respond with the slogan which the new group of independents has used with a fair degree of success in the recent elections: "Apartheid cannot be reformed; it must be abolished!"

What is implied by the abolition of apartheid? "The extension of democratic rights to all!" is the liberal response. "No, to abolish apartheid is to end domination not only in the political, but also in the economic sphere," argue the members of the resistance groups and the social democrats within the establishment. But whereas social democrats and most democratic socialists believe or hope that this change can be brought about by transforming existing structures, there are other groups who believe that apartheid can only be eradicated by 'smashing' the political and economic structures of domination. It is the views of these groups that are considered here.

It is not easy to establish who really believes that liberation can only be attained by the total eradication of existing structures. Political activists have seldom shown an aversion to hyperbole. Many of those who call for destruction in fact hope to retain the productive base and transform it. On the other hand, there are strategists who believe in understatement and speak mildly of social transformation when their intention is far more radical. It is wrong, therefore, to categorise groups or individuals on the basis of their rhetoric. Instead, one has to consider the concrete programmes to which they are committed.

There are at least five different groups who believe that the elimination of apartheid calls for the destruction of both the economic and the political systems. Firstly there are the Trotskyites, who see apartheid as a system of racial capitalism: racism will survive as long as capitalism does. Then one finds a group which, for lack of a better term, will be referred to as traditional Marxist-Leninists. Thirdly there is that section of the African socialists whom I have chosen to describe as African socialist nationalists. (For the sake of correct classification the adjectives added are essential in the last two cases, for many Marxist-Leninists and African nationalists do not in principle reject a negotiated settlement which will leave much of the economic system intact. In this discussion we are only concerned with those who oppose any compromise.) Fourthly, there are growing numbers of 'Pol Pot' types of cadres that may be loosely affiliated to one political organisation or another, but which are in fact developing a character and a momentum of their own. Finally, there is a small but committed fundamentalist Muslim movement.

Although it will not be surprising if the last two groups play a crucial role in determining the denouement of the South African drama, their economic programmes are not likely to be implemented, either because they are nonexistent (in the case of the 'Pol Pot' youth), or because the group's zeal and commitment cannot compensate for its lack of numbers (South Africa is not going to become a fundamentalist Islam state modelled on Iran).

WHY THE STRUCTURES MUST BE 'SMASHED'
The Trotskyites
There is a long tradition of Trotskyism in the Cape. It used to be an elitist movement with a limited grass-roots influence. However, during the past year or two it has, for a number of reasons, been acquiring a wider influence. Firstly, the alliances formed in the Forum movement with AZAPO and other groups have resulted in Trotskyite ideas being incorporated into the programmes of a

wider group of people than had been the case before. Secondly, the Trotskyite criticism that ANC strategies for making South Africa ungovernable were not founded on a proper analysis of the strength of the government, and were counter-productive because they would lead to greater repression, has strengthened the Trotskyites in two ways. They have been given some leeway by a government which, with its traditional divide-and-rule tactics, is at present not suppressing nonviolent radical groups opposed to the ANC with as much vigour as in the past. This argument has also gained them support from some of those who have become disillusioned with UDF promises that the government would soon collapse and are finding the Trotskyite analysis to be better informed, or more 'scientific', to use Trotskyite terminology. Thirdly, some able Trotskyite thinkers, in particular Dr Neville Alexander, have used the new opportunities to adopt a more activist line. Although they continue to shy away from what they disparagingly call the populism of the UDF, there is more emphasis on bringing their message to a wider audience.

In South Africa the Trotskyite approach represents a strange mixture of radical objectives and conservative noncollaborationist strategies. This can be explained by a deep faith in the Marxist historical materialist laws. Premature action is rejected as adventurism, both because it exposes the people to unnecessary suffering, and because it may in fact, as it has done in Russia, put a true socialist revolution at risk. It may free South Africa from the bonds of international capitalism only to make it a captive of Soviet communism.[10]

History, moving inexorably forward, will break the chains of racial capitalism if the workers are permitted to fulfil their mission. The danger is that the petty-bourgeoisie leadership of the ANC and the UDF will, after its initial struggle, negotiate a settlement which will effectively undermine progress towards true socialism.

Traditional Marxist Leninism
Whereas the Trotskyites wish to avoid a repetition of the Russian experience, the *traditional* Marxist-Leninists are committed to emulating it. They actively pursue a revolution which will 'smash'

the structures of domination and, under the leadership of the vanguard party, will transform South Africa into a socialist state.

In contrast to the Trotskyites, who are vague in providing details of how and when socialism is to come about, traditional Marxist-Leninists have little doubt about the nature of the transition. A vanguard party will have to gain control and smash all the counter-revolutionary forces. The Zimbabwean process of compromise has to be avoided. All the big industries, the banks and the agricultural sector will be nationalised.

The accusation is often made by Trotskyites and other opponents that these traditional Marxist-Leninists are in fact Stalinist. Traditional Marxist-Leninists scorn talk of the workers taking over control of the factories by retorting that when the people's government governs, the unions must also be subjected to its discipline. Dreams of the redistribution of land to farming co-operatives or black peasants are rejected as utopian and foolish. (Why create a Kulak class? Where are the black peasants in any case? Look at the failure of the social-democratic induced experiment with co-operatives in Tanzania!) State-run farms are the answer.

Social democratic schemes to redistribute the savings on military expenditures are, according to the traditional Marxist-Leninists, devoid of any realism. The counter-revolutionaries, supported by world capitalism, will launch an even more determined attempt to sabotage the revolution than they did in Nicaragua. High military expenditure will be needed to combat these contras. Democratic socialists' hopes that there can be a transformation via a democratic evolution have no foundation in reality. It is naive to assume that capitalism will ever permit a true democracy to evolve, for democracy will lead to the abolition of capitalism. Social-democratic compromises, in any case, would leave capitalism intact. Dialectic logic calls for the resolution of contradictions, not for marginal adjustments. Structures of domination must be 'smashed', even though the cost in the short run may be high.

The African socialist nationalists
African socialism has many different versions. The African socialists within the ANC often seem to have social-democratic or demo-

cratic-socialist types of goal. Many PAC and AZAPO activists, and some members of the ANC, although nominally also committed to socialism, seem to be more concerned with the transfer of power to black South Africans or 'Azanians'. In spite of socialist rhetoric it is, in the case of this group, not capitalism as such to which they object, but white economic dominance. Their position is similar to that of the Afrikaner national socialists of the thirties and forties who explicitly defined capitalism as the system under which the English owned most of the means of production.[11] The concern now, as then, is to transfer economic power to a specific group, not to destroy capitalism as such, and their arguments are often couched in racist rather than class terms.

In principle, an African socialist-nationalist programme implies a less radical transformation of society than more radical socialist programmes – the crew is changed, but the ship continues to sail on its old course, to use a metaphor which critical Marxists often apply to this type of programme. However, it is not capitalism which whites are defending, but the privileges acquired under capitalism. To bring about this type of shift in power and wealth, a destruction of the power of the dominant elite is as much a precondition as in a Stalinist type of transformation.

AN ASSESSMENT OF THE RADICAL
REVOLUTIONARY 'SOLUTION'

Should the present government, or a right-wing successor, persist with a siege economy to the bitter end, it is likely that either a traditional Marxist-Leninist policy or an African socialist-nationalist policy will be adopted in the wake of the revolution. The victorious revolutionary government will most probably institute a one-party state and will take over the control of the devastated economy. Authoritarian structures of command, established during the period of war, will form the basis of the new government, and the economic devastation will be such that a great degree of government involvement in the economy will be inevitable. There will not be much need for social democratic types of compromise, because power will have shifted completely to the revolutionary forces.

If one is to judge by the present balance of forces, it is probable that the new government will be of a Marxist-Leninist, rather than what I have called an African socialist-nationalist, nature. However, as the experience of Zimbabwe has shown, one cannot predict at this early stage how support may shift during the years ahead. A shift towards the PAC and AZAPO could take place quite rapidly, if for example the ANC's nonracism is rejected by millions of blacks who could turn to black racism after having suffered much at the hands of whites during a protracted civil war.

It is rather senseless at this stage to give an assessment of the specific economic programme likely to be adopted after the revolution. Suffice it to say that serious questions could be raised regarding the economic rationality of a number of the traditional Marxist-Leninist strategies mentioned above. It is of greater immediate relevance to question the strategy of opposing any negotiated settlement until the structures of domination have been totally dismantled.

It is generally accepted that a modern war cannot be won on the battlefield alone. To ensure victory one also needs to undermine the economic system of the enemy. In the case of a civil war this, however, becomes a self-destructive policy. The greater the resistance groups' success in destroying the economy, the greater the problems they will face in a post-revolutionary government. This is one of the reasons for the argument, accepted in some circles of the ANC, that economic pressures should not be aimed at destroying the economy but merely at forcing negotiated settlement onto a reluctant government. It is clear that the price to be paid in terms of human lives and suffering, both during the conflict and in the post-revolutionary years, will be very high indeed. Only the most cold-blooded will demand destruction of the economy if a negotiated settlement is a feasible alternative.

An economic system
compatible with a negotiated settlement

In the midst of polarisation between the Left and the Right, influential sections within government, big business and the ANC are pinning their hopes on a negotiated settlement. From discussions and interviews it is clear that there is more support for real negotiation than public rhetoric would have us believe. In spite of very different motivations and aspirations, a wide spectrum of individuals would prefer a negotiated settlement to a destructive civil war.

The details of the economic system which may emerge from such negotiations have not often been spelt out in any detail. At present three types of solution are on the table. The first position holds that one can entrust most of South Africa's problems to a free market. This is argued, for example, by the influential *Financial Mail*. Secondly, there is a range of solutions which could be labelled social-democratic. All entail a significant redistribution of resources to the black community (often in the form of social investment financed out of growth) and an extension of democratic political rights to all groups, together with the maintenance of the present structure of production. A third set of solutions can best be described as democratic-socialist and entail the extension of political democracy to all, together with a significant degree of socialisation of the means of production – a phrase which, as is shown below, means rather different things to different democratic socialists.

FREE MARKETEER VISIONS OF THE FUTURE

South Africa has a long tradition of opposition to the apartheid system, based on the contention that it is economically extremely wasteful. For years influential liberal spokesmen such as Professor W. H. Hutt (once head of economics at the University of Cape Town), Dr Ralph Horowitz and Mr Michael O'Dowd (a director of Anglo American) have contended that economic rationality calls for the abandonment of apartheid legislation.[12] The reforms adopted in the wake of the Pretoria economists' conversion to neo-conservatism were a clear victory for this school of thought.

The central argument of the free marketeer school is that government failures are far more serious than market failures. Hence it is best to leave the regulation of most spheres of human activity, with the exception of defence, security and education, to the market. When governments start interfering in the economy, they usually serve the interests of particular lobbies, often at a high cost to society at large.

Further contentions are that apartheid regulations interfere with the optimal allocation of resources. For example, job reservation was in the interest of white workers, but it pushed up costs for the employers and denied black workers many employment opportunities. Similarly, economic measures undertaken in the name of African socialism in the rest of Africa have often served the interests of small elite groups. The urban workers, for example, benefited from policies for keeping the prices of agricultural products artificially low, but this was at the cost not only of the peasantry, but of everyone, including in the long run the urban workers, for such policies undermined agricultural production.

Quoting surveys taken among blacks in Soweto regarding the preferred economic system, the free marketeers argue that although blacks claim to favour socialism, their choices regarding the type of economic activity they would prefer indicate that they in fact favour a free market system. Some free marketeers argue that blacks have lived under a socialist system all these years, as some of the restrictions imposed on blacks are very similar to those implemented in socialist countries.

Free marketeers are loath to give the central government of a future South Africa too much power. They suggest either a federal system along the lines proposed by the Progressive Federal Party, or a type of canton system. This would permit socialist types of system in specific areas, but, it is claimed, the free market would show itself to be superior in such a competition between regions, and would therefore become the dominant system of a democratic South Africa.[13]

Critique of the free market solution
Marxist critics of the free market argue that apartheid is the fruit of capitalism, given the specific historical conditions of South Africa. As proof they refer to the extremely high rate of economic growth (on average about five per cent per annum) South Africa experienced during the period 1920-1970. If apartheid were economically irrational, this rate of growth would not have been attainable.

Radical critics have been particularly enraged by the free marketeer contention that black South Africans have been living under socialism for years. While it cannot be denied that the only countries which have imposed similar restrictions on the migration and economic activities of their citizens in recent decades are to be found in the socialist bloc, it is absurd to contend that these similarities turn apartheid into socialism.

Socialist systems usually attempt to promote the interests of the working class and the poor in general. In South Africa the reverse is true, at least as far as black South Africans are concerned. After the National Party first came to power in 1924 in a coalition with the Labour Party, a number of measures were introduced to increase the standard of living of the 'poor whites', often at a high cost for the poor blacks. Gradually a 'whites-only' social democracy developed in South Africa. After 1948 further measures were implemented which favoured white workers, farmers and traders at the cost of black South Africans.

Should democratic rights, after a negotiated settlement, be extended to all South Africans, it may well be that black workers would decide to use their political muscle to claim the usual benefits for workers in a social democracy, rather than to do away with capitalism as such. If one is to judge by the experience of other countries, it does not seem as though the extension of democracy will lead to the abolition of all private ownership of the means of production. However, it is highly unlikely that the free marketeer system will be acceptable. If the workers spare the goose that lays the golden egg, they will do so in order to lay claim to the eggs. A free marketeer regime which frowns upon significant attempts to redistribute income has no chance whatsoever of being acceptable to most black South Africans. Therefore it is wishful thinking to believe that a negotiated settlement along the lines the free marketeers propose is at all possible.

DEMOCRATIC SOCIALISM

The realisation of the socialist dream

Many of the supporters of the Freedom Charter – the programme for economic transformation which was accepted, inter alia, by the ANC and the Congress of Democrats at the historic meeting at Kliptown in 1955 – believe that South Africa could become the first truly democratic-socialist country in the world. For here, in contrast to other countries which have experienced socialist revolutions, the capitalist economy is already fully developed.

Democratic socialists argue that societies ought to be democratic not only in the political but also in the economic sphere. After all, people's lives are often affected far more directly and far more dramatically by economic decisions taken by industrialists than by the decisions of elected politicians.

'Economic democracy' usually implies the 'socialisation of the means of production', but it is not always clear how these goals are to be reached. For some (the 'workerists' who are strong within the trade unions) this implies that democratically elected workers' councils run the factories, and that these bodies constitute a first level in a system which elects a workers' government;[14] for others the implication is that a representative government also takes over the control of all the larger companies in addition to its usual tasks. A third position is that the people themselves have the right to make decisions regarding the question of the control of industry, agriculture and mining through a Swiss type of referendum system.[15]

A critique of democratic socialism

Both Marxist-Leninists and free marketeers argue that a democratic-socialist economy will be highly inefficient. Economic decisions need to be taken by experts. The critics of this system contend that if the workers or the democratically elected representatives of the people were to make economic decisions, far too much would go into immediate consumption and the investment needed for sustained growth would simply not be possible.

Again we need not, however, spend much time considering the economic merits and demerits of this system. Although the writer of this chapter had himself argued in favour of a particular version of democratic socialism, it is utopian to believe that any kind of democratic socialism would be accepted at the negotiation table in the foreseeable future. It is likely that a type of democratic socialism would continue to get considerable support from the black trade unions, but it will have no chance whatsoever of being accepted by some of the most powerful establishment groups. Negotiations will not, at this stage of the conflict, lead to a democratic socialist type of settlement.

A SOCIAL DEMOCRACY – THE UNEASY COMPROMISE

Traditional social-democratic lobbies do not exist in South Africa. The dominant white trade unions wish to maintain white privilege, and the black trade unions would prefer to see a more radical transformation of South Africa. Nevertheless, a wide spectrum of people have expressed an interest in a democratic system which leaves the present structure of production largely intact but which redistributes resources, usually from growth and for purposes of social investment.

Whereas businessmen often prefer the term 'social market', stressing the fact that the market rather than government bureaucrats will take the most important decisions, it is clear that they are willing to live with a northern European or Scandinavian type of social democracy. Similarly, some government technocrats who speak of a democratic settlement with moderate blacks (usually excluding ANC supporters as radicals not willing to make any compromises) and who argue for redistribution with growth, would in fact be quite sympathetic to a conservative social democracy. UDF and ANC supporters usually think of social democracy in more radical terms and see it as a first step towards a democratic socialism.

Support for a social democracy, broadly defined, has thus been expressed by some individuals within government circles, by influential members of the UDF and by certain members of the ANC. One wing of the Progressive Federal Party has put forward its own conservative version, calling it 'capitalism with a human face'.[16]

Although there is a wide spectrum of support for a social democracy, support from members of the establishment is often only lukewarm. Some see it simply as the lesser of the socialist evils, others as the best bargain which could be struck under present circumstances. Such reluctant support has, however, always been the strength of a social democracy. It provides a middle ground for the coexistence of opposing interest groups.

223

In this section the extent to which a social democracy can meet the economic expectations of the different groups in South Africa is considered. The conclusion is that this is the only type of system which could emerge from a negotiated settlement, under the present circumstances.

To understand what sort of social democracy may emerge in South Africa, one needs to consider the aspirations and fears of the various groups and classes. In this respect the interviews with both establishment and resistance actors who favour, or are willing to accept, a social democracy, have proved to be particularly useful. Even though those interviewed may, when accepting a social democracy, represent a minority within their group, they understand which concerns will be of crucial importance for the group they represent.

EQUALISING THE SOCIAL AND
INFRASTRUCTURAL INVESTMENT
Growing support for social investment

'No more gutter education!' has been the slogan of black youth ever since the Soweto uprisings of 1976. Since then other demands have been added. In many townships, action committees have sprung up with demands for better housing at lower rents, a better transport system and, occasionally, better medical services. As a prominent UDF leader remarked after a visit to Scandinavia, these are demands which social democracies have historically shown themselves most capable of meeting.

Present policy is, as we have seen, to provide these social and infrastructural investments wherever it is deemed important in order to buy political stability. This is a highly inefficient process, and is opposed by influential members of the government technocracy. Many establishment economists strongly support an economically rational social investment programme. In particular, a rapid improvement in the quality of black education is seen as a precondition for a resumption of South Africa's historically high rates of growth. A study co-ordinated by Lombard[17] showed that the shortage of skilled labour is the most serious obstacle to a higher rate of growth. The conclusion is clear: not only has Bantu Education contributed to political instability, but also to severe structural economic problems.

Another group of economists, predominantly from Afrikaans universities, concluded in a study which was recently released by the government-financed Human Sciences Research Council that the reduction in the South African rate of growth has its roots, amongst other things, in the low per capita investment in black education. In addition, they recommended more investment in black housing and in medical services for black communities, (particularly in preventive fields as a matter of urgency).[18]

Not only the economic necessity of more social investment to benefit black communities but also the moral rectitude of investment in these communities is gaining some acceptance in Afrikaner establishment circles. Verwoerd's policy was to invest only as much in black education as was contributed directly to the fiscus by black taxpayers. In a recent debate in parliament the Minister of Finance, Barend du Plessis, countered a Conservative Party outcry that the government was spending far more on the black community than was warranted by black tax contributions by arguing that it was a sound and just fiscal principle that the poorer members of the community should be supported. He justified this by referring to the redistribution which has taken place from English- to Afrikaans-speaking South Africans (the 'whites-only' social democracy discussed above).

The fact that an influential section of the business community supports redistribution in these areas is clear not only from the statements of various company chairmen,[19] but in particular from the work undertaken by the Urban Foundation. This organisation has made a number of investments in an attempt to improve black urban housing and to change government housing policies. In recent years it has also endeavoured to improve black education. Many of the bigger companies have, in addition, made direct contributions to improve black housing and black educational opportunities.

The above information is not intended to convey the implication that what is being done in the social investment field is sufficient (the contrary is true), nor that there is widespread support within the establishment for more redistribution from the privileged to the poorer groups. However, it is significant that influential groups within the establishment have come to realise, often because of determined struggles by the disadvantaged communities themselves, that redistribution (for purposes of social investment) is not the dirty word dogmatic free marketeers would have one believe. Clearly, a negotiated settlement which demands more action in these spheres will not be met by a blank refusal, as would inevitably have been the case ten years ago, particularly if redistribution were to take place mainly from growth.

Redistribution: An evaluation
Those committed to the free market system argue that significant redistribution by the state will inevitably undermine the rate of growth of the economy. However, the history of social-democratic countries seems to prove that the contrary is true. Indeed, there is little doubt today that the large-scale social investment made in the Scandinavian countries and in Germany were major factors which contributed to economic success in these countries. Also in the case of the NICs (i.e. new industrial countries), educational and other investments in the social infrastructure which were made during the past three or four decades seem to be paying very high dividends.

There is obviously a danger that these investments can be financed by taxes which are so high that they destroy sections of the economy. However, assuming the reallocation of some government expenditure (for example, security expenditure could probably be cut down to its relative size in 1960, if political consensus can be reached) and additional taxes on luxury goods, for example progressive taxes on homes and cars, and given the much higher rate of growth which could potentially be realised by a social-democratic South Africa (see below), expenditure on social investments of crucial importance to black South Africans could be doubled in a very short period.

The politics of redistribution out of growth
There is undoubtedly the potential for some type of consensus in this field. The long-term economic self-interest of most groups in

South Africa demands much higher spending on black needs. However, this is a controversial political issue. As various studies, such as the one by the University of Cape Town economist Charles Simkins[20] have shown, it is not possible at present to equalise social investment in the different population groups. In addition, in fields such as education there are not sufficient qualified experts to provide the quality of education needed to all.

Any changes of policy put forward by a government elected by whites which fall short of providing equality in all fields overnight will be rejected by most black South Africans. Political unrest may well continue in the face of social investment policies which may in fact be optimal. Only a democratically elected government, representing all South Africans, could be granted a period of grace by the black majority when it pleads for time to correct the inequalities of the past. Only a government which is trusted by the people could thus bring the peace and stability needed for a social democratic type of reconstruction and for growth.

UNEMPLOYMENT – THE SOUTH AFRICAN TIME BOMB

In South Africa, black unemployment, which is estimated at somewhere between 20 and 30 per cent, could reach 50 per cent by the end of the century if the economy continues to stagnate as it did during the first half of the present decade.

There is consensus today over a very wide spectrum that this problem needs to be given the highest priority. Whereas government economists argued in the 1970s that the reduction of inflation was far more important than any attempt to tackle unemployment, various government departments have now launched programmes aimed at providing short-term employment for the unemployed. Again the concern is, however, with security aspects rather than with social consequences. Evidence shows that the cities in the Eastern Cape, which have been rocked by political instability to a much greater degree than most other parts of the country, have unemployment rates which even at this stage are in the vicinity of 50 per cent. Government employment projects in these areas often aim at buying political stability rather than at finding long-term solutions.

Given a rate of increase in the labour force of more than 3 per cent, estimates based on past patterns of unemployment show that the economy needs to grow at more than 5 per cent if there is to be a reduction in the proportion of the labour force unemployed. A growth rate of about 6 per cent is needed for absolute numbers to decline.

Only a negotiated settlement could possibly make growth rates of this magnitude attainable, as is increasingly being realised by some technocrats within the government who wish to see a negotiated settlement. It is accepted that the South African government is sitting on a time bomb. The specific measures taken now to reduce unemployment will be of little or no significance if a settlement which leads to a higher rate of economic growth is not reached. Very high rates of unemployment, which have been shown to be political dynamite, will spread throughout the country.

Although this time bomb may eventually blast the white South African government from power, demographic realities are increasingly causing concern in resistance circles also. The new government will inherit a country in which more than half the labour force will be unemployed, in which 80 per cent or more of those who have entered the labour market will still not have had any permanent employment after five years, and in which many will have turned to crime to survive.

The rate of undernourishment of black children, with all its destructive consequences – for example on the children's intellectual capacity – is even today estimated to be somewhere between 10 and 30 per cent, and it may be as high as 40 or 50 per cent before liberation dawns. Clearly it is in the interest of all South Africans that this time bomb be defused without further delay.

THE RELATIONSHIP BETWEEN
INCOME REDISTRIBUTION AND ECONOMIC GROWTH

Whereas there are indications that it would be relatively easy to reach a consensus regarding the importance of social investments and the eradication of unemployment, there are conflicting perspectives concerning the relative importance of the redistribution of income and of a higher economic growth. Those within establishment circles who favour social democratic types of policy hope that these will lead to a higher rate of growth. The resistance actors, on the other hand, generally seem to be far more concerned with the redistribution of income and wealth. The question is whether this difference in priorities can threaten a possible social-democratic consensus.

Both neo-classical and Marxist economists believe that these two objectives are in conflict. The tenet that capitalist growth leads to the immiserisation of the working class is one of the cornerstones of traditional Marxist economists. Neo-classical economists, on the other hand, have no doubt that attempts to redistribute income undermine economic growth.

It is not difficult to find historical examples to support both these points of view. In the initial stages of economic growth a surplus needs to be mobilised. This primitive accumulation, as Marxists call the process, often leads to the impoverishment of one or more classes of a society. If there is too much concern during this 'take-off' phase with the redistribution of income, the economy may also never get off the ground. It is for this reason that Lord Bevan contended that there would have been no industrial revolution in England had there been a democracy in the eighteenth century.

However, it can hardly be disputed today that capitalist development has in the long run often led to sustained increases in the working-class standards of living, and although dogmatic free marketeers may wish to close their eyes to the evidence, it is clear that the type of redistribution of income brought about by social investment has, in the case of the European social democracies, contributed to the sustained high rates of growth in these economies. On the other hand, it cannot be denied that certain types of redistribution of income have clearly had a negative impact on growth.

There are a number of economists who argue that under present circumstances in South Africa redistribution need not undermine growth. Indeed, some contend that redistribution is a prerequisite for higher rates of growth. We have already taken note of the argument that the South African economy would benefit from the types of social investment which would be made under a social-democratic form of government. In addition, some economists have pointed to the beneficial demand effects of an increase in the relative size of black income.

The economist Anthony Black believes that the inability of South African industry to develop a capital goods industry must be explained in terms of the unfair distribution of income. The demand for many types of goods is too limited to justify the local production of machinery needed to produce the goods; hence the fact that South Africa's dependence on imported goods has not declined, in spite of many years of import substitution. In a paper delivered at a recent conference in Amsterdam, Black contended that a rapid growth in the relative size of black incomes will create the mass market needed for the development of a local capital goods industry.[21]

A paper by Simon Brand and Jan Dreyer,[22] prominent establishment economists who are respectively in charge of the Development Bank of South Africa and the Central Bureau for Economics and Statistics, does not comment upon the desirability or otherwise of income redistribution. It merely shows that a process of income redistribution associated with urbanisation need not lower potential rates of growth. It thus refutes the right-wing contention that income redistribution necessarily has negative consequences. From this conclusion it follows that economically rational income redistribution would lead to higher rates of growth, to the extent that it eliminates political obstacles to growth.

If one assumes that it is possible, under this type of social-democratic government, to attain an economic growth rate of between 6 and 7 per cent per annum, and assuming further that the income of the wealthier classes will grow at only about 1 per cent per annum, everything could be plain sailing. The per capita income of the poorer groups would improve at an annual rate in excess of 10 per cent and income inequalities would rapidly diminish. By the turn of the century the situation could be similar to that which existed in southern Europe in the sixties, and two decades later it would have approached that of the Scandinavian countries.[23]

It would seem as though the goals of redistributing income and increasing the economic growth rate need not be incompatible. On the contrary, in the South African context they could be complementary. Even if the growth rate attained during the first decade or two were slightly in excess of 5 per cent, it should be politically feasible for a democratic government committed to this type of programme to carry it through. This scenario will, however, only have a fair chance of succeeding if a number of crucial, and at times very difficult, political decisions are made at the outset.

DIFFICULT COMPROMISES

In the preceding sections it was argued that many of the objectives of the resistance groups and of influential members of the establishment are not necessarily in conflict, and could be accommodated in a social-democratic system. The most controversial issues have, however, been left until last. Some of the economic objectives to which the resistance movements are committed directly threaten the interests of powerful sectors of the establishment. If compromises regarding these positions cannot be reached, there is no possibility whatsoever of a negotiated settlement in the foreseeable future.

In the Freedom Charter it is stated that the mineral wealth of the country, the banks and the monopoly industries shall be transferred to the ownership of the people. The talks which English-speaking business leaders have had with the ANC in recent years seem to have confirmed their worst fears that this resolution is interpreted literally. To these businessmen, several decades of siege economy seem preferable to a negotiated settlement which leaves the door wide open for nationalisation. Similarly, the farmer who is told that his land will be taken from him will fight to the bitter end, and the civil servant who is told that he will not only be fired but will face a Nuremberg-type trial, will happily spend six months a year on the border rather than accept a settlement which puts his career and possibly his very life at risk.

If compromises regarding these issues are not reached, there is little or no likelihood of an early settlement. Is it, however, politically realistic to assume that economically rational compromises are feasible? At least some of those interviewed believed that it may be in the interest of the resistance groups to reformulate their position if there really seems to be a possibility of serious negotiations.

Firstly, there are clearly pragmatic considerations which may lead to a modification of present positions. After all, if agreement on how these extremely sensitive issues are to be handled cannot be reached, there will be no negotiated settlement. In the absence of a compromise, the resistance to change by the establishment could delay a transition to a democratic government for decades. There will be little joy in nationalising gold mines which have little profitable gold ore left, and in taking over industries which have been destroyed by years of war and economic isolation.

Another set of reasons for reconsidering the implementation of specific programmes has to do with economic realism. For example, in the presentation of a paper[24] dealing with the role of Armscor in a liberated South Africa, Professor Gerard Wittich from East Berlin argued that a post-apartheid government will be very hard put to find personpower merely to take over the existing state corporations. It will not be possible, he argued, for such a government to begin to take over effective control of the four or five really large companies which control so large a proportion of the South African economy.

Instead of nationalising all land, a Zimbabwean type of farming policy in which the productive white farmers are not only permitted to continue to produce their goods, but are encouraged to produce more, while black farmers or co-operatives are simultaneously established on farms previously owned by absentee landlords and in other areas, may seem to be the only feasible economic policy for a post-revolutionary government. It would not be in the interests of anyone to carry on with a long and destructive conflict because of the resistance movement's intention to socialise or nationalise the land and the large companies, when these goals are not tenable in any case.

The shortage of skilled personpower, caused partly by the Bantu Education situation, is not a problem which will disappear with the abolition of apartheid. On the contrary, it is likely to become an even more serious issue should the economy resume its historically high rates of growth in the wake of a negotiated settlement. The skills which are disproportionately in white hands will thus be at a particular premium. More than any constitutional guarantee in a social democratic type of negotiated settlement, this reality would provide the assurance that the new government would not adopt policies which could lead to a large-scale emigration of exactly those people that the economy needs the most.

In the case of the civil service the same type of argument can be put forward in respect of the technocrats. As far as the less-skilled civil servants are concerned, the danger of any radical policy change is that the displaced civil servants would become the backbone of a contra movement. Since the successful implementation of a social democratic type of policy will lead to a fairly rapid expansion of the civil service in any case (most of the social investments made will, for example, be done collectively rather than privately), it again makes little sense to propound radical changes in this sphere when they are unlikely to be implemented should a negotiated settlement be reached within the next decade. In the case of the police and the military it will clearly be particularly difficult to reach a compromise.

The preceding set of considerations does not imply, though, that it is reasonable to expect that the economic sphere will and ought to be left untouched in a post-apartheid phase. Indeed, some form of worker participation and possibly government representation on the boards of directors of big companies, the redistribution of land not productively farmed and a policy of positive discrimination are probably minimum demands which will have to be met. A South African social democracy will only gain acceptance if it goes significantly further than the redistribution-with-growth policies which establishment supporters are propounding. At least some members of the establishment are beginning to consider the possibility of compromises in these areas.

At this stage it is not possible to present any details of possible compromises which could be reached with regard to the controversial economic issues. Neither the establishment nor the resistance members have given serious consideration to these questions, nor has sufficient research been done to ask for responses to possible strategies. At best it can be concluded that there is at present an indication that compromises will be considered by both sides.

The establishment of a social democracy is clearly not going to be an unproblematic exercise. However, if there is to be a negotiated settlement, it is likely that it will be along these lines.

A UNILATERAL SOCIAL DEMOCRACY?

Would it be possible for a social democracy to be implemented unilaterally once a settlement has been reached between the government, the Labour Party and traditional black leaders, including Buthelezi? (The ANC would, under such a settlement, be excluded on the grounds that it does not reject violence.)

It seems unlikely for two reasons that a negotiated settlement which excludes the UDF and ANC could lead to long-term economic progress, even if an economic policy commensurate with a social democracy were to be adopted.

Firstly, as was noted earlier, the compromises implicit in a social democracy will not be acceptable to the people if the government does not have their full confidence. Only a settlement which includes the UDF and the ANC could, under present circumstances, ensure the internal stability that is a precondition for the successful implementation of a social democratic type of policy.

Secondly, the relatively high rates of economic growth which are a prerequisite for a successful social democracy could be realised only if South Africa were to regain full access to international markets and credit. It is unlikely that the international pressures on South Africa would be significantly reduced should an important group such as the ANC be excluded from a settlement. In addition, a whole range of positive international measures to support relatively rapid rates of growth will probably be essential for such policies to succeed. Indeed, in order to improve the chances of success for a social democratic type of settlement, it would make good sense for all South Africans to demand concrete guarantees of international support for the new South Africa as part of the settlement package. Access to the markets of the European economic community and the United States, the reconsideration of South Africa's international debts and negotiated agreements to provide the new South Africa with aid on the scale of the Marshall Plan are all possible benefits of an internationally recognised settlement.

Attempts to 'go it alone' are bound to fail. A social democracy requires internal stability and international acceptance and support.

Expanding conflict or a negotiated settlement?

It was argued above that if there is a long and destructive conflict before the present government loses power, it seems most likely that a Stalinist type of transition will take place. War demands authoritarian structures of command, and the economic chaos and destruction caused by a long period of armed conflict and sanctions would undermine the case for social-democratic reconciliation. Furthermore, a radical young generation which had grown up in townships under constant siege would be emotionally less inclined than the old guard to consider any compromise. It was also argued that a siege-economy strategy may enable the present government to hold on to power for considerably longer than the opponents of the government would care to admit.

As is often the case in situations of conflict, the extremes gain strength from each other. The radical programme of rigid Marxist-Leninists are put forward by the government as a justification for resisting change to the bitter end. The siege-economy approach in its turn justifies the position of those on the left who claim that there is no room for compromise.

Is there, under these circumstances, a reasonable chance that there will be a negotiated settlement before the productive capacity of the economy has been destroyed by a long period of sanctions and military conflict?

THE SOUTH AFRICAN GOVERNMENT AND NEGOTIATION

The attack by the South African army on what it claimed to be ANC bases in Harare and Lusaka at the time when the Eminent Persons Group was visiting Cape Town on behalf of the Commonwealth in an attempt to get negotiations off the ground, was a clear indication of dominant thinking within government circles regarding negotiations.[25] In this section two questions will be addressed:

What are the reasons for the reluctance to negotiate, even though the likelihood of escalating economic sanctions has been clearly spelt out? Under which circumstances is it likely that negotiations will be given serious consideration?

It is clear that the government embarked on its siege-economy programme with a certain degree of reluctance and that there is still much ambiguity with regard to the future. The original vision was one of incremental reform, incorporating more and more groups into the political system, doing away with the discriminatory measures unique to South Africa, and in the process gaining increasing international acceptance. All groups were to be represented in the South African government, but political control was to remain in 'responsible hands'. The combination of these reforms would bring political stability and economic progress to all South Africans. It would not be a Western democracy, but would become one of the more successful and progressive third world countries.

When it became clear that the reforms which were being implemented did not meet the expectations of large sections of the black population and did not achieve the international acknowledgement which the government expected, but led instead to escalating internal resistance and increasing international pressures, the government decided that it would proceed alone. It would 'restore order' on the home front, and would rather face a siege than give in to international pressures. The reform programme would not be abandoned. Instead, more efforts would be made to incorporate 'moderate' blacks into the political process, and political stability would where possible be bought by social and infrastructural investment.

If the conclusions reached above are correct, the siege economy, if the government should commit itself fully to it, will eventually fail, but only after an initial and possibly quite extended period of success. In the end negotiations will be unavoidable. At that stage, for the reasons discussed, a social democracy is unlikely. The resistance groups, sensing victory, will be in no mood for compromise.

Although the siege-economy strategy seems to be on the ascendant at present (late 1987), there are influential groups within the government who would prefer to see a negotiated settlement along the lines of a relatively conservative social democracy. The recent acceptance of the South African Transport Workers Union, after the initial dismissal of all 18 000 members, partly reflects the strength of the union, but also indicates that a willingness to compromise is still there.

Those within the government who are considering a negotiated settlement do not, however, seem to believe that it is possible to reach it with the ANC, as the administration is constituted at present. Some hope to incorporate the majority of blacks into a democratic-socialist system which excludes the ANC with its 'totalitarian Marxist tendencies', whereas others hope that a deal can be struck with the nationalist wing of the ANC, excluding the Communist Party with its radical goals. If these strategies for negotiation should fail, most of the social democrats within the government would opt for a siege economy rather than 'surrender to the ANC extremists'.

THE ANC AND NEGOTIATIONS

ANC and UDF spokesmen have declared at various stages that it is no longer a question of negotiating a settlement concerned with the nature of future economic and political systems; the question of how power is to be transferred is all that is at issue. The government, on the other hand, has indicated that it would enter into negotiations only with those who foreswear violence. The ANC has refused to take this step, arguing that it would deny itself one of the few avenues along which it can exert pressure on the government to take negotiations seriously. Does it follow from these two stands that negotiation is not possible in the foreseeable future?

Judging from opinions expressed by ANC members, including members of the Communist Party, it is clear that a wide spectrum of opinion within the ANC accepts that, should there be negotiations, not only the issue of the transfer of power, but the actual nature of the future society will be open for discussion. Is there any chance, however, that the social democratic type of solution which at present seems to be by far the most radical the establishment would consider, will be accepted by the ANC, and will the Communist Party have to be excluded from any negotiations if there is to be a settlement?

There is no doubt that many of the ANC members who have Marxist sympathies would strongly object to the types of compromise suggested above. Furthermore, there is much evidence that the South African Communist Party has been traditionally far more hard line than the Euro-communists. However, it would be wrong to conclude from this that the Communist Party would necessarily reject a negotiated settlement along the lines envisaged in the preceding section. Both the communists and the nationalists have a hard core of radicals who are fully committed to the belief that the structures of domination will have to be 'smashed'. Both groups, however, also have members willing to compromise. A Communist Party statement, that the nature of the new society which will emerge will depend on the relative strength of the classes at the stage of transition, can surely be read to imply an acceptance of a social democracy should transition take place under the present circumstances.[26]

At present the major obstacle to a serious consideration of alternative economic strategies within the ANC seems to be a lack of significant research into the technical constraints and possibilities of the South African economy. Whereas the establishment has done a fair degree of in-depth research about possible future scenarios, the ANC has, for understandable reasons, been more concerned with political and strategic issues. Only very recently have members of the ANC and groups close to it started to consider some of the detailed economic implications of a transition. It is possible that this process may itself lead to a willingness to accept compromises.

This does not imply that it is highly likely that the ANC will give serious consideration to a compromise solution. However, it is wrong to argue that simply because the ANC has a strong communist wing compromises are not possible before the SACP is excluded. Indeed, on certain issues Marxists may be more willing to compromise than nationalists. In addition to those whom the Trotskyites have branded Stalinists, there is a group that seems to be more pragmatic. Given more research and more understanding of economic realities, the bridge between the establishment and the ANC may not be as large as both sides seem to believe.

A PREDICTION

The South African drama has two possible denouements. In the one, the government, although it occasionally considers negotiation, clings to power to the bitter end. Its prediction that the ANC will establish a radical Marxist government will then, as we have argued above, most likely prove to be self-fulfilling.

The other possibility is that both sides will begin to realise that a long and drawn-out conflict during the next few years will serve the interests of no-one, and that a political and economic compromise will be reached after negotiations which will be at times very difficult.

Which of these two resolutions is the most likely? Economic rationality argues for the second scenario, but political momentum seems to favour the first. A firm prediction can, however, not be made. In the final analysis the outcome will depend on the choices which both the establishment and resistance participants make during the next few years.

7 The United States and the world

JOHN MARCUM, HELEN KITCHEN
AND MICHAEL SPICER

The United States and other external participants

South Africans of all political persuasions monitor external reactions to their country's protracted political crisis with varying degrees of hope, anger and despair. They try to predict the short- and long-term impact of external policy responses on political and economic conditions in South Africa. Many opponents of the apartheid system assess responses with the view that the United States, Western Europe or the Soviet Union (taking into account their divergent economic interests, ideological motives and threat perceptions) have the power, if not the will, to hasten, shape or block progress toward fundamental political change.

It is with a mixture of defiance and concern that the governing National Party watches the policy initiatives of Western powers who refuse to accept today's South Africa as an integral part of the 'free world'. Groups on Afrikanerdom's extreme right now assume that the West is hostile, and they tend to view all international interactions with increasing suspicion. Incrementalists who share Western values and visions of a democratic, pluralist future for South Africa worry that Western sanctions may render such goals less attainable. Anti-government resistance forces perceive the West and Japan as economically linked to the support of the status quo, but they nonetheless actively seek support from those states as well as (notably in the case of the African National Congress) from the Soviet Union and associated states.

South Africa constitutes an intractable distraction for external powers embedded in a global system that is seized by enormous trade deficits and economic imbalances and by momentous issues concerning security and disarmament. Until recently, most states have approached their relations to South Africa with essentially the same economic and strategic reasoning that shapes most of their own interstate relations. They assumed that historical and economic logic would serve their interests by gradually integrating a unified South African nation within a modern, Western-oriented economy which is immunised against Soviet/communist influence.

Over a period of time, however, the continuing exclusion of a majority of South Africa's population from political power on racial grounds has generated a mixture of militant and populist anti-apartheid activism which has become a significant force in some Western countries. In the United States, where racial exclusion is now widely viewed as an exceptional affront to human dignity, relations with South Africa have become a test of the United States' moral character for many people. The argument that the traditional notions of 'national interest' must give way in this instance to an exceptional moral imperative, directly challenges the 'realist' school of foreign policy theorists and practitioners. Dissension over their counsel, for example Henry Kissinger's thesis that "a foreign policy that makes human rights its cornerstone invites revolution",[1] has led to lurches, lulls and inconsistencies in United States policy.

Although the policies of the United States, as well as those of South Africa's other major trading partners, have been neither consistent enough nor potent enough to induce the desired fundamental reform, they have not been without effect. A largely observed international arms embargo and other Western sanctions are exacting not only short-term military and economic costs but, more significantly, long-term opportunity costs in the form of lost investment, constraints on technology flows and the emigration of skilled professionals. The National Party may win elections, circumvent trade sanctions, expel investigative journalists, block external funding for opposition groups and otherwise successfully defy external 'interference' in its 'internal affairs'. But in time the price could prove devastating for South Africa (and for the whole southern African region), and could also impose heavy penalties on any successor government in South Africa and on its ability to foster a more just and equitable society.

The present and prospective role of the world community as a constraint and influence on South Africa may be best analysed by focusing on four actors, or clusters of actors: the United States; Western Europe and Japan; the Soviet Union and associated states; and South Africa's frontline neighbours.

THE UNITED STATES

For the United States, more than for any other Western country, South Africa has become a significant domestic political issue. Because Americans have a high level of sensitivity to racial scenes of police violence, to news of arbitrary arrests and to the enforcement of discriminatory laws which remind them of their own nation's recent past, South Africa has drawn large numbers of city councillors, state legislators, trade unionists, university administrators and others who do not normally address such issues into 'foreign policy making'.[2]

The widespread perception that successive United States administrations have failed to lever or stimulate fundamental changes in the South African system has sparked further grass-roots efforts to reorient and drive United States policy. In January 1987, an independent Advisory Committee to the Secretary of State (established by President Reagan in response to 1986 congressional guidance) reported that the situation within South Africa had "moved in a direction sharply at odds with the hopes and expectations of the architects" of United States policy. Although failing to agree unanimously on policy prescriptions, the committee's twelve members despaired of 'fundamental change' under "a process managed and led by a National Party government"; and concluded that unrest and violence in urban and rural areas raised doubts about the government's ability to halt 'political disintegration'. They also perceived 'evidence of increasingly bitter anti-Americanism among South African blacks' as a threat to long-term United States interests; and noted the significant growth of citizens' groups, including TransAfrica and the Free South Africa Movement, which had rendered 'apartheid a major public issue'.[3]

Another factor in the preoccupation of the United States with the South African situation has been the 'can do' problem-solving approach characteristic of American thinking. The solution to South Africa's trauma has appeared quite straightforward to many

– simply repeal all apartheid legislation, release Nelson Mandela from prison, unban political organisations and negotiate a new constitution. Ipso facto, the South African issue should therefore be susceptible to solution, with but a push and some arm-twisting by the United States. Such causal optimism has long befogged much American analysis of United States–South African relations.

In the years immediately following the Second World War, United States policy toward South Africa was based on the assumption that the country would experience a gradual extension of Western political norms. South African forces had fought for the Allied cause in both Europe and North Africa in the Second World War, an air force unit served alongside United States forces in Korea and Oak Ridge technology and training helped South Africa build its first nuclear reactor. In due course, however, the imposition of rigid apartheid as the law of the land after 1948 undermined hopes for evolutionary liberalisation and led the United States to join (1962-1963) in an arms embargo as part of an international effort to mount external pressure on Pretoria for change. Though there have been fluctuations in emphasis which ranged from cajoling to condemning, an official approach known as 'constructive engagement' gradually emerged as the core of United States policy. As first set forth in a State Department release of July 1973, 'constructive engagement' – a term later amplified by and associated with the Reagan administration's Assistant Secretary of State for African Affairs Chester Crocker – was defined as "a policy of systematic communication with the leaders of all of South Africa's racial groups" and "a programme of actively encouraging and supporting the efforts of private American firms operating in South Africa to upgrade the pay, conditions of work, job opportunities and fringe benefits of their black employees".[4]

The underlying assumption remained optimistic. Despite political 'differences' the United States attached 'value' to its economic relations with South Africa and looked "forward to the day when, her racial problems solved and the rights of all its citizens protected, South Africa (would) play an increasingly important role on the continent of Africa and in the world generally".[5]

Typically, each successive United States administration assertively raised expectations that it would be more successful than its predecessor in hastening South Africa along the liberalisation path. Inevitably, each would be judged by the shortfall in its achievements, a shortfall which, aside from a lack of strategic thinking, reflected both a limited commitment and limited power to shape the course of events.

In focusing initially on the goal of facilitating Namibian independence under internationally acceptable terms, the Reagan administration sought to demonstrate in its first years that a solicitous pursuit of a regionally applied policy of constructive engagement could produce a sequence of concrete and progressive results. However, in unilaterally linking the withdrawal of South African forces from Namibia to a simultaneous withdrawal of Cuban troops from insurgency-torn Angola, United States policy makers dismantled collective Western diplomatic pressure[6] and provided a rationale for prolonging South Africa's military presence in Namibia. By 1986, the Reagan administration had deferred to conservative domestic forces, had become an open supporter of anti-government insurgents (UNITA) in Angola and had found its diplomatic efforts to achieve a Namibian settlement sidelined. Partly as a result of these actions, Angolan dependency on an enlarged Cuban military presence was intensified. The administration was left unable to claim any tangible success for its regional policy except in Mozambique, where its good offices helped to produce a nonaggression pact between that country and South Africa (the Nkomati Accord of 1984), as well as an expanding political/economic opening to the West.

A paradox of United States policy is that for some time it was arguably more influential with regard to circumstances within South Africa itself. Though the political reforms of the Botha presidency removed some important but still marginal building blocks of apartheid (the ban on mixed marriages, the pass laws, restrictions on university admissions) as distinct from the more central ones (the Group Areas Act, homeland citizenship, franchise prohibitions), they did seem to gather momentum, to raise hopes and to permit an enlarged scope for organised opposition. In the view of some United States and South African government observers, discreet United States pressure was a contributing factor to this apparent trend toward liberalisation. But the gap between what the National Party government and the black political leadership considered a reasonable scope, pace and process of reform led to an increasing incidence of violent confrontation which pulled millions of American television viewers into the vortex of the South African racial drama.

Anti-apartheid activism

As Pretoria resorted to increasingly coercive measures in order to restore its authority, pressure from a media-sensitised American public for sanctions 'to force' South Africa to become more liberal assumed unprecedented proportions. This growing American restiveness found expression and reinforcement, in part, through the activities of committed anti-apartheid organisations such as the American Committee on Africa, the Washington Office on Africa, TransAfrica, and the Interfaith Center on Corporate Responsibility (ICCR).[7]

These political action groups, which endorse very generally what they perceive to be ANC and United Democratic Front (UDF) visions of a unitary, nonracial democracy with simple majority rule and a redistributive economy, have been quite specific about what they believe Americans should do to hasten an end to the apartheid system. In their opinion they should press for the withdrawal of all United States firms, end licensing and other agreements that provide access to United States technology, ban bank loans and restrict South African imports. Their reasoning is that these actions will weaken the South African economy and thereby motivate whites to seek political accommodation with the black majority. Accordingly, they have mobilised pressure on United States companies and banks through divestment, consumer boycott and shareholder actions. They have organised popular campaigns at local and state levels in support of legislation designed to persuade United States firms to pull out of South Africa and have lobbied at the national level for sanctions legislation. They also helped to inspire the anti-apartheid activism which surged on United States campuses in the mid 1970s, and which has risen and fallen with the level (and portrayal on American television) of violent unrest in South Africa over the ensuing decade.

By mid-1987, university and college divestment action had resulted in the sale of over $600 million in stocks of companies doing business in South Africa. This protest-driven action, in turn, helped trigger moves by state and local legislative bodies to mandate divestment of public pension funds from such stocks. At the end of 1986, the holdings of city, county and state employee pension funds totalled over $650 billion as compared to $57 billion held in university and college portfolios. By 1987, a growing list of divestment laws had compelled the sale of some $20 billion of public pension fund-held stock over the next five years. This represented approximately 1 per cent of all company stock in the United States. It happened because state and local legislators responded to the combination of anti-apartheid lobbying and South African unrest.

At the same time, what was even more alarming for United States business were the decisions taken by some state and local governments (including New York City and Los Angeles) which made it increasingly difficult or even impossible for companies with operations in South Africa to bid successfully on state and municipal government contracts. In voting for or against such measures, interviews in diverse cities and states suggest that legislators were not responding to voter pressure. They report that their constituents rarely raised questions about South Africa. By assuming a clear anti-apartheid posture, however, legislators took the precaution of protecting themselves from potential attack for being 'soft on racism'.

Legislators at all levels, like most anti-apartheid activists, leave detailed political prescriptions for the future to South Africans. What little thought they have given to visualising a post-apartheid society has been prodded forth by opponents of sanctions, who ask whether economic destabilisation might not lead South Africa 'to go Communist'. As with United States businessmen operating in South Africa, it is not surprising that their response affirms a preference for a South Africa with a free market economy shorn of all racial barriers without being rigidly prescriptive.

246

The United States business community

As a political agent lobbied by anti-apartheid activists, the United States business community has perceived and presented itself increasingly as a force committed to the rationality of equal opportunity and racial integration. Even if United States corporations did not always implement these principles in a timely or thorough fashion, their nominal adherence to them helped to render official policies of discrimination illegitimate. United States businessmen generally articulate a cautious reformism and are wary of a rapid implementation of majority rule lest it provoke right-wing counter-revolution and/or black one-party rule. They argue the need for a transitional phase to bridge the way into majority rule.

In the view of some United States bankers and corporate executives, such a transition phase could create a set of interests and values among South African blacks which would overlap those of business and encourage rejection of political demagoguery. To this end, they accept that all laws restricting freedom of association must be eliminated. With South Africans of all races free to live where they choose, to send their children to whichever schools they choose and to purchase property or run a business where they choose ('choices' which beg the questions of accessibility and which ignore the time it would take to close the economic gap grounded in racial cleavages), universal suffrage and majority rule would become feasible.

Other United States businessmen interviewed, however, believe it impractical to think that political rights for blacks can be withheld until the socio-economic gap between black and white has narrowed. In their view, an acceptable transition phase would be one that provided constitutional protection for individual and group rights. Some even more sceptical corporate executives (recognising that their preference for a free market economy in which gradual redistribution would ameliorate inequalities may be an unrealistic hope, and noting a rise of antipathy toward capitalism among blacks who associate the term with apartheid) observe philosophically that United States firms operate around the world under a variety of political and economic systems. So long as any

247

South African government allows them reasonable management autonomy and profit and eschews confiscatory tax rates, they will be prepared to conduct business in South Africa.

Conservative activism

Latecomers to the South African debate are such groups on the right of the United States political spectrum as the Heritage Foundation, the American Legislative Exchange Council, the Conservative Caucus and the Liberty Foundation (formerly the Moral Majority). Adherents of these organisations, and their media outlets, accept that South Africa must rid itself of apartheid, but believe that the process should be incremental so as not to jeopardise political and economic stability. In their view, President Botha has made progress toward ending apartheid and is obliged to move carefully in order to avoid a devastating conservative white backlash.

Although they are partial to decentralisation and to built-in protection for minority groups, conservative activists envisage the Inkatha movement, homeland leaders and black township councillors negotiating with the white government to create a future political structure. Like some (but, as noted earlier, not all) United States businessmen, conservative activists fear that attempts to install centralised majority rule would bring chaos – white rebellion, a splintered National Party and opposition from many coloureds and Indians. This school of thought would replace what it views as the 'ethnic socialism' of present-day South Africa with a free enterprise economy which would create sufficient wealth to improve the living standards of blacks without reducing the wealth and economic security of whites. Believing that economic growth would lead to an extension of political rights to blacks, conservatives typically argue for increasing United States economic and diplomatic ties with South Africa. They would also reframe the South African debate in geostrategic – as opposed to racial – terms, believing the 'most important question' to be whether a mineral-rich South Africa, located adjacent to 'the Cape route', ends up as an ally of the West or as a satellite of the Soviet Union.

A crescendo of political activism climaxed in 1986 with the enactment of what is officially termed the Comprehensive Anti-Apartheid Act. Overriding President Reagan's veto, Congress translated a package of sanctions into law which notably banned imports of South African textiles, iron, steel, coal, uranium, agricultural products and all goods produced by South African government-controlled corporations, and which terminated landing rights for South African Airways in the United States.

The passing of the 1986 sanctions act – the strongest unilateral sanctions package adopted to date by any of South Africa's major trading partners – marked a watershed in United States-South African relations. When added to the negative assessment of constructive engagement by the administration's own Advisory Committee and to divestment action by well over a hundred United States firms, it gave anti-apartheid activists the impression that they had prevailed. Even conservative political leaders such as Republican Governor George Deukmejian of California seemed to join the activist ranks as he successfully urged the regents of the University of California to divest funds totalling over $3 billion from firms 'doing business' in South Africa. Deukmejian asserted, without feeling the need for explanatory analysis, that if such action were taken throughout the country, it would force the South African government to abandon apartheid.

This 'leap of faith' assumption, possibly based on the questionable hypothesis that the political shock caused by a 1985 refusal of international banks to roll over South African loans implied a critical vulnerability to trade and investment sanctions, pointed to a weakness shared by anti-apartheid and conservative activists, legislators and businessmen. Few, if any, had done much strategic thinking or feasibility testing of their policy prescriptions. It seemed to matter only that one took the 'right' stance. The moral climate, suffused by racial and/or anti-communist emotion, was largely intolerant of deliberate or deliberative processes. There was no sense of obligation to expand upon and 'reality test' the logic of why one's strategy would work, and at what costs, over what period of time or by what criteria for success.

Where did this leave things? What strategic choices were still open to United States policy makers in the wake of the Comprehensive Anti-Apartheid Act?

It did seem that American options had narrowed and American leverage had further diminished. Exercise of United States influence by means of increased economic and diplomatic involvement (that is, expanded engagement) was, in the prevailing mindset, a spent option. Military intervention by an overextended and debt-burdened superpower was not then, and probably never had been, a politically feasible option. Massive assistance for educational and economic programmes for the emancipation of black South Africans or for construction of transport and communication infrastructure to enable neighbouring states to escape dependency on South Africa had become hostage to executive branch and congressional preoccupations with trade and budget deficits. This left the virtual certainty of continued economic sanctions, with debate centred on whether or not to expand them. Anti-apartheid groups were bound to press for expansion, arguing that the screws should and could be tightened until the South African government deferred before such external pressure.

What would this entail? How would one know that sanctions were working? The advocates of sanctions did not elaborate an agreed list of such signals. But if they had, the list might presumably have included concrete evidence of economic stress (for example, declining investment and trade, rising unemployment) and, subsequently, leaving aside whether such a causal link was ever likely or indeed even possible, some moves to initiate talks with resistance leadership, to dismantle key structures of apartheid and to halt military and economic intervention against neighbouring states. Equally, the haste with which *Forbes* magazine blazoned its cover (9 March 1987) with the assertion that 'Economic sanctions aren't working' could be attributed to an American tendency to focus on short-term consequences or the lack thereof.

In fact, the sanctions adopted were both limited and inexpensive. They should not have been expected to have great impact. They left United States firms free to pursue business by adjusting to commercial modes which had been employed successfully by the

Japanese for some time: reliance on licensing, franchising and sales agreements free from capital entanglement. And it was predictable that a wave of near-simultaneous divestment decisions would, in the short run, benefit those who hold the political and/or economic power in South Africa. It afforded opportunities for bargain buy-outs, removed externally imposed constraints on sales to military and security agencies, and freed successor firms from Sullivan Code fair-employment obligations.

Ironically, United States business, which in the past had some-times been slow to pursue the kind of aggressive fair-employment practices long recommended by critics and the United States government, had acceded to domestic pressure and finally begun to challenge apartheid at its core. Corporations had, for example, taken to providing appropriate housing to key black employees in white residential areas – just at the moment when decisions to with-draw had begun reducing the United States presence, and with it the South African government incentive to tolerate United States 'interference'. What limited the influence of the United States even further was the irritating but non-debilitating effect of low-cost sanctions which rendered the South African government less disposed to grant visas, issue passports and permit external fund-ing destined for educational and economic programming which is necessary to prepare the way for an equitable post-apartheid so-ciety.

Assessing the new conjuncture, Princeton's Henry Bienen con-cluded that the United States had embarked upon "a policy that involves partial sanctions over a long period of time", which por-tends a general distancing from South Africa, and requires a realis-tic acceptance of the limits of American influence. But "as violence increases within South Africa," he predicted, "American constitu-encies will fragment over the 'what-is-to-be-done' question. A pol-icy of disengagement will be as fraught with difficulties and open to attack as the policy of constructive engagement has been."[8]

In a tandem of speeches given in late 1987 as they approached the end of their "watch", Secretary of State George Shultz and Assistant Secretary Crocker acknowledged "frustration" in the face of "grim realities", warned against "debilitating pessimism", and set forth a to-be-hoped-for vision of a democratic South Africa grounded in universal suffrage, individual rights, multiparty elections, and a free economy. While arguing that "meaningful reform" ceased and the cycle of violence and counterviolence increased in the wake of the 1986 sanctions, they nonetheless accepted that Americans were deeply divided over how to facilitate the realization of their widely acceptable vision.

Crocker, in particular, lamented that the South African government had been "slow" to respond to a "unique opportunity" afforded in part by well-intentioned American policy. He decried an "adolescent tendency" among South African protagonists of all persuasions "alternately to cultivate or scapegoat" foreigners. Sobered by experience, he and Secretary Shultz seemed to be advising those who would succeed them after the 1988 United States presidential election against unrealistic expectations or promises. In Crocker's words: ". . . we know now – more than ever – that the fate of South Africa is not in our hands".[9]

Long-term prospects

Sanctions may assume an altogether different significance in the long run. Opportunity costs in terms of investment, technology and markets not acquired – what might be termed invisible sanctions – could prove critically debilitating. With a rapidly expanding population, limited water resources and dependence on depleting gold seams, South Africa must run just to stand in place economically. Diversion of the country's creative energies and material resources into the open-ended military and security expenditures required by a siege-state scenario would blight its economic future. If gradual but inescapable marginalisation within a highly competitive world economy and progressive geopolitical isolation are to be avoided, South Africa must invest massively in the development of its human capital.

By September 1987, *The Wall Street Journal* was reporting that although sanctions had prompted Pretoria "to tighten repression and become even less responsive to United States influence", they had already begun to show "signs of long-term dividends". Economic analysis indicated that sanctions were "inhibiting what

252

would have been more-robust growth, creating long-range pressures for Pretoria". They were holding growth to a 2,5 to 3 per cent annual rate, a percentage point below what it might have been without sanctions, and well below the 5 to 6 per cent "needed to keep up with population growth and to cut unemployment". In addition, *The Wall Street Journal* concluded: ". . . blacks in South Africa and the rest of the continent who once interpreted President Reagan's resistance to sanctions as American support for apartheid are developing new confidence in the United States".[10]

Even in the medium term, United States pressure on Israel – pressure stemming in part from the exigencies of a seasoned but troubled black-Jewish political alliance in United States domestic politics – to curtail economic, technological and military collaboration with South Africa could prove costly. For Israel, that largely concealed collaboration represents thousands of jobs and hundreds of millions of dollars annually. Yet maintenance of the present level of co-operation with South Africa, in defiance of an investigative press and an inquiring United States Congress, might not be worth the risk of alienating political opinion in a country upon which Israel depends for billions of dollars in annual assistance.

As long as violence and repression are perceived as the dominant motif in South African politics, United States public-sector pressure to sustain and expand sanctions and the private-sector propensity to withdraw or avoid new entanglement is bound to continue. Sceptics point to the American public's notoriously short attention span in foreign affairs, and to the episodic nature of campus and other anti-apartheid activity. They note that expanded sanctions would cross the threshold of serious economic costs to the United States. They point out that, despite the promissory wording of the Comprehensive Anti-Apartheid Act, a financially pinched Congress (in the absence of committed presidential leadership) did not significantly increase funding for black South African educational programming. Indeed, with a diminution of support from corporations relishing relief from the difficulties of investor responsibility in South Africa, the number of scholarships available for university study in the United States under the Institute for International Education's South African Education Pro-gram (SAEP) decreased in the aftermath of the sanctions enactment.

Given the sheer magnitude of economic and security issues confronting United States policy makers in the form of trade deficits, disarmament negotiations, an increasingly unstable Middle East, Central American conflicts and random crises from the Philippines to Chad, the United States seems unlikely to give intense, consistent priority attention to South Africa. The temptation to conclude that divestment and disinvestment, low-cost trade sanctions, sports and cultural boycotts and political distancing has ended United States complicity with or obligations concerning apartheid could prove powerful – especially with intensified media censorship drastically reducing the amount of emotive print and television coverage of the South African scene.

Nonetheless, the conscience-prodding and relentless unfolding of what has come to be perceived globally as a kind of morality play of our time will simply not let Americans escape. They will probably not respond with a comprehensive or coherent overall strategy. They are likely to be chronically frustrated and confused by the intractable nature of South African issues – soluble, if at all, only by negotiation between the major rival actors: the government and the resistance. But what if, in Henry Bienen's words, "black leaders who want to negotiate cannot appear at the table because of violence and intimidation? What if the South African government is too split and paralysed to negotiate?"[11] Will the United States dismissively turn its back and walk away? The South African issue has probably been too deeply assimilated into domestic political life in the United States for this to happen. It also seems unlikely that such complexities will erode the perception of South Africa as a morality play or encourage new forms of engagement. What is more likely is a fitful, incoherent, but persevering pursuit of policies which tend to ostracise and penalise South Africa and South Africans in a rather undifferentiated and strategically chaotic manner.

At the same time, the commitment of major foundations, universities, churches, a few corporations and even local governments to support educational and economic programmes developed in col-

254

laboration with black community-based organisations such as the South African Committee for Higher Education, the Educational Opportunities Council, the Equal Opportunity Foundation, a range of black trade unions and others will persist. Established programmes which assist a level of up to 500 black South African students and trainees in the United States are likely to continue. United States research centres and universities will go on addressing South Africa as 'a problem to be solved'. A remorseless series of descriptive and prescriptive studies and polemics will continue to testify to an enduring fascination with and engagement in the South African challenge.

As the political and economic frustrations and costs of a partial sanctions policy mount, however, Americans are likely to become increasingly agitated by other 'business as usual' countries which seek to serve their national interests by eschewing or circumventing sanctions and disengagement. In confronting assertions that sanctions do not work, anti-apartheid activists will stress that to work they must be multilateral. Ideology may meld with economic self-interest to generate strong efforts by the United States to prevail upon South Africa's traditional trading partners as well as upon new prospects for trade and technology exchange such as the Newly Industrialising Countries (NICs) of the Pacific Rim, to adopt policies conforming with its own. The previously cited 1987 report of the Secretary of State's Advisory Committee on South Africa pointedly recommended that "the President begin urgent consultations with our allies (especially Britain, Canada, West Germany, France, Japan and Israel) to enlist their support for a multilateral programme of sanctions".[12]

WESTERN EUROPE AND JAPAN

European and Japanese interests do not include the domestic racial dimensions featured in the United States. Their interests are principally economic and are only slightly modified by general human rights concerns. Given the increasingly multiracial character and the attendant racial tension in British society, together with the enduring presence of a large number of exiled South African anti-apartheid activists, however, the United Kingdom is a partial exception. There, South African issues are beginning to feature in borough politics and a growing drive exists to pressurise British companies to divest.

The heavier the investment and trade involvement, the more cautious the Europeans and Japanese are in approaching the topic of sanctions. Apart from any principled conviction, such interests are the major reason for Britain's strong opposition to sanctions at the United Nations and within the Commonwealth, and they explain why Prime Minister Margaret Thatcher has steadfastly rejected the pro-sanctions advice of such bodies as the Commonwealth's Eminent Persons Group and most Commonwealth leaders. By contrast, the Scandinavian countries, with only minor economic interests at stake, call for assertive, draconian and principled action.

Within the European Community (EC) a lowest common denominator or consensus approach has neared the limits of low-cost action and has slowed down. In Europe, even more assuredly than in the United States, resistance seems set to grow as pressure for more stringent measures appears likely to entail serious costs. Both Europe and Japan are necessarily sensitive to United States policy stances, however, and will not wish to compound trade disagreements of a more central importance with confrontation over South African policies. Similarly, Israel and the Asian NICs will have to consider the trade-offs most soberly.

As a compulsive trade-surplus builder, Japan could find itself a special target of United States rancour. In 1986, despite a decline in yen terms, Japanese two way trade with South Africa climbed to $3,59 billion, just behind the figure of $3,64 billion for the United States, South Africa's premier trade partner. Japanese trade in 1987 was roughly $4 billion, well ahead of the Federal Republic of Germany which moved into second position and of the United States in third, where South African imports were cut by the 1986 sanctions measures. Japan is conscious of the risk of angry economic retaliation if it should be seen to profit unfairly from the principled actions of sanctions and disengagement. There are signs that Japan is informally seeking to adjust its trade levels with South Africa in a way which will preserve strategic minerals and metals imports. The response of black Americans to injudicious comments by Japanese leaders, who have compared the advantages of Japan's homogeneous society favourably against the racially heterogeneous society of the United States, has already shown how volatile the issue might be.

Another factor which is internal to South Africa and which may intensify pressure for multilateral distancing is the prospect that an increasingly hard-pressed government, relying on co-option and coercion of blacks in order to stay in power, might turn to the private sector for direct assistance. In such circumstances, Pretoria may ask business to assume political responsibilities that the government decides it is unable to carry out at permissible cost. For foreign firms, such policies could heighten the onus of doing business in South Africa and could add a new incentive for collective withdrawal.

If concerted United States/Western European/Japanese action were to materialise, the impact of sanctions would be increased significantly. In theory a more plausible type of collective action might be co-operation around a positive-aid programme for frontline states which would be aimed at deterring South African destabilisation policies and placing extra pressure on the country. This collaboration would focus on endeavours such as the construction, operation and protection of the Beira Corridor trade route for landlocked states in the region now perilously dependent on South Africa as the regional economic hub. To be effective, however, and to create a new reality from the deep-rooted interdependence of the region, such collaboration would require the investment of hundreds of millions if not billions of dollars, coupled with security assistance sufficient to block regional threats to stability. Assistance of this magnitude is not in sight at present, although the Commonwealth seems to be trying to co-ordinate Western policy in this direction. Conceivably, a major racial flare-up and an increase in repression could ignite United States public opinion and force the issue on the Western alliance.

In the meantime, South Africa is certain to manipulate the contradictory elements of Western policy with some effect. On the one hand, some of the costs of sanctions imposed on Pretoria can be passed on to other parties, notably the frontline states and black South Africans, before they impinge on the government and its direct support group. On the other, measures designed to reduce the dependence of the frontline states on South Africa may, if they are presented in any way as preparatory to the imposition of sanctions by these countries, be seized upon by elements in the South African government who have backed destabilisation as validation for their position.[13]

THE SOVIET UNION

For the Soviet Union, South Africa constitutes both a political opportunity and a political risk. Backing for the ANC may have secured the Soviets an uncertain client, but the relationship could also become an impediment to United States-Soviet rapprochement. Hence, Soviet actions and even Moscow's rhetoric are characterised by a growing measure of caution.

An example of note was provided by comments made by Dr Victor Goncharov, deputy director of the Africa Institute of the Soviet Academy of Sciences, at an international conference in Harare, Zimbabwe in June 1987. Firmly rejecting the view that the African National Congress is 'the long arm of the Soviet Union', Goncharov set forth the following line of reasoning:

- He pointed out that the ANC was founded in 1912, a half-decade before Russia's Great October Revolution.
- He argued that the acceptance by the United Nations that apartheid is a crime against humanity justifies assistance to resistance forces, including military assistance.
- He observed that the Soviet Union gives advice on occasion to the ANC but does not undertake to dictate on strategy, tactics or the basis on which it should enter negotiations if the prospect of peace talks develops.
- He said that the Soviet Union has "no 'vital' interests" in the region and no desire to "interrupt . . . traditional ties between some countries of Southern Africa and some of the Western powers".
- He envisaged a time (post-Reagan) when the 'relative disinter-

est' of the two superpowers in the region could potentially result in "Soviet-American co-operation on resolving the crisis both in South Africa and the region".

- He emphasised that the United States and the Soviet Union should not interfere directly in South Africa, either in a unilateral or joint manner (i.e. by 'sending in their own armed forces').
- He cited the Secretary of State's Advisory Committee Report of 1987 as providing a possible 'basis for discussions' between the superpowers.[14]

Partly because the Soviets were disillusioned by the 1960s association with African ventures in socialism (Ghana, Guinea, Mali), today's officials and other spokesmen take the position that socialism for South Africa, where the majority of blacks remain in precapitalist and/or uneducated dependence, is a distant goal. Moreover, the Soviet Union, like its superpower competitor, now finds itself economically and militarily overextended. Given the responsibilities it has already assumed toward such client states as Cuba, Angola, Ethiopia and Afghanistan, Moscow is not eager to assume the additional economic burden that an ANC-ruled South Africa might present. Refuting the crude 'total onslaught' scenario presented by Pretoria, the USSR is seeking to cultivate relations with African states and groups of nonsocialist as well as socialist orientation. Indeed, its pragmatism now includes efforts to establish contact with liberal whites in South Africa. Strong aversion is increasingly expressed to 'anarchism' such as is manifested by the excesses of township 'comrades'; the possible rise of anti-white racism; and any solution that does not recognise the lasting importance of white participation in the economy.

In the long run, however, the Soviet Union may be inclined to seek advantage from the instability, frustration and anti-apartheid fervour of South Africa's neighbours. It will continue to support ANC and SWAPO rebels and the security forces of regional states, notably Angola. It will thus exact an attritional price from South Africa in the form of military expenditure and manpower diversion away from economic and social needs. For an opportunistic although cautious Soviet Union, policy toward South Africa will continue to be two-pronged: relatively low-cost support for a low-level war of attrition and simultaneous pragmatic overtures to South Africa's nonsocialist elements (including on-going collaboration with private sector precious metal and mineral producers) which leaves its future options open.

In line with the Gorbachev position that it is not the intent of Soviet policy on South Africa to promote a *destructive* revolution, Soviet analysts in the late 1980s express concern that American assumptions to the contrary could, within a South African context of growing political polarisation and violence, lead to mutually undesired superpower confrontation. Accordingly, they have increasingly signalled a desire to clarify intentions, seek common ground, and attempt to accommodate differing interests before becoming caught up in a regional collision potentially very damaging to prospects for improved Soviet-American relations.

SOUTH AFRICA'S NEIGHBOURS

South Africa's neighbours are politically fragile, economically vulnerable and militarily weak. Pretoria's combined policies of pre-emptive strikes, support for anti-government rebels, heavy-handed control of transport lines and selective economic rewards for good behaviour keep these countries off guard, distracted and dependent. In the short term, South African dominance in the region is assured.[15] The limits of this dominance are evident in Angola, where expanding air and anti-air defences (including Angolan-piloted MiG-23s) are raising the price of South African intervention, and in time may press South African influence back to the Namibian border.

The history of military confrontation between South African forces and Angolan nationalists of the MPLA dates back over two decades to the period when South African helicopters transported Portuguese troops in the south-eastern sector of the country, a region later to be controlled by South African-aided UNITA forces. It is within this context that the MPLA government in Luanda agreed to host political offices and training centres for both the ANC and Namibia's SWAPO. While the ANC maintains its political headquarters in the easily accessible capital of Zambia, training is provided to its military arm by the Soviets and others in the obscurity and inaccessibility of rural Angola.

Whether the MPLA's commitment to the ANC might be considered expendable to the cause of an elusive overall settlement of Angolan-South African differences is something about which MPLA leaders drop no hints – and indeed may be a matter to which they may have given little consideration. Angolan officials affirm, instead, a continuing loyalty to their association with the ANC, an association that has persisted for more than two decades and is reinforced by a common dedication to nonracialism and a common support from the Soviet Union and its allies.

Unless and until there is a larger international settlement, with internal processes of negotiation and change which can serve to defuse regional tension, Angola and South Africa may be expected to remain gripped and depleted by a state of intermittent hostilities. Just how depleted this condition is, will be evident from reports that South African assistance to UNITA insurgents totalled some $1 billion by late 1986,[16] and from predictions that famine and cholera threatened Angola with massive human disaster. Some 55 000 Angolan children died from war and war-related causes in 1986 alone.[17]

Soviet influence with the Luanda government and with the leadership of SWAPO's small, externally dependent insurgent organisation will probably remain significant for the foreseeable future. The best-trained and best-equipped SWAPO units have been utilised in recent years to help the MPLA combat UNITA insurgents and thereby protect its Angolan sanctuary. SWAPO's 'rejectionist' policy, its refusal to participate in an 'internal settlement' outside of structures and processes guaranteed by international supervision (under United Nations Security Council Resolution 435), may simply prolong its Angolan dependency and political exile. At the same time, the costs for South Africa of avoiding an international settlement which might bring a perceivedly Marxist-oriented SWAPO to power may continue to exceed $1 billion a year, meaning a significant displacement of funds otherwise available for the educational, health and other domestic programmes essential to the construction of a more equitable, productive and stable order within South Africa proper.

The deteriorating quality of life in South Africa's contiguous Portuguese-speaking neighbour, Mozambique, illustrates how readily a fledgling, undeveloped state, suffering from a severe skills shortage and governed by inexperienced and poorly advised leaders often pursuing ill-judged policies, can be crippled by insurgency which is externally catalysed and funded. Having come to independence in 1975 with a colonial legacy of 90 per cent illiteracy, Mozambique seems destined to see its 'second independence generation' even less educated than its first. The plight of Zambia illustrates how dependence on commodities of volatile value – in this case copper – in addition to inappropriate economic policies, is leaving other neighbouring states vulnerable to economic disaster. And once reduced to chaos, it is not clear how these countries and the fractious forces of either their governments or the opposition movements which seek power can piece them together again.

For South Africa, the consequences could logically mean prolonged political instability, economic malaise and foreign intervention along its own and Namibia's borders. The extent to which the South African government will perceive this as a threat is difficult to predict. By helping to reduce its neighbours to humbled wastelands, Pretoria impoverishes and diminishes its own future. But history shows that the logical consequences of actions are not readily perceived by fearful, reactive, survival-oriented authorities. This may be even more true if the short-to-medium term alternatives appear equally unattractive because of a perception that a less tough stance would only precipitate sanctions.

The FRELIMO government of Mozambique, like its MPLA counterpart in Angola, continues to anticipate an eventual collapse of apartheid rule in South Africa. But in the meantime (probably a very long meantime), it cannot allow itself to risk potentially disastrous tests of strength with its neighbour. Turmoil, which is partly South African-induced, has forced the government to turn inward, to concentrate on sheer survival and to accept Pretoria-dictated terms for neighbourly relations. Hence the survival of the Nkomati

Accord in 1987 even after such low points in the relationship as Mozambique's allegations of South Africa's complicity in the death of President Samora Machel in an air crash on South African territory in late 1986 and in several major civilian massacres in 1987.

Zimbabwe's relative economic strength and political stamina under the leadership of its stern and determined Executive President, Robert Mugabe, pose the single most formidable obstacle to total South African dominance of the southern African region. Rumours that Zimbabwe might expend scarce resources earned by its agricultural and chrome production on sophisticated warplanes from the Soviet Union or elsewhere must inevitably be a cause for South African concern so long as the SADF lacks comparable external access to the acquisition of aircraft. On the other hand, drought, ethnic tensions (Shona versus Ndebele and intra-Shona), limited foreign investment, a critical shortage of foreign exchange, uncompetitive industry created under the siege economy of Ian Smith's Rhodesia of UDI days, heavy reliance on South African trade and communication routes and supportive military action in Mozambique place severe limits on Zimbabwe's capacity to challenge, for the foreseeable future, South African regional pre-eminence. Hence the extremely reluctant retreat in 1987 from the commitment undertaken in 1986 at the Commonwealth Conference to impose sanctions on South Africa.

The real threat to South Africa from the frontline region, however, will be the region's ability to survive and move, albeit painfully and with setbacks along the way, toward the goal of independence from South African transport and communications lines. A shift toward a long-range policy focus on the part of Western Europe, the Commonwealth, the North American countries and the World Bank seems increasingly to centre on building the economies of the nine Southern African Development Co-ordination Conference (SADCC) states.

Undramatic but functionally crucial projects to restore or improve transport routes such as the Limpopo (Maputo-Zimbabwe), Nacala (Mozambique-Malawi) and Beira Corridor (Mozambique-Zimbabwe) railways, a northern transport road (Malawi-Dar es

Salaam), and port facilities (Maputo, Beira, Dar es Salaam) are all commanding increasing attention. The entry of British military training teams and other Western commitments to Mozambique's security threatens to escalate the cost of South African support for sabotage of the Beira and other Mozambique-centred initiatives, by creating the risk of a collision with Western military and economic interests. More broadly, and for the longer term, the Commonwealth Secretariat has reportedly been studying the feasibility of sending a Commonwealth force to southern Africa to act as a disincentive to South African destabilisation and to increase pressure on that country.

To the north, if the Angolan government should ever gain effective control over the Benguela railroad, Zaire and Zambia would be able to reorient their trade away from South Africa. The regional political and economic advantages of a Benguela opening are of such potential significance that some observers believe that a future United States administration would be inclined to forsake its alignment with the UNITA insurgency in favour of pursuing long-term interests via diplomatic, cultural and economic ties with a nominally Marxist-governed Angola.

All the hope generated by the SADCC regional development approach relies on a very shaky premise – that requisite funding will be forthcoming. As noted earlier, hundreds of millions, if not billions of dollars would be needed. Prospects for obtaining such funds in competition with other security and diplomatic priorities appear dim.

Conclusion

Long-term trends nevertheless suggest a slow withering of South Africa's regional ascendancy. While this withering will probably take place in the context of regional decline there may be counter-trends. Post-Banda Malawi will be less compliant. When finally delivered by political negotiations or by military collapse or victory from paying for a continuing war, Angola should find its oil wealth to be dramatically empowering. Western countries may increasingly intercede to defend modest but developing economic interests in the region.

A chronically violence-prone South Africa will find itself faced with an emigration brain drain of key professionals and a decreasing access to the swiftly changing universe of knowledge which is essential for the proprietary technology upon which any prosperous or 'winning' nation must, in these times, be built. This is not to argue that South Africa will not retain the capacity to withstand outside pressures from the region and/or the superpowers. It is not to underestimate the ability of an essentially reactive South Africa to interrupt, delay and derail through pre-emptive strikes, retaliatory raids and transport squeezes. It is rather to suggest that the tide of history runs against South Africa, that the outreach of its power is likely to decrease, that it could descend into the status of a 'military fortress' bled by regional and internal conflict – a 'ghastly' scenario.[18]

The external world is preoccupied with heady problems that leave the South African issue competing feebly yet distractingly for attention. Even in the United States, where the 'exceptionalism' of the South African issue has rendered it *the* foreign policy issue for black Americans, the matter generates but fitful commitment and energy. Still, the issue retains a volatility, keeps breaking back into public consciousness, and defies those who insist that it is just one more human rights question.

If outside influence, notably that of a quick-fix-prone United States, is eroding, the ability of South Africa to maintain a place in the mainstream of the world economy beyond the short-term may be even more so. The external world may deflect more of its limited attention and energy to providing development support, however inadequate, to South Africa's beleaguered and alienated neighbours, because it is frustrated in its attempts to influence the course of events within the country. This may or may not be enough to arrest regional decline into impoverished, chaotic human misery.

United States and Western European availability for brokering roles in quest of an internal solution will hold for some time to come. But invocations to anti-communist solidarity in the cause of 'free world' values may prove less and less effective as South Africa relies more and more on internal coercion, and as black opinion is progressively embittered and radicalised by government refusals to negotiate with representative black leaders. This may prove all the more true should Mikhail Gorbachev's *glasnost* alter the paradigm of superpower relations and free United States policy from the blinkers of monocausal threat perception in the form of obsessive anti-communism.

External perceptions of South Africa's future grow gloomier with the advancement of time. External parties will look to strategies of damage limitation, focusing on how to limit regional chaos and destruction, how to prevent the projection of racial conflict into their own societies, societies which are caught between the moral exigencies of human solidarity and the inadmissible costs of intervention, and how to limit the opportunistic intrusion of Soviet influence. A rejected outside world will not and cannot save an unregenerate white-ruled South Africa from the wasteland that it is capable of inflicting on itself and its neighbours. At most, the United States and the rest of the world will provide an interactive context of constraints and opportunities within which South Africans will determine their own future.

8 South Africa in comparative context

PETER L. BERGER AND
BOBBY GODSELL

The South African debate is replete with appeals to comparative experience. All actors make use of analogies. Most defend their beliefs against their opponent's analogies by asserting South Africa's uniqueness, and indicating the consequent inappropriateness of the analogy at hand. All countries are the unique product of their own history and circumstance. This uniqueness does not vitiate appropriate comparison. In this chapter we seek to distinguish helpful from unhelpful appeals to experience.

Unhelpful analogies: the world's last colony

Colonial analogies represent an unhelpful appeal to experience, which are used by diverse actors. A mindset is evident in Western concepts of South Africa that sees conflict and change in South Africa as a delayed last chapter in the post-Second World War process of decolonisation. Those holding this view define the essential 'problem' in South Africa as the fact that people with the wrong skin colour are in power. An implicit 'Africa for the Africans' notion underlies it. To change the skin colour of those occupying Pretoria's corridors of power is seen as the essential challenge. The inevitability of change derives from the historical trend based on the pattern of decolonisation in Africa and elsewhere.

WHY IS THIS TYPE OF ANALOGY UNHELPFUL?
South Africa is not a colonial society. It was given effective self-government by Britain in 1910, and obtained the same sovereign status as Canada, Australia and New Zealand in 1933, with the advent of Dominion status. Any doubt about the real autonomy of South Africa in relation to Britain should have been dispelled by

267

the fierce debate which surrounded South Africa's decision in 1939 to enter the Second World War on Britain's side. In 1961 the last affiliation with Britain was severed when South Africa became a republic outside the Commonwealth.[1]

These details of constitutional status are important because of what they indicate about the nature of power in South African society. Power is held by a segment of the indigenous population. The task facing those who seek fundamental change in the present government does not lie in persuading a colonial authority that the costs of continued occupation outweigh the benefits, but rather in helping one section of a population wrest power, by force or persuasion, from another. This is a much more difficult exercise.

In the process of dislodging a colonial overlord, economic, military and political costs had to exceed their benefits. The speed of the decolonisation process in Africa indicates just how dramatically and rapidly the balance of interests did change. From 1950 to 1955 a single territory obtained independent status (Libya). From 1955 to 1959 six territories joined independent Africa. In 1960 sixteen further independent countries emerged, with sixteen more being added in the following eight years.

Whilst this is not the place to debate the nature of colonialism, suffice it to say that Europe's rapid withdrawal from the African continent raises important questions about both Leninist concepts of imperialism and more recent dependency theories.[2] In military terms, decolonisation has mainly involved campaigns of endurance on the part of indigenous guerrilla forces, and exhaustion on the part of the colonial power. The military stakes were seldom high.

In contrast to this colonial pattern, conflict in South Africa pits one section of the population against the other. Although the four million whites are a demographic minority, they have access to significant power: a mobilisable army of some 400 000; a police force of some 50 000; and considerable administrative and financial resources.

RHODESIA REVISITED

A domestic form of the colonial analogy is that which compares South Africa with Rhodesia/Zimbabwe. The analogy is used most

268

frequently by groups on the right of the South African political spectrum. In recent years the Herstigte Nasionale Party (HNP) has made use of street posters with the slogan 'Remember Rhodesia'. For these groups the lesson of Rhodesia is that conciliation and concession proved to be a slow form of suicide for Rhodesia's white population. Rhodesia is seen as another in the sad sequence of forlorn struggles by white settler societies against the 'logic of Africa', and against the perfidious behaviour of colonial powers, particularly Britain. The moral that the Right draws from its Rhodesia parallel is 'fight, don't compromise'. For example in response to the May 1987 white election slogan of the National Party 'Reform Yes, Surrender No', the Conservative Party responded with 'Rhodesia Reformed And Surrendered'.

Left-wingers also make the Zimbabwe analogy. At times it is made to indicate the inevitable direction of change in South Africa. At other times it is used to suggest that the most radical or militant expression of black nationalism is the form which will eventually triumph. Buthelezi is equated with Zimbabwe/Rhodesia's Abel Muzorewa, and Oliver Tambo with Robert Mugabe.

This analogy is unhelpful, whether encountered in either its right- or left-wing clothing. Firstly, Zimbabwe was a colony. Throughout its march to independence Britain played a central role in its political affairs. It was against Britain that Rhodesia's Ian Smith rebelled with his unilateral declaration of independence in 1966. It was with Britain that the failed constitutional talks took place. It was Britain that formulated the demand for 'no independence before majority rule' (NIBMAR). Britain proposed and chaired the constitutional conference held at Lancaster House, which led to internationally recognised independence. South Africa has neither the encumbrances nor the advantages provided by such an external colonial point of reference. Secondly, South Africa's ethnic demography differs from that of Zimbabwe in a very significant way. A white:black ratio of 1:5 is very different from 1:20 as it was during the Zimbabwe conflict. (It is now of the order of 1:70.) The presence in South Africa of significant 'coloured' and Indian communities also provides for a very different pattern of racial politics than that which obtained in Rhodesia. Thirdly, both history and economics demarcate South Africa and Zimbabwe. White settlement and black/white interaction have a much longer history in South Africa – three hundred years in South Africa, effectively one hundred in Zimbabwe. More importantly, South Africa has a much more developed industrial economy. Whereas no more than one in five black Zimbabweans were in formal (wage) employment at independence in 1980, at least five out of ten black South Africans are so employed, and probably as many as four out of the remaining five are mainly dependent on migrant remittances. South Africa's urban industrial proletariat is large. The political consequences of this are already evident in the powerful union movement which has emerged in the ranks of black workers, and which is already shaping the process of political change.

It is dangerous to equate patterns of change merely because they occur in the same region, and even more so because their key actors share a skin colour. Inevitably such comparisons ignore the structures of political power in the societies they equate. This is well illustrated when the politically powerful comparison of Buthelezi and Muzorewa, Tambo and Mugabe is examined.

Abel Muzorewa was drawn into politics as a symbol of unity between Rhodesia's two major black nationalist movements, Joshua Nkomo-led ZAPU and Ndabaningi Sithole- (later Robert Mugabe) led ZANU. Muzorewa entered without his own political organisation or following. The organisation which he came to lead, the African National Council, was essentially intended as a ZANU/ZAPU alliance. When this alliance failed, and the Zambia-South Africa talks between the Rhodesia government and ZANU and ZAPU also failed, Muzorewa remained in the political arena and entered into a process of negotiation and then of coalition government with the white Rhodesian administration.

In contrast Buthelezi heads a political organisation and enjoys a political constituency which even his most fiery critics concede is significant. He is a powerful force in his own right. Though his rejection of the strategy of armed struggle separates him from both the (South African) African National Congress (ANC) and the Pan Africanist Congress (PAC), he has not entered into any alliance with Pretoria. Were he to do so its nature would be very different

270

from that of the Smith/Muzorewa administration. Its outcome could be as different.

ALGERIA REVISITED

An analogy which is even more prevalent in contemporary debate is that of Algeria. Alistair Horne's *A Savage War of Peace: Algeria 1954 to 1962* enjoys wide readership and seems to evoke feelings both of *déjà vu* and of foreboding amongst South African readers. The comparisons drawn include those of Algerian *pieds noirs* attitudes and actions; failed attempts at reform (especially socio-economic reform); and parallels between French and South African counter-insurgency strategies.[3] A sense of foreboding is often attached to the rise of urban terror.

Algeria, of all colonial analogies, is compelling in the similarity between its ratio of settler to indigenous populations (one to eight in Algeria's case), the 'depth' of settler society, and especially in the potential costs of change through armed struggle (where estimates of fatalities vary from one to four million, with a further one million resettled to metropolitan France).[4] Ethical parallels can also be usefully drawn between the equally repugnant tactics of terror of the Algerian resistance movement, the FLN, and the torture of the French army, and those practised in the name of rebellion and repression in South Africa.[5]

However, the predictive quality of this analogy is seriously impaired by one critical difference. Charles de Gaulle lived in Paris, not Algiers. This fact, above all others, renders the speculation of the so called 'De Gaulle option' fanciful. It requires one kind of calculus to persuade a leader and a government to surrender even a much-treasured colony, and quite another for the abdication of power in one's own territory.

SELMA IS NOT SOWETO

Another analogy that has undermined the understanding of conflict in South Africa is the comparison, often implicit, made by many Americans between that country's civil rights struggle and racial conflict in South Africa. The analogy is seductive. Race prejudice must have a familiar ring for many Americans. Both the nature of segregationist practices and more especially the rational-isations which are used to justify them, project Americans back into their relatively recent past. The analogy has a hopeful moral. Though the struggle for full civil rights for Americans of colour was dramatic and difficult if seen in its most recent phase from the Supreme Court ruling on school integration in 1954 to the passage of the Civil Rights Act in 1964, it was relatively bloodless and comparatively short. The United States civil rights struggle also indicates just how quickly entrenched racial attitudes can change, as both the political and economic progress of black Americans in the Jim Crow southern states indicates.

Why is it mistaken to confuse Selma with Soweto?
The first answer is because the demographic ratios of white to black in South Africa are very different from those in the United States. Indeed, they are almost exactly reversed in the two soci-eties. Secondly, it is because the civil rights struggle essentially completed a process which had much earlier and bloodier origins. The American Civil War was fought to decide whether America could exist as half-slave and half-free. The negative answer to this question achieved in 1865 set the nation on a course of full equality of all its citizens. Thirdly, the forces opposing each other in the United States civil rights struggle were very different from those in contest in South Africa. In the United States, local communities and local politicians opposed the Federal Courts, the Federal Government (as represented in the end by Federal marshals), the media, the churches and many other national institutions. None of this diminishes the heroic nature of this struggle. It was, however, a struggle to achieve recognition and application of the nation's constitution in one region of the nation; it was a resolute effort to fulfil and complete a century-long programme.

In South Africa by contrast, the issue of one or two nations is on the agenda. The challenge is not to complete a programme of national values, but to change these values, laws and practices fun-damentally. In this struggle state institutions are most often oppo-nents of change. The powers of the courts are severely circum-scribed by the doctrine of parliamentary sovereignty, inherited from Britain. The media are divided, and the electronic media back only government-supported change. The struggle in South Africa is primarily about power, and who shall exercise it, rather than about racial desegregation – not that these two issues are entirely unconnected.

The misleading nature of the Selma analogy is well illustrated by the historical development of the Sullivan Code. In its earliest form the Code laid great stress on racial desegregation, for instance on factory 'rest and comfort' facilities, and on affirmative action measures in recruitment and promotion. In the first edition of the Code no reference was made to the already central question of worker representation and trade unions. It is important to note, however, that the Code quickly evolved to address trade union issues, and indeed in its most contemporary form it incorporates the issues of political change more comprehensively than any other employment-related Code. Nevertheless the false start can, at least in part, be attributed to a confusion between Selma and Soweto.

Perhaps a more serious hazard inherent in this analogy is its tendency to underestimate what is at stake in the contest for South Africa, and therefore the lengths to which the sides, perhaps particularly the present government, are likely to go in order to resist naively framed demands for change. At issue in South Africa is who will rule, and how political power will be exercised. Such a struggle is more fundamental than bus or shop desegregation, or even voter-registration campaigns. The degree and nature of resistance, especially to demands for the 'transfer of power', should consequently be expected to be altogether more determined. And who will play the role of federal marshals?

There are helpful points of comparison between the American and the South African experience of combating racial discrimination. The malleability of racial attitudes, as demonstrated in the United States, should encourage all South Africans who seek to escape the shackles of prejudice. The economic dynamism of the American South demonstrates the economic benefits of deracialisation. Indeed, as racial barriers are breached in South Africa, both of these phenomena are becoming apparent.

273

As South Africa has become an international 'flashpoint', comparisons with other contemporary international dramas are inevitable. A number of similarities between apartheid South Africa and the Shah's Iran suggest themselves. Both countries exhibit an absence of either full or effective democracy. In both countries control is maintained with considerable degrees of coercion. Both in the Shah's Iran and Botha's South Africa, ambitious programmes for social and economic reform were instituted to pre-empt campaigns for political power.

The most powerful application of the Iran analogy in the South Africa debate lies in the unexpectedly rapid overthrow of the Shah. The regime had seemed invincible. It was rich, militarily strong and had powerful international allies. If such a regime could be destroyed by popular sentiment and a grim-faced Ayatollah, why not South Africa? The question is important, and deserves serious debate. Many detailed points of difference can be noted between the two societies. For this purpose three will be mentioned.

The first difference is the presence of a powerful mobilising set of beliefs in Islamic nationalism. The role of Islam in the Shah's overthrow is clearly central. The authentic Islamic character of the Shah's regime was disputed. Many of his reform programmes offended (or could be made to offend) traditional visions of an Islamic society. Islamic opposition to the regime and its reforms had a specifically anti-modern quality which had appeal both for traditionalists and those elements of the newly urbanised who drew the least benefits from Iran's sudden and disruptive modernisation.

Secondly, in the final months of the Shah's regime in particular, his behaviour was inconsistent, hesitant and ineffective.[6] The Shah's will to govern was inconstant from the start of his rule.

Thirdly (and almost certainly related to both the points above), the Iranian Army proved to be an ineffective and unreliable instrument of control.

Whilst an argument can be made for an analagous role for religion in the South African struggle, this role is much more ambiguous. Christian religious communities support, oppose and ignore the present regime. The Dutch Reformed churches are largely supportive of the present regime, the South African Council of Churches is deeply committed to its replacement, and the 'independent' churches, particularly the Zion Christian Church, occupy a sort of political no-man's land.[7]

It is very hard to portray the behaviour of South Africa's present rulers as anything but determined, consistent and tough. There are no Hamlets in the South African cabinet.

However, the most important difference of all lies in the military establishments of the two societies and their relationship to the political establishment. The lines of conflict are drawn in South Africa along the lines of race. The defence force is predominantly composed of white South Africans, and is almost completely white in its leadership. Whereas Islamic nationalism and anti-Shah sentiment could and did undermine the Iranian Army's willingness and capacity to impose order (it is said that troop contingents in Teheran had to be changed fortnightly in the final phase of the struggle against the Shah), no doubts exist about the loyalty of the generals or troops to the present South African government. Indeed, the only suggestions of disloyality come from organisations to the right of the present government, who claim some support in the military.

PHILIPPINE-STYLE PEOPLE POWER

The collapse of the Marcos regime in the Philippines, and its replacement by the Corazon Aquino administration, were bound to produce comparisons with South Africa. There were moments in early 1986 when people were speaking of Winnie Mandela in Corrie Aquino terms. Indeed, the role of massive popular protest in the undermining of Marcos is impressive. The crumbling of a seemingly all-powerful regime in the face of this protest raises the question once again : Why not in South Africa?

There can be no doubting the existence of popular sentiment which seeks an end to the apartheid era. Nor is there any lack of organisations and symbols to mobilise this sentiment. In fact, South Africa's history records mass demonstrations on many past occasions. Perhaps the decade of the fifties presents the most dramatic evidence: the march of some 17 000 women on the Union

275

Buildings in Pretoria; the defiance campaign during which some 10 000 went to jail through deliberate individual acts of non-compliance with apartheid laws; the anti-pass campaign of 1959; the bus boycott and the potato boycott.

These mass actions brought a severe response from the state. Gradually, mass mobilisation has become more and more difficult. Whilst meetings of thousands of people can and do still take place, massive open-air rallies, and especially marches, have become almost impossible. However, even when they did take place, although they often provoked severe state reaction, they have at no time brought the administration close to the point of abdication. It seems difficult to imagine a scenario in which mass demonstrations, national strikes and campaigns of non-co-operation would succeed in transferring power in South Africa.

Why?

Again the role of the military in the two societies is very different. Whilst demonstrations of hundreds of thousands, if not millions of people in the street played an important role in the change of the regime in the Philippines, it was ultimately the defection of the Army Chief of Staff, General Ramos, and a number of other senior military leaders which led to the transfer of power. Such an event is simply impossible to imagine in any leftwards change of regime in South Africa.

There is also a deeper difference. The Marcos regime could be described as a network of individuals held together by loyalty to and patronage from Marcos. The Marcos regime represented the dictatorship of an individual. In South Africa power is exercised by white South Africans. Within this group one political party has consistently won all elections since 1948. South Africa's present government is the hegemony of a significant minority group. To break this hegemony, the group in charge (white South Africans) have either to be defeated on the battlefield or persuaded that some new form of the exercise of power is in their best interests. Street demonstrations seem an unlikely avenue to achieve either of these ends.

Though analogies with Iran and the Philippines have operated only at the most superficial level of public debate, they have informed a critical dimension of change in South Africa – the time scale of change. Just as events in both Iran and the Philippines developed over a short period of years, and even months, to a dramatic and decisive point, so people within and without South Africa await the imminent apocalypse. The media speak of a country in crisis. Often an assumption in both description and analysis is that "things cannot continue in this way much longer". Various specific predictions of change within months and years have been made, and all have proved, thus far, unrealistic. By any standard of moral measurement, and certainly by comparison with a fully developed liberal democracy, South Africa is a state in crisis. The present State of Emergency makes this explicit. However, a glance back into history suggests that the crisis is chronic and not acute. And there is no indication on the horizon to suggest that a 'resolution' is imminent.

Two assumptions underlie analogies of the Iranian and Philippino type: one analytic, one normative.

The analytic assumption suggests that undemocratic governments are inherently unstable. This is often expressed as an observation about South Africa that "it is impossible for a minority of four or five million to rule a country of thirty million". Seen historically, such an assertion is simply wrong. Government by consent is the exception and not the rule. This is true at this moment of history, just as it has been at every other moment. Small minorities have succeeded in ruling large majorities for very long periods of time. In this century, Franco's Spain, Salazar's Portugal and Stalin's Russia all provide examples of highly repressive regimes which have lasted for decades.

The normative assumption often linked to the sentiment that tyranny must end is that the overthrow of an evil, repressive regime will necessarily bring social progress. History again suggests no such necessary rule. Indeed the two countries discussed above, Iran and the Philippines, suggest the widely different outcomes that a repressive regime's demise might occasion. By every observable indication, Iran is less free now than it was under the Shah. In contrast, the Aquino regime in the Philippines seems altogether more benign than its predecessor.

277

Those who not only seek, but also predict, the imminent demise of white hegemonic power in South Africa need to explain how this end will come about. In so doing they need to indicate why the new pattern of power which follows, will be better. To fail to do the first is quixotic. To fail to do the second raises the prospect of a future defined by unintended and possibly unpleasant consequences.

Some less common but more useful comparisons

Thus far we have surveyed some of the most common and misleading comparisons which have been made in the debate about South Africa. We wish now to turn to two novel analogies which throw an interesting light on current debates.

THE MEIJI RESTORATION IN JAPAN

Political change in South Africa must mean the end of white hegemony. Black South Africans must gain meaningful and effective access to political power. White politicians and white-defined political institutions will become one agent amongst many. They will lose control of politics, though they may well retain a significant influence.

The end of the hegemony of a small powerful group was achieved in Japan in 1868. In that year a pattern of government which had persisted over some seven centuries was ended. In this pattern power had been exercised by an overlord, or Shogun, in association with a network of underlords, or daimio. These essentially feudal lords or chieftains in turn made use of a warrior class, or samurai, to exercise control, collect taxes and govern their territory. During the seven centuries in which Japan was governed in this way there was fluctuation between feudal anarchy and feudal centralism. During the 268 years of the Tokugawa shogunate a rigid feudalism developed. The samurai became a hereditary elite which provided a powerful civil service. In the caste order craftsmen were ranked below the peasantry, and merchants below the craftsmen.

Feudal rule in Japan was undermined from without and within.

278

For centuries Japan, by reason of geography and through its own determined efforts, had maintained itself in isolation from Asia and the world beyond, interrupted only by relatively brief military excursions and invasions. With the growth of exploration and maritime trade, Japan's isolation became more and more difficult to defend. In 1853 Commodore Matthew C. Perry from the United States landed in Edo Bay. He demanded trading rights and, later, special legal rights for American citizens resident in Japan. France, Germany and Britain made similar demands. Facing modern navies, the Japanese shogunate had little alternative but to agree.

Japan's shogun regime had already been severely undermined by economic change. Throughout the nineteenth century a money economy had been developing. Money and markets breached feudal barriers and inverted caste ranks. When rebellious samurai seized control in Kyoto it was not only to avenge the loss of national sovereignty, but also to cut the links with a feudal past.

It is the manner of this break with the past which is of special relevance to debates about change in South Africa. Firstly, the change, though under external and internal pressures, was executed from within the ranks of the ruling class. Secondly, the change was cast as a restoration rather than a revolution. The shogunate was deposed in the name of a fifteen-year-old Emperor. Thirdly, great care was taken to give existing elites, and especially the warrior class, a stake in the new order. This was done in a number of ways, perhaps pre-eminently by exchanging aristocratic privilege for entrepreneurial opportunity.

It is important to complete the story by indicating that in the remaining decades of the nineteenth century Japan plunged itself into modernity with astonishing energy and amazing results. The new rulers of Japan – the men of the Meiji, or enlightenment – moved quickly to modernise economic and military institutions. Barriers to occupations and economic activity were removed. The nation began its investment in human capital which would give it the best-educated population in the world.[8] By the turn of the century the country had been transformed. Dramatic economic growth was under way, and this was able to support a modern military capable of inflicting a humilating defeat on Czarist Russia in 1905, then invade Korea and China and ultimately pose a serious military challenge to the United States.

Comparative experience must be seen as suggestive and not prescriptive. We cannot learn by attempting to duplicate experience from another time and place. Rather, wisdom is gleaned when we ask whether functional equivalents might exist in our own context. In this light one might ask a number of interesting questions about the Meiji analogy.

Is the apartheid order being undermined by the changing nature of economic activity within South Africa?

There is much to suggest that it is. The need to admit black workers to the ranks of skilled and semi-skilled employees has made union organisation of black workers possible, and has given blacks power in the market place. The demographic significance of the black consumer has created new interests in burgeoning black wealth and well-being, and has given black South Africans an economic clout only now being recognised, and yet to be exercised in an organised way. A nonracial work force and a nonracial market place increasingly make racially exclusive social and political institutions anachronistic.

Is the apartheid order being undermined externally?

This question is more difficult to answer. Superficially of course, South Africa must be a strong contender for the title of least favoured nation. Time and again the country is the combined focus of East/West/North/South international condemnation. To what extent does such unambiguous verbal opposition undermine the government's confidence and efficacy? Perhaps far from undermining its resolve, this ubiquitous criticism strengthens it.[9] A more persuasive case can be made for the corrosive quality of international economic pressures. Again this is not unambiguous. Recent economic performance must be seen in the context of isolation rather than contact. Yet because the South African economy, particularly in the fifties and sixties, has already become a significantly differentiated economy with substantial domestic manufacture of a wide range of goods, its involvement in the world economy is both more differentiated and more complex. Two dimensions of current international economic links illustrate this point. The divestment of local subsidiaries by major Western companies has increased the demands on South African managerial, technical and professional management. This increased demand must lead to greater black South African participation in these occupations. Equally, the South Africanisation of manufacturing – now in areas beyond the crude import-substitution of previous decades – is likely to increase the skill levels demanded from the work force. Such enhanced skills will in turn increase the bargaining power, as well as the productivity, of these workers.

Do groups who seek fundamental change exist within the ruling class?

The answer to this question turns on what both analyst and actor understand by fundamental change. Certainly the economic component of apartheid ideology has been abandoned by those in power. The deracialisation of the labour market is almost complete.[10] Current economic planning uses an administrative paradigm which clearly transcends grand apartheid.[11] However, in the social domain, and more emphatically in politics, racial division and racial hegemony remain central.

What could play the role the imperial restoration played in Japan as the introduction to a period of fundamental political, economic and social transformation?

South African society is peculiarly devoid of national symbols – symbols which mean something to all thirty million or so inhabitants. Religion seems the only possible source of such symbols. At present, however, religion serves to divide as often as it unites.

In what way could key elements of today's ruling class be introduced positively to post-apartheid society?

To the extent that the end of apartheid is presented to white South Africans in terms of surrender, they must be expected to resist to the end. In all but a Khmer Rouge type of transformation, which seeks to deny the realities of a modern industrial state, the role of most whites in the economy will remain vital. Increased economic growth will make already scarce skills even more valuable. If the answer is elusive, the question is provocative.

DENG XIAOPING'S CHINA

Japan's Meiji restoration presents an encouraging parallel. Contemporary China suggests a depressing one. If this parallel has any validity, it lies in the difficulty of modernising and liberalising a highly regulated society without placing the control of the ruling group in jeopardy. Many will hope that the reforms of Deng and Botha do destroy current patterns of power in both societies, as it is pre-eminently these patterns which need to be destroyed. We share this view. However, it seems too much to expect of these leaders that they will actually reform themselves into oblivion. The best we can hope for is the prospect of unintended positive consequences.

If a parallel can indeed be drawn between mainland China and South Africa, and we are not sure that it can, it lies in the attempt to liberalise aspects of these societies without putting the essentials of political power under threat. The Chinese rulers are anxious to enhance the degree of economic rationality and efficiency in their society. This has already necessitated diminished governmental control in some aspects of society. The Chinese rulers seem unwilling to pay a price for such liberalisation, however, if the price means the significant demise of the Chinese Communist Party's grip on political power. The Botha regime wants at least to multiracialise, if not deracialise, many aspects of South African society, from the economy to the performing arts, sport and many public institutions. It has thus far shown no appetite, however, for loosening the control that whites continue to exercise over the reins of political power.

Yet both societies seem to be discovering that the consequences of 'reform' are not always as anticipated. Neither can they always be controlled, contained or even reversed. The prime initiative for change appears, in China, to emanate from within the ruling class. Reformist measures have set up an interaction with other groups in the society (students for example) which may promote or retard further change.

282

To those who exercise power in their capacity as officials of the Chinese Communist Party, measures which reduce the role and power of this institution automatically reduce their own power. An analogy can be drawn between the hegemony of the Communist Party in China and the self-defined white exclusivist institutions in South Africa.

A second interesting analogy is to be found in the extent to which economic and political goals may diverge in these two societies. Liberalisation (or deracialisation and deregulation, to use language less prone to meet cognitive closed doors in South Africa) seems imperative if the modernising and growth goals of both societies are to be addressed. Yet if the political imperative is continued hegemonic control by the existing rulers, these goals will conflict with political needs. The acknowledged need by the present power-holders to create areas of segmental autonomy will create autonomous areas of action. Actors in such areas may wish to use their autonomy in ways which make those at the centre uncomfortable. The conflict between a desired nonracial regional authority in Natal-KwaZulu, and the government's racially defined structures of metropolitan government (i.e. the Regional Services Councils) well illustrates this tension. In the Chinese context the debate about Hong Kong's 1997 incorporation into mainland China provides a similar example.

Present indications seem to suggest that the prospects for the emergence of democratic political institutions in China are slim. Does this suggest an analogous difficulty in moving beyond apartheid's political institutions in South Africa?

A choice of words: totalitarian versus authoritarian regimes

Nondemocratic regimes can be divided into those organised along totalitarian, and those organised along authoritarian lines. In totalitarian states, the ruling group makes a total claim on society. All aspects of social organisation are rendered subordinate to the ruling political institution. The party controls all arenas of human endeavour through ideologically linked and subordinate organisations. Hitler's National Socialist regime well illustrates this. The Nazi Party co-ordinated Nazi youth, teacher, scientific, artistic, labour and employer bodies. In the end the only partially autonomous organisation remaining outside the organic grasp of the party was the army, and this not for want of attempts to render it subordinate. In authoritarian regimes, political power is exercised undemocratically: that is, outside of any institutions making rulers accountable to the ruled. However, society is not accommodated in a matrix of institutions all created by, or under the control of, the political elite. Areas of organisational autonomy exist – though none powerful enough to challenge or change the political elite.

It is important to note that this distinction is analytic and not moral. Some authoritarian countries may be more brutish and unpleasant than some totalitarian states. (A contemporary example of such a situation would be authoritarian Iran in contrast to totalitarian Russia.)

South Africa clearly belongs in the authoritarian and not the totalitarian category. Political power is exercised undemocratically, but the 'space' exists for churches and unions and artists and academics to operate outside governmental frameworks. This fact is important both in terms of the strategies for change available, as well as for their chances for success. The 'space' suggests that it may be easier for South Africa to break out of the apartheid paradigm than for China to break away from a centrally managed society. New paradigms require new institutions and new people. In a totalitarian state such new institutions immediately threaten the existing order, merely by their existence. The emergence of Solidarity in Poland challenged the state-recognised union movement, and indeed threatened the role of these state-supported unions as well as the Communist Party to which these unions owe allegiance. The emergence of trade unions for organising black workers in South Africa did not have this problem.[12] The degree of political freedom that does exist in South Africa, however circumscribed, holds out the hope of new needs being able to result in new institutions. The emergence of new political parties and coalitions within the presently enfranchised is an example of this.

Where first world and third world meet?

Another common set of symbols used to describe and explain South African realities is found in the frequently employed first world/third world analogy. In terms of this analogy South Africa exhibits the characteristics of both first world and third world countries.

Clearly supporting evidence for this analogy can be found. In many respects South Africa does appear like an Australia superimposed on a Nigeria. White fertility rates exhibit a first world pattern of very slow growth, with white schools facing a decline. South Africa's spatial reality combines modern cities, which look like Boston and Sydney, with typical third world squatter settlements and rural wastelands.

However, this analogy is also misleading. It underestimates the interaction between the rural and urban, industrial and feudal dimensions of South African reality. The imputed coincidence of first world and white, and third world and black realities is also dangerously misleading. This neat overlap conceals more than it illuminates. If modern/pre-modern fault lines are to be drawn they need to include parts of Soweto (certainly Diepkloof Extension, but probably larger areas) in the modern sector, and exclude some deep rural white areas.

Equally the 'economic dualism' model often paired to this first/third world analogy is misleading. Little evidence of any real subsistence economy is to be found. Most South Africans are critically dependent on formal cash employment, either directly or through migrant remittances, or informal economic activities which depend on the formally employed.

Similarly the 'two cultures' model is false, at least in part. Heribert Adam has recently suggested that the common conception of South African society as a culturally and ethnically plural society is open to question. Ethnic diversity cannot be disputed. However, if culture is understood in terms of the way in which ordinary people live their lives, and the aspects of social reality most valued, then cultural pluralism is questionable. Evidence abounds of an emerging industrial culture. Modern clothing, housing, food and especially patterns of reaction cut across both geographic separation and race. The capacity of this homogenising industrial culture to modify ideology was well illustrated by the threatened Warner Brothers' removal of major American movies from the South African circuit. White South Africans were faced with a simple choice: either surrender racially segregated movie houses or lose access to these films. Local municipal governments had to take this decision. In the end, from Pietersburg to Pretoria, whites chose Rambo over racial segregation.

The dependency/modernisation debate

The interaction between South Africa and the rest of the world has been the focus of a theoretical debate in which South Africa has served as an exemplary guinea pig for two opposing approaches to social change.

Dependency theory, originally developed by a group of neo-Marxist social scientists in Latin America, sees the world as one huge drama in which the central ('metropolitan') capitalist powers control and exploit the less-developed regions of the world ('the periphery'). In this view, lack of development is not an unfortunate occurrence, an accident of history, but the necessary (and in large part intended) consequence of development. In the words of Andre Gunder Frank: 'the development of underdevelopment'. Put simply, it is not just that there are rich and poor countries; rather some are poor because others are rich. Cast in terminology derived from Marxism and from the Leninist theory of imperialism, dependency is a gigantic elaboration of Proudhon's famous dictum that property is theft. This constellation of relationships is seen as endemic to capitalism, at least in its mature form, and the only way out of it is a transition to socialism.

If this interpretive scheme is applied to South Africa, its peculiar racial features can ultimately be explained in terms of the functional requirements of capitalism in South Africa. An essential requirement has been the maintenance of a large, cheap labour force, made docile by political repression and social segregation. Apartheid is not some sort of historical happenstance, but an intrinsic feature of the capitalist system in South Africa – 'racial capitalism', as it is often described. Apartheid is not the result of a psychological aberration that one must deem irrational (in the manner in which American psychologists have dealt with 'racial prejudice'), but is rather a thoroughly rational arrangement if capitalism is to be maintained in South Africa. Consequently, only a transition to socialism will provide a real remedy to the country's racial ills.

Modernisation theory, originally developed by American social scientists in the 1950s (though based on various theories of classical sociology, in particular those of Max Weber and Emile Durkheim) puts less emphasis on capitalism and on economic factors as such. The main engine of change in the contemporary world is the revolution in human life brought about by technology and its concomitant transformations (as in Weber's 'rationalisation'), or by making the world more rational. The sum total of these changes is modernisation – an increasingly rational, technologically driven reorganisation of every aspect of life, including the economy, but also including every other institutional sphere and, very importantly, human consciousness (values, beliefs, morality, religion) as well.

Applied to South Africa, modernisation provides a very different perspective. South Africa is a country in the throes of modernisation, which follows the same patterns as elsewhere, though these patterns are, of course, modified by local conditions (including racial demographics). Here apartheid is seen as indeed a sort of historical accident, extrinsic to the overall historical process of modernisation. More than that, apartheid is an irrational intrusion into the logic of history. Insofar as capitalism is a very modern economic system, apartheid is an irrational intrusion into the logic of capitalist development – distorting the efficacy of market forces, introducing a political system that hinders capitalist development and fostering mental attitudes that constitute 'obstacles to development' (analogous, say, to caste values in India or shamanistic beliefs in a primitive society). Consequently, the abolition of apartheid will allow all modernising institutions in South Africa, including its capitalist economy, to function with enhanced rational efficacy.

This is clearly not the place for an extended critique of either theoretical approach. We are critical of both, though less so of the second. Both approaches are overly rationalistic in their perception of human society: dependency theory exaggerates the rationality of the capitalist system, modernisation theory the rationality of everything. Both are intellectual children of Enlightenment philosophy and thus of the myth of progress. We tend to the view that history applied to South Africa is a much messier affair. Both approaches distort, though the first distorts more than the second. It is arguable that, as dependency theorists argue, the origins and the early period of South African capitalism went very well with, and perhaps even required, something like apartheid. This argument rapidly loses plausibility as one gets closer to today. The approach must assume, minimally an implicit conspiracy between the economic and political elites of the country. Yet, at least since 1948, the South African situation has been marked by sharp antagonism between these two elites. The argument is forced to ignore substantial dents made in apartheid society precisely by the maturation of South African capitalism. Finally the argument must leave aside all empirical evidence regarding socialist systems, which evidence provides little if any comfort to the notion that socialism is conducive to racial amity, or for that matter, greater economic and social equality in general.

Modernisation theory applied to South Africa also distorts, because it tends to gloss over the peculiar features of the South African situation. It tends to judge rationally in systems terms – that is, something is deemed rational or irrational in terms of the overall society, itself understood as a functioning system. This overlooks the fact that what is irrational to one group (say, English-speaking businessmen) may be very rational indeed to another group (say, Afrikaans-speaking bureaucrats). Another way of putting this is to say that modernisation theory tends to overlook or at least de-emphasise the power of vested interests in society. Many groups with strong vested interests could not care less how their actions affect the entire society as a functioning system. Also, modernisation theorists tend to have too facile a view of the 'obstacles to development', those putatively irrational values, beliefs and emotions that move living people – for example, pride in nation or in ethnic group (be it among Afrikaners or Zulus), racial fears (so prominent in the minds of white South Africans) or the rage manifested in the actions of the 'comrades'.

Finally, both dependency and modernisation theories have some heuristic value in indicating that South Africa is part and parcel of the contemporary world despite its distinctive features, and as such is subject to forces operative elsewhere. Dependency theory, while largely falsified in its major presuppositions, retains some usefulness in drawing attention to the international economic forces impinging on South Africa, and to the vested interests present in any modern economy. Modernisation theory, while distortive and overly optimistic in its view of the modernising process, is useful in drawing attention to certain global processes, such as industrialisation, urbanisation, or changes in mindset brought about by literacy and the mass media, which – despite many local variations – are at work throughout the contemporary world.

The apartheid paradigm

Thus far we have looked at the way in which South African realities are explained, or might be explained, in terms of the experiences of other societies. However, in addition to the appeals to the experiences of others, there is a way of thinking about conflict in South Africa itself which needs to be questioned. Conflict in South Africa is almost universally seen as a struggle between white and black political interests. The whites have power now. The blacks want it. Underlying this concept are two critical assumptions:

- Firstly, political interests in South Africa are defined by skin colour.
- Secondly, these racially defined interests are inherently in conflict.

These assumptions lie at the very heart of the *apartheid-gedagte*. However, they hold sway far beyond the ranks of apartheid's supporters. They have become built into the way in which almost everybody experiences South Africa. They have become part of the grammar of political debate. It is as common to hear resistance speakers proclaiming that 'blacks' want X or Y as it is to hear the spokesmen of the Right articulating the aspirations of 'whites'.

HOW ACCURATE ARE THESE ASSUMPTIONS?

They certainly do not stand up well to the test of critical reason. When one asks what 'black' or 'white' political interests are, one finally confronts either a concern about culture or language rights, or concern about material interests concealed in cultural clothing. If conflict in South Africa were really focused on language rights it could be easily resolved. To the extent that material interests are dressed up in racial terms they are not only concealed but also distorted.

As Schlemmer suggests in Chapter 1, present government concerns relate more to the preservation of a certain materially defined way of life than to cultural interests. Again we must ask, what way of life? To the extent that white voters are concerned about the preservation of orderly suburban life, the combating of crime, the preservation of income and the avoidance of (even higher) taxation, these are surely common middle-class aspirations. Do the attitudes of a growing number of middle-class black South Africans differ from these aspirations? If most white South Africans want a growing and efficient economy, a dependable civil service, social services that work and a physically secure living and working environment, what is there to suggest that their black counterparts differ?

In asking these questions we do not mean to suggest that the political interests of South Africans are uniform: obviously a debate rages about what constitutes the good, and how the goals of liberty and prosperity and justice can best be achieved. What we question is whether the crucial cleavages *necessarily* follow the lines of skin colour.

If few today would argue for biologically determined political interests, many more would point to the subjective and experiential foundations of racially defined conflict. The tragic success of apartheid has been to become a self-fulfilling hypothesis. Because

290

race and class experiences have been engineered to run along parallel tracks, elements of identity in race and class interests are apparent. And race is such an obvious and convenient label – it provides a highly attractive filing system for human experience. To the extent that actors construct their social reality in these terms, conflict acquires a racial form.

However, the contrast between contrived and essential definitions remains a vital one – especially with regard to future prospects. A careful examination of South African history provides many examples which undermine the concept of racially defined interests. The organisations that have opposed racist rule in South Africa have always had whites in their leadership ranks. At present whites play important roles in the ANC, SACP, UDF and CO-SATU. If they have been able to break the biological determinism of their skin colour, this must remain a possibility for others.

What is significant about the apartheid model, is that as with all models, its definition of the problem excludes certain solutions. If political interests are racially defined and racially antagonistic, then by definition a nonracial democratic future is impossible. The options are only an oppressive white minority government or an oppressive black majority government. Einsteinian physics cannot be conceived in the language of Newton. As long as we use Newtonian language we exclude Einsteinian insights. Equally, as long as actors debate South Africa in racially deterministic terms, they prevent themselves from moving beyond apartheid.

South Africa beyond apartheid: is it possible?

Finally, what does comparative human experience suggest about South Africa's future? Is progress towards a nonracial democracy possible, or must the future be seen in terms of Greek tragedy?

Once again conventional wisdoms are misleading. "Where in history have a privileged minority voluntarily handed over power to a majority?" is the despairing question often posed. The question is asked rhetorically. It presumes the answer: 'Never!', which answer is not only historically wrong, but also historically absurd.

Either the question must be understood in such a way as to render it meaningless, or else its negative answer would deny the emergence of the modern world.

The emergence of industrial societies, at first in Europe, has seen political power and economic opportunity move from the hands of a feudally defined elite to a mass society. Universal enfranchisement in the political arena, the abolition of occupational barriers as well as the rise of labour organisations in the economic field, have fundamentally altered the way power is exercised in these societies. In some countries this change has been accompanied (or more often preceded) by a violent change of regime. In many more it has occurred incrementally through actions either initiated, or at least accommodated by, existing ruling groups. These actions have diminished the political power and material privileges of this ruling group.

Did these ruling groups change voluntarily, or under force of circumstance? The distinction, in its extreme, is meaningless. The historical record shows that in some societies change was initiated, encouraged and facilitated. In others change was resisted to the point of armed conflict.

Perhaps the most interesting contemporary example of such a process is the democratisation of Spain, where the move to democracy was initiated from the top. Change here cannot be seen as coerced by either internal or external pressures. The move occurred against a background of bitter struggle and ideological polarisation, reaching its climax in the Spanish civil war. The result has been a pluralist democracy, in which totalitarian movements on the right and left have been effectively marginalised. If democracy can come to Franco's Spain, why not to Botha's South Africa?

Two related but distinct questions suggest themselves:

- How can a ruling group be induced to relinquish control?
- How can such a process be moved toward democracy rather than towards new forms of nondemocratic rule?

Two cases mentioned earlier, that of Meiji Japan and of Deng Xiaoping's China, recall a practical observation. There are really only two ways in which a ruling group can be induced to relinquish control: they can be coerced, or they can be seduced. Coercion as a possible strategy of change may be ruled out in the South African case, at least in the foreseeable future, because of the realities of military power. Hence a formula must be found by which power-sharing is made palatable to those elements of the ruling group who are to be the objects of the exercise. In Meiji's Japan this was done by giving the disposed aristocracy the kind of financial compensation (mostly in the form of government bonds) that gave it an economic interest in the new order. It was, if you will, a vast act of bribery. As such, it was eminently successful, to the point where a sizeable number of the old gentry became financiers and entrepreneurs in the new capitalist system. And this transition from feudalism to capitalism was legitimated by an ingenious ideological trick, by which the old samurai ethos (loyalty, discipline, frugality) was transformed into a remarkable analogue to the so-called 'Protestant ethic' – that is, into a value system conducive to modernisation. The 'Emperor system' was focal in this.

Deng Xiaoping's China is, as yet, a more ambiguous case of this political logic – partly because it is still very much in its beginning, partly because we don't know just how far the present leadership intends reform to go. The formula thus far appears to guarantee political power while taking away some economic privilege – as some observers have put it, trying to have a market economy while retaining a Leninist polity. This is a difficult feat. One suspects that one or the other part of this formula will have to give in time. The perusal of just about any issue of the *Beijing Review* gives its reader a vivid idea of the ideological tensions that this project has engendered.

A ruling elite is very rarely moved to relinquish control by attending to moral arguments – if only because most people who have power and privilege are coolly confident that they are morally entitled to these. Rather, in the absence of compelling coercion, a ruling group will relinquish control when they believe that it is in their interests in the longer term so to do. Such a conclusion requires a high measure of analytic capacity: to act on such a conclusion effectively requires an equally high measure of political will and acuity.

If one wants a less contemporaneous but instructive example beyond those discussed above, the great compromise (*Ausgleich*) of 1867 which created the Austro-Hungarian state provides one. Until then the Austrian oligarchy had exercised unitary control over the entire Habsburg realm. Both external and internal pressures induced this ruling group to conclude that a continuation of the status quo was no longer practicable. The major external pressure was the Austrian defeat by Prussia in 1866. Internal pressures came from the increasing clamour for equal rights by subject nationalities, among whom the Hungarians were the largest, most cohesive and vocal. The *Ausgleich* involved a substantial relinquishment of control by the Austrian elite (power-sharing if you will). The compromise was struck with another elite, the Hungarian gentry. The resulting dual state served the interests of both. The two parts of the Austro-Hungarian state developed quite differently: the first toward a pluralistic democracy; the second toward a unitary state based on Magyar hegemony. Both experienced pressures in ensuing decades. It is by no means clear, though, that the overall arrangement was doomed to fail: the Austro-Hungarian state collapsed after defeat in war. If it had either avoided or won this war, a good argument can be made that it would have moved toward a wider and more democratic compromise – an enlarged *Ausgleich* – in which Slavic nationalities would have participated.

Let us return to our second question: How can a relinquishment of control take on a democratic character, rather than merely exchanging oligarchies?

There is a large body of literature somewhat grandiosely labelled 'democracy theory', which dissects the conditions and putative requirements of democracy in a broad comparative perspective. The literature cannot be reviewed here. Suffice it to say that it is inconclusive: it does not render a recipe or cure for ending authoritarianism. Comparative experience, however, certainly indicates that this transition can be made.

Whilst none of the above render 'solutions' for South Africa, a few conclusions are suggested.

In most cases nonviolent change conducive to a relinquishment of control by a ruling group requires time. Rapid, cataclysmic change is likely to lead to the substitution of one oligarchy by another, not to a democratic regime. Revolutionary cataclysms create new tyrannies. In South Africa such a cataclysm is highly unlikely. The formula must be seduction rather than the quick knockout blow. Evidence suggests that significant, perhaps even decisive, elements within the ruling group have decided that the maintenance of the status quo is too costly. Whether an *Ausgleich* results, or a long painful and bloody deadlock, will be determined by the imagination, skill and courage of political leadership on both sides of the present power divide.

Breaking the apartheid mould: new institutions, new leaders and above all new symbols

If comparative experience suggests that Armageddon is not South Africa's necessary destiny, then it also implies that the overcoming of apartheid requires new institutions, with new types of leadership and above all a new symbolic legitimacy.

Apartheid institutions are the institutions of racial mobilisation. Post-apartheid institutions must be the institutions of nonracial mobilisation. Apartheid institutions have used feudal forms of power and authority. Post-apartheid institutions will have to evolve democratic forms of power and authority.

In practical terms, a post-apartheid South Africa will be organised around the concerns of any modern industrial state: prosperity, liberty and justice. These goals will of necessity be nonracially defined. Already the shift in paradigm is apparent.

The debate which has begun about the role of universities such as those of the Witwatersrand and Cape Town is essentially a dispute about the political and vocational tasks of a university in a modern state. Politically, the debate contests essentially liberal and Marxist conceptions of the role of education in society. Vocationally, it pits the role of equipping graduates with useful skills against the 'awareness-raising' role of education. These debates are not racial in character.

295

Capitalism versus socialism:
which road to development?

Another example of a debate which, though often conceived in racial terms, will outlast and indeed overshadow the deracialisation of politics in South Africa is the capitalist/socialist debate. The present fusion of the issues of racial access to power and the best method for organising and managing national resources, (as expressed in the phrase 'racial capitalism'), serves to obscure perhaps the most crucial set of issues facing the South African nation: which road to development? White political hegemony has encouraged an economic illiteracy in South African politics. The vocabulary of the present government would suggest that South Africa is currently organised along capitalist, or even libertarian lines. In a country where state regulation is central to most aspects of the lives of black South Africans in particular, this is clearly not the case. The vocabulary employed by the resistance groups suggests that South Africa is basically a rich country: the problem is that wealth is concentrated in the wrong hands. In fact South Africa is a comparatively poor country. With a gross national product per capita one-seventh that of the United States, the redistribution of existing wealth could do no more than modestly expand the circle of the privileged. If the nation is to aspire to decent housing, health, education and employment opportunities for all thirty-five million citizens, a sustained period of significant economic growth will have to be achieved. As the country has a population growth rate of about 2,3 per cent per annum, levels of growth in GNP consistently above these levels will be necessary, something not achieved in the decade of the 1980s. To achieve such levels of growth will require the effective management of domestic economic resources, as well as successful participation in the world economy. Which system of economic management, capitalist or socialist, will achieve this?

The capitalist/socialist debate in South Africa has been an essentially backward-looking debate. The debate has been concerned with the nature of the relationship between economic and political structures – the role that capitalism has played in the emergence and maintenance of apartheid. The debate will take on a new form as it turns to future choices. This debate should be informed by contemporary comparative experience.

The twentieth century has provided considerable empirical evidence as to the performance of the two systems. Capitalist forms of organisation, in which the means of production are held mainly in private hands, have been more successful in producing wealth, alleviating poverty and achieving equality than socialist systems. Capitalism also appears to be a necessary but not sufficient condition for democracy, understood as a system of restrained and accountable government.

An even more important burden of evidence exists to suggest that countries develop best when they engage the world economy through trade and investment links, again held in private hands. The phenomenal economic growth achieved by Japan and the East Asian 'little dragons' fundamentally challenges the core-periphery analysis of dependency theory. Three decades of independence on the African continent lead to the same conclusion drawn in negative terms: centrally directed economies whose link with the world lies chiefly in development aid do not grow.

The East Asian experience requires careful study. Whilst there can be no doubt about the role of private ownership in these societies, they do not conform to libertarian notions of minimal or laissez-faire government. Governments have made highly significant investments in social capital such as housing and education. Close relationships have often existed between business and government. Neither have these societies practised free trade policies. However, these societies remain impressive examples of essentially capitalist growth.

The extent to which South Africans effectively address the challenges of economic growth will determine the real benefits that new political institutions will be able to deliver to all South Africa's people.

An open future

There are some grounds for hoping that the process of building new nonracial institutions can succeed. Though South Africa's history is replete with racial division, significant traditions of non-racialism also exist. Such a tradition is apparent in the so-called English-speaking churches. The decision in 1986 by the Dutch Reformed Church to declare racism a sin, and open its own membership to Christians of all races expands and strengthens this resolution. A nonracial ethic which is derived from the exigencies of the market place is at work in the economy. Most universities and private schools have been deracialised. Significantly, all political organisations opposing apartheid promote this ethic of nonracialism. The new Independent Nationalist movement have drawn a line between themselves and traditional Nationalists essentially on this issue.

However, it is clear that change beyond apartheid requires not only new wine, but also new wineskins. What is needed is not only new political parties, but a new political process. In such a process the nature of leadership will be different. Leaders will appeal to ideological rather than ethnic allegiances. In so doing they will change the symbolic reality of South Africa. They will help to manufacture the symbols of national unity that will enable South Africans to develop a loyalty to the land and to the nation.

Neither paradise nor Armageddon awaits South Africa. Instead, a slow and often painful march towards modernity is on the agenda. A nonracial democratic and prosperous society *is* possible. South Africans simply have to make it happen.

Footnotes

1 – South Africa's National Party government (pp. 7-54)

1 The author would like to acknowledge the contributions of others to this chapter. The section on the South African security agencies is very largely based on a paper prepared for the South Africa Beyond Apartheid project by Bobby Godsell: 'The Role of the South African Security Agencies in the Process of Political Transformation', May 1986. Ms Karin Roberts gave valuable assistance to the author in conducting some interviews, by assisting in taking notes in interviews with senior government officials and politicians, and in preparing other notes for consideration by the author.

2 List of persons interviewed:

Cabinet Ministers: P. J. Clase; J. C. Heunis; F. W. de Klerk; M. A. Malan; Dr G. Viljoen; and A. J. Vlok.

Deputy Ministers: T. J. Alant; G. Marais; R. P. Meyer; R. B. Miller; H. J. Tempel; and C. J. van der Merwe.

Members of Parliament: C. Coetzer; H. J. Kriel; I. Louw; W. C. Malan; J. H. W. Mentz; A. E. Nothnagel; P. de Pontes; R. S. Schoeman; A. T. van der Walt; Dr J. J. Vilonel; V. A. Volker; and L. Wessels.

National Party office-bearers (mainly chairmen of constituencies): I. Bosman (Pretoria East); J. Celliers (Dundee); H. Klopper (Durban); G. Krog (Durban); T. Kruger (Koedoespoort); E. Lombaard (Pretoria West); C. Meiring (Linden); A. Odendaal (Newcastle); B. Pearce (Durban); G. MacGregor (Howick); J. Steenkamp (Durban); C. Vosloo (Empangeni); F. Steyn (Winterton); and F. van Deventer (Secretary of the Federal Congress).

Others: Other interviews included discussions with General Jannie Geldenhuys, Head of the South African Defence Force, two senior officials of the National Intelligence Service, as well as a large number of less formal interviews conducted in the course of other research.

Five of those interviewed formally were approached on two occasions; the second interview being part of the 'reality testing' phase of the study.

3 See also the analysis of voting trends in Schlemmer, 1987a.

4 As already acknowledged, this section draws heavily on the South Africa Beyond Apartheid project's paper by Bobby Godsell, 'The Role of the

South African Security Agencies in the Process of Political Transformation'. The conclusions drawn are this author's, however.

5 Interviews with Minister Vlok and Deputy Minister Meyer in particular.
6 See, for example, the article by Heitman in the *Sunday Times*, 5 July 1987.
7 See the paper prepared for the South Africa Beyond Apartheid project by Neuhaus, 1987.
8 For the most recent promotions see the *Sunday Times*, 7 June 1987.
9 See also the South African Institute of Race Relations *Quarterly Review*, July 1987.
10 See, inter alia, the budget speech by the Chairman of the Central Witwatersrand RSC. Stadler, 1987, concedes this point in an otherwise critical book.

2 – The right wing in South African politics (pp. 55-94)

1 This paper is an abbreviated version of a longer research paper compiled for the South Africa Beyond Apartheid project. It is based on a survey of contemporary right-wing literature and interviews with leading right-wing politicians and analysts, many of whom were interviewed on several occasions. Interviews were conducted with: Dr A. P. Treurnicht, leader of the Conservative Party; Mr Jaap Marais, leader of the Herstigte Nasionale Party; Mr Eugene Terre'Blanche, leader of the Afrikaner-Weerstandsbeweging; Professor Carel Boshoff, chairman of the Afrikanervolkswag and of SABRA; Mr Clive Derby-Lewis, chairman of the Stallard Foundation, the Conservative Party spokesman on economic affairs and member of the party's National Executive; Professor Barney Uys, a lecturer in engineering at the University of Pretoria and the right wing's election statistician; Mr Z. B. du Toit, former editor of the HNP's official newspaper, *Die Afrikaner*, and now on the editorial staff of the CP's newspaper, *Die Patriot*; Mr Hendrik Verwoerd and Mr Ben van den Berg of the Vereniging van Oranjewerkers; Professor Alkmaar Swart of the Executive of the Oranjewerkers and the executive of the Afrikaner-Weerstandsbeweging; and Professor J. C. Schabort, leader of the Blanke Bevrydingsbeweging. No attempt was made to canvass the views of rank-and-file right-wing supporters. It is sometimes argued that the rationally articulated ethnic nationalism of the right wing's leadership does not reflect the political opinions of their supporters. To some extent this is true of all political movements. No attempt was made to check this thesis as far as the right wing is concerned. However, it was interesting to note that in a survey of 252 Bushveld farmers in the Northern Transvaal, conducted by Professor Pierre Hugo of the University of South Africa, many respondents sponta-

neously used the same political and ideological arguments as those of right-wing leaders. (The results of this survey are contained in an unpublished memo made available to me by Professor Hugo.)

2 $\dfrac{1981 \text{ NP support} - 1987 \text{ NP support}}{1981 \text{ NP support}} \times 100 = 25\%$

3 There were eight seats in which the CP's and HNP's combined total exceeded the NP's votes. In two other constituencies, Roodeplaat and Krugersdorp, the NP's winning margin was so narrow that it is almost certain that a united right-wing effort would have captured these seats. Internecine feuding cost the right-wing parties considerable support at the polls – a common phenomenon in elections.

4 For example, Bloemfontein North (24,27%), Bloemfontein East (38,55%) and Waterkloof (18,9%).

5 According to Uys, this is a conservative calculation based on the results in constituencies such as Wonderboom and Gezina which are largely inhabited by public servants.

6 During the interviews, I was told that the right wing had managed to take control of several school committees in the Pretoria area, including Menlo Park High School. Shortly afterwards the committee made national news by refusing to allow a black athlete to participate in a sporting event at the school.

7 These estimates are made by Professor Barney Uys, who specialises in analysing statistics for the right wing and is considered to be an expert on the subject by all parties and organisations on the Right. He is known for his caution, and his predictions have often clashed with those of politicians. His statistics on the AWB were categorised as 'the most plausible' during interviews with other right-wingers (for example, Du Toit and Boshoff).

8 The HNP demands total assimilation and accepts only one official South African language – Afrikaans. The AWB has begun actively to recruit English-speaking members, through press advertisements (for example, *Sunday Star*, 23 August 1987).

9 The right wing draws no distinction between a 'united' and a 'unitary' state – an important constitutional distinction.

10 There are some variations on this theme. Some HNP members and the BBB do not recognise Bophuthatswana, arguing that 'the Tswanas already have Botswana'. The CP and the HNP support the notion of a 'coloured' homeland, but differ on their policy towards South Africa's one million citizens of Indian origin. Some support an 'Indian homeland' somewhere in Natal, while others believe that Indians must either find a political home in the 'coloured homeland' or return to India. None question the unilateral right of whites to decide on the future of these groups.

11 These quotations are taken from two articles by Arnheim published in

303

Finance Week (7-13 November 1985 and 14-20 November 1985). All right-wingers interviewed referred to these articles, which summarise some of the key arguments of Arnheim's book, *South Africa After Vorster.*

12 Of the NP's 133-member caucus, 123 are elected and ten nominated.

13 This calculation is based on the following assumptions and election statistics: of all voters, 60% were Afrikaans and 40% English. Of the Afrikaans voters 4% supported the PFP; 2% supported the NRP; 42% supported the CP; 5% supported the HNP; 1% supported the Independents; 5% spoilt their papers and 47,3% supported the NP. Uys stresses that this calculation is the most optimistic possible for the government, as it is largely based on election results. The NP fielded candidates in the vast majority of constituencies, giving most of its supporters a chance to cast a vote. This was not the case with the CP and even less so with the PFP and Independents.

14 Following the 1987 general election, at least 19 NP-held seats are officially considered marginal – and particularly vulnerable to the right wing. Of these, 12 are in the Transvaal, one in Natal, five in the Orange Free State and one in the Cape. The CP believes that it can easily win these seats if an election is held in 1989.

The Right also bases its calculation on an average 2% right-wing swing per year. On this basis it believes that it can win at least 43 more seats if an election is held in 1992.

3 – Exile and resistance: the African National Congress, the South African Communist Party and the Pan Africanist Congress (pp. 95-124)

1 This analytic account is based on personal interviews with ANC and PAC representatives, internal ANC documents, evidence from trials and the police, public statements, speeches, broadcasts and publications issued by the movements, as well as the growing journalistic and academic literature on the subject. For South African legal reasons many quotations are not attributed to specific sources or persons. Most undocumented quotations are either from public statements or interviews, particularly those held at the ANC/IDASA Dakar meeting in July 1987, or the Internal Commission Reports (Cadre Policy, Political and Ideological Work, Strategy and Tactics) of the ANC National Consultative Conference, June 1985 in Kabwe, Zambia.

This paper is aimed at presenting a more accurate assessment of the banned resistance movements to a South African audience which receives only censored and propagandistic information. I am indebted to Kogila

Moodley, Colin Bundy and Michael Savage for their critical comments, and to the Centre for Intergroup Studies at the University of Cape Town for an academic home during 1986-1987.

2 For figures I rely partly on Tom Lodge, 'State of Exile: The African National Congress of South Africa, 1976-86' in *Third World Quarterly*, January 1987: 1-27, and a wide range of sources cited therein. I also had the benefit of listening to various lectures by Lodge as well as private conversations with him. For further data see Stephen M. Davis, *Apartheid's Rebels*, 1987.

3 See particularly the statements by former AZAPO president Saths Cooper (*Frontline*, September/October 1986) and the writings of Neville Alexander (1985), *Sow the Wind*.

4 Here too are different emphases among ANC and SACP adherents, as evidenced in an article in a SACP journal that "People's democracy means the dictatorship of the people". How South African disinformation can distort ANC policy is perhaps best illustrated by an SABC Commentary after the NECC and the ANC had argued consistently for a return to school: "Indeed," declared the SABC (Commentary, 24 March 1987), "the return to school in black areas is one of several manifestations of rejection of ANC policies by a significant number of black people". The return, against widespread feelings in favour of a continued boycott, proved precisely the influence of the ANC, guided by strong community pressures from parents, teachers and churches, particularly in the Eastern Cape.

5 When members of the British Anti-apartheid Movement (AAM) imposed a total boycott on all South African cultural exports, including bans on anti-apartheid plays such as Robert Kirby's *Bijer's Sunbird*, the ANC warned against the tendency to equate everything South African with the apartheid regime. The movement rejected a blanket cultural boycott. In line with UDF spokesman Murphy Morobe, it advocated a flexible approach, dependent on whether or not the person was broadly allied with the 'progressive forces'.

6 Such imperatives, quite apart from the explicitly stated intent of nonracialism, put the lie to the National Party scares that "there would be no place for whites in South Africa if the ANC succeeded in its struggle" (John Wiley, former Minister of Water Affairs and the Environment, as reported in the *Cape Times*, 23 March 1987).

7 For a further elaboration see Heribert Adam and Kogila Moodley (1986): *South Africa Without Apartheid*, Chapter 4.

8 An additional reason for the expulsion was the charge that the group stole the secret address list of SACTU.

9 See Winrich Kuhne (1986): *Sowjetische Afrikapolitik in der 'Ära Gorbatschov'*.

10 Goncharov, *Work in Progress*, 48: 7. See also the much-discussed paper by Gleb Starushenko of Moscow's Africa Institute, who recommends that the ANC should offer 'comprehensive guarantees' to whites (*Africa Analysis*, 12 December 1986, and the *Weekly Mail*, 9-15 January 1987). The SACP dismissed this suggestion as a private opinion which does not represent the views of the CPSU or the Soviet government. It was reported that "at the conference the ANC delegation and many Soviet scientists took issue with Starushenko in a comradely manner". The rebuttals do not alter the fact that in the pragmatic Gorbachov era, some experts in the Soviet Union have doubts about the past ANC/SACP strategy. For a similar conclusion see also Kurt M. Campbell, *Soviet Policy Towards South Africa*, 1987.

11 For the two examples, see the *African Communist*, (106)3, 1986.

4 – The politics of internal resistance groupings (pp. 125-163)

1 While this chapter reflects a single authorship, it is largely a product of numerous contributions. For instance, the material on education and the churches is a result of the research and papers presented by James Leatt, while Jakes Gerwel, Reuel Khoza, Vincent Maphai and Paulus Zulu contributed the material on the UDF, the black professionals, Black Consciousness and street resistance respectively. The chapter is therefore a synthesis of the above six papers, although this author takes full responsibility for the way in which these views are projected.

5 – The incrementalists (pp. 164-199)

1 Deep-level, hard-rock gold mining would have been impossible in South Africa without access to very considerable amounts of 'start-up' capital. This required the formation of the mining-finance house, which in turn became the logical channel for the re-investment in secondary industry of mining profits.

2 For example, all business representatives interviewed for the South Africa Beyond Apartheid project accepted that extensive state intervention was not only likely but indeed required in order to create a society of really equal individual opportunities.

3 Whilst business was of course not alone in seeking this change, it was one, if not the major, of the key groups in effecting this change. The 'campaign' to end the pass laws was both designed by and 'coached' through its stages by the Urban Foundation, and included the commissioning of research to

provide a body of evidence supporting abolition, and both private and public lobbying. See Bernstein, 1986: 39-40.

4 A dramatic example of this was P. W. Botha's vitriolic response to the FCI stance on the second State of Emergency in 1986. This response has played an important part in the organisational and financial problems currently being experienced by that organisation.

5 Since the Zambia encounter there has been little evidence of an ANC shift in attitudes towards the economy (and especially divestment), and no evidence of a shift in its attitude towards violence as a strategy for change.

6 See Cadman and Godsell, 1987: 2.

7 All opinion surveys have found substantial support for Inkatha in the Natal region, whilst support outside of Natal (for example in the Witwatersrand) has varied from significant to marginal. See Cadman and Godsell, 1987: 23-26.

8 See Cadman and Godsell, 1987: 2.

9 Buthelezi quoted in Kane-Berman, 1982: 152.

10 Pre-eminently, Inkatha's president is also KwaZulu's chief minister, whilst the movement's general secretary is also a KwaZulu cabinet minister. In fact, the entire KwaZulu cabinet are also members of the central committee of Inkatha.

11 For example, whereas all polls show significant support for the ANC, there is equal evidence of a popular rejection of change through violence, despite the fact that the ANC is committed to the armed struggle.

12 See Lodge, 1983. This is also the common finding of a diverse group of opinion polls. (See Cadman and Godsell, 1987: 23-26.)

13 See, for example, Inkatha's statement of belief, which endorses 'respect for individuals', 'individual equality before the law', 'the rule of law' and that the "development of trade unions, guilds and associations should be encouraged by the enactment of enabling legislation and courts of arbitration" (quoted in De Kock, 1986: 176-177), and the movement's support for the KwaNatal Indaba Bill of Rights, which, as a prototypical liberal Bill of Rights, provides for individual liberty and freedom of movement, thought, conscience, religion, opinion and expression (quoted in De Kock, 1986: 155-161).

14 De Kock, 1986: 176-178.

15 This change in style involved a move away from the characteristics of a crusading protest movement towards a more conventional 'parish pump' political identity.

16 This group of voters has clearly moved into the National Party camp, as the PFP loss of seats such as Wynberg, Walmer, Albany, Hillbrow, Pietermaritzburg North and South, Bezuidenhout and Edenvale indicated, along with the loss of NRP seats in Durban Point, Umbilo, King William's Town and Umhlanga.

17 Twenty-two elected to the PFP's nineteen. Each party will gain one or two nominated members.

18 Interview with General Secretary Fred Peters, January 1986, quoted in Zille, 1986: 2.

19 For example, the party's ten-point statement of principle provides: "that the rights of the individual are paramount and the state exists to serve the individual". Quoted in Zille, 1986: 4-5.

20 In other conversations with the writer, the party's deputy leader, Mylie Richards, has suggested that a coloured boycott of the 1948 general election contributed to, if it did not cause, the National Party victory.

6 – The economics of conflict and negotiation (pp. 200-239)

1 Anthony Giddens, *Central Problems in Social Theory*. Marx's famous dictum is changed fundamentally by the addition of the final phrase.

2 See O'Dowd in Leftwich, *South Africa: Economic Growth and Political Change with Comparative Studies of Chile, Sri Lanka and Malaysia*, 1974, and Houghton, *The South African Economy*, 1973, 3rd ed.

3 The popular mono-causal explanations of the nineteenth century have maintained a dominance of the social sciences for far too long. Implicit in much of what is argued in this paper is an acceptance of Giddens's theory of structuration.

4 A typical example of this narrow concern with constitutional arrangements is to be found in the book by Arend Lijphart, *Power-Sharing in South Africa*, 1985, Policy Papers in International Affairs, No. 24.

5 It is interesting that the Vorster era saw reforms, under the leadership of Fanie Botha, then minister of Labour, which created space for the black trade union movement, whereas most of P. W. Botha's reforms are aimed at furthering the interests of black entrepreneurs.

6 See J. A. Lombard, *Freedom, Welfare and Order: Thoughts on the Principle of Political Co-operation in the Economy of Southern Africa*, 1978.

7 See for example, F. J. du Plessis, *Persoonlike Besparings in Suid-Afrika: Staan Ons Tans Voor 'n Krisis?* which is the publication by Potchefstroom University of a lecture delivered on Thursday, 29 August 1985, and in particular see a lecture delivered by him on 25 March 1986 and published in the same series under the title *Die Vryemarkideologie in Perspektief*.

8 Tony Bloom claimed in a BBC series on South Africa broadcast in December 1986 that the Rubicon speech was of crucial importance for the decision of many bankers to withdraw.

9 See J. P. Dreyer and S. S. Brand, ''n Sektorale Beskouing van die Suid-Afrikaanse Ekonomie in 'n Veranderende Omgewing', a paper delivered at

the 1986 Bi-annual Conference of the South African Economics Society, and subsequently published in the *South African Journal for Economics*.

10 See Neville Alexander, *Sow the Wind: Contemporary Speeches*, 1985.

11 In the thirties and forties members of the secret Afrikaner Nationalist organisation, the Broederbond, at times defined socialism as the system under which the English own all the means of production.

12 See W. A. Hutt, *The Economics of the Colour Bar: a Study of the Economic Origins and Consequences of Racial Segregation in South Africa*, 1964 and M. O'Dowd, 'A Capitalist Approach to the Amelioration of Poverty', 1984.

13 See L. Louw and F. Kendall, *South Africa, the Solution*, 1986. Although Winnie Mandela's preface seems to imply support for this programme, she subsequently denied that this was her intention. More importantly, there is simply no other acknowledged leader within the ANC or UDF who seems to be remotely sympathetic to this type of system.

14 See, for example, J. Maree, 'The Past, Present and Potential Role of the Democratic Trade Union Movement', York Conference paper, Institute for Southern African Studies, September 1986.

15 See P. le Roux, 'Die Uitdaging van die Demokratiese Sosialisme' in *Die Suid-Afrikaan*, No. 7, Herfs, 1986. Strictly speaking, 'economic democracy' rather than 'democratic socialism' would be the correct description of the proposed system, but in the South African context such an economic democracy would probably lead to the implementation of a democratic-socialist system.

16 In Chapter 5 on the incrementalists, the impression is created that social democracy is a system generally accepted by the Progressive Federal Party and big business. This does not accord with my observations. Within these circles there seem to be important, probably even dominant groups that favour a free market type of approach. However, it is clear that many would be willing to accept a social democracy as a system rather than a more radical socialist solution. The official PFP position is contained in a document entitled 'Economic Democracy: A Charter for Social and Economic Progress'. Details of this charter, which was drawn up under the chairmanship of Harry Schwartz, were published under the heading 'The PFP's Alternative Economic Democracy' (*Deurbraak*, May 1985: 7). This document is a balance between the conservative social-democratic position of the chairman, and the free market conviction of some of the other members of the commission.

17 See J. A. Lombard, *Socio Economic Prospects for the Eighties*, 1981.

18 HSRC Investigation into Intergroup Relations, *Growth, Equity and Participation*. Work Committee: Economics and Labour, edited by Godsell and Le Roux.

19 See, for example, A. Rupert, 'A Plea for Co-existence', the Chairman's address delivered on 28 August 1986, Rembrandt Group Limited.
20 See C. Simkins et al., 'Justice, Development and the National Budget', second Carnegie Enquiry into Poverty and Development in Southern Africa, Post Conference Series No. 6, Cape Town, 1985.
21 See A. Black, 'Industrialization, Economic Crisis and the Question of Redistribution in South Africa', *SAERT*, Amsterdam, December 1986.
22 See J. P. Dreyer and S. S. Brand, "n Sektorale Beskouing van die Suid-Afrikaanse Ekonomie in 'n Veranderende Omgewing', a paper delivered at the 1986 Bi-annual Conference of the South African Economics Society, and subsequently published in the *South African Journal for Economics*.
23 These estimates are based on my own calculations.
24 See G. Wittich, 'Research Priorities for Socio-Economic Planning in Post-Apartheid South Africa Manufacture (Parastatals)', a paper delivered at the conference of the *SAERT*, Amsterdam, December 1986.
25 See *The Commonwealth Eminent Persons Group on South Africa. Mission to South Africa: The Commonwealth Report*, 1986.
26 It is possible, of course, that this more accommodating position is based on tactical considerations rather than on any change in conviction.

7 – The United States and the world (pp. 240-266)

1 *The New York Times*, 18 January 1979.
2 See Steven Metz, 1986: 'The Anti-Apartheid Movement and the Populist Instinct in American Politics', *Political Science Quarterly* (101)3: 379-395.
3 U. S. Department of State, 'A U. S. Policy toward South Africa', *The Report of the Secretary of State's Advisory Committee on South Africa*, Washington D. C., January 1987: 38.
4 U. S. Department of State, 'South Africa: Background Notes', No. 8021, Washington D. C., July 1973.
5 Ibid.
6 The Cuban linkage was rejected by the United States' partners in the so-called Contact Group (Britain, Canada, France and West Germany) that had been seeking to persuade South Africa to accept an internationally sanctioned settlement in Namibia.
7 This and the ensuing paragraphs on political activism in the United States are based on interviews and research conducted by David Hauck and Shelley Green.
8 Henry Bienen: 'A New Policy – Selective Engagement', *Orbis*. Philadelphia, 1987: 17-31.

9 See the speeches by Chester A. Crocker, 'A Democratic Future: The Challenge for South Africans', CUNY Conference on South Africa in Transition, White Plains, N.Y., 1 October 1987; and Secretary of State George Shultz, 'The Democratic Future of South Africa', Business Council for International Understanding, New York, N.Y., 29 September 1987.
10 Robert S. Greenberger, 'U. S. Trade Sanctions on South Africa Starting to Pay Long-Term Dividends', *The Wall Street Journal*, 21 September 1987.
11 Bienen, op. cit.
12 'A U. S. Policy toward South Africa', 1987: 13.
13 See J. P. Hayes, *Economic Effects of Sanctions on Southern Africa*, 1987.
14 *Work in Progress*, 48, July 1987.
15 South African power reached its geographic apogee in 1964 when forces led by South African mercenaries succeeded in catapulting Moise Tshombe to power in Zaire. The subsequent collapse of Portuguese rule in Angola and Mozambique (1974-1975) and the demise of white Rhodesia (1978) reduced South Africa's political, if not military, power in the region.
16 *Los Angeles Times*, 24 September 1986.
17 According to a 1987 study of the United States Committee on Refugees.
18 Clem Sunter, 1987: *The World and South Africa in the 1990s*. Cape Town: Human & Rousseau, Tafelberg: 51 and 102.

8 – South Africa in comparative context (pp. 267-298)

1 The sovereign status of South Africa and its noncolonial character are accepted by resistance groups and by other African states, and indeed by the Organisation of African Unity, as evidenced in the 1969 Lusaka Manifesto.
2 Peter Wickins notes: "To draw up a balance sheet of the costs and benefits of colonialism, both for colonies and for colonisers, defies human ingenuity because of the impossibility of their quantification or even of identifying their nature ... While no doubt the imposition of political control was thought by the occupying powers to serve their economic interests, directly through immediate economic advantage or indirectly through the protection of strategic interests or the furtherance of national prestige, both of which have an economic aspect, it does not follow that the allocation of human and material resources to empire brought greater gain than would have accrued to their use in a different way. The only certainty is that some did very well out of imperialism and that equally others lost their money or their lives" (Wickins, 1981: 205). The balance of economic advantage

311

seems clear in the final stages of colonialism. Wickins notes that "in the last years of their rule the colonial powers consciously did a great deal for their colonies that was disinterested" (Ibid: 205). This is dramatically illustrated by the Constantine Plan in Algiers. This five-year plan, launched in 1958, had as its objective the transformation of Algeria into an industrialised nation, with a standard of living equal to metropolitan France. Though the plan fell far short of its targets, it nevertheless involved France in a very significant transfer to Algeria (see Horne, 1977: 305 onwards). The key motivations for the very sudden Portuguese withdrawal from Africa were cited as the excessive economic and military costs of continued colonisation. One account puts the cost of Portugal's fifteen-year military encounter with Frelimo in Mozambique at three billion pounds (sterling) and 5 000 fatalities (Hanlon 1984: 43).

3 For example, Philip Frankel attributes enormous (almost certainly exaggerated) influence to the writings of a key French military strategist in Algeria: "... the ideological and strategic spirit of the South African military is particularly and peculiarly Francophile in character and if there is any single figure whose writings have had a formative influence in how the current generation of Defence Force leaders interpret the world in relation to counter-insurgency, it is above all, the French general, Andre Beaufre, whose various works are the basis of virtually every lecture at the Joint Defence College – the primary institution for socialising South Africa's military elite, one of the main contact points for communication between government, the private sector and the state security apparatus, and, since the early seventies, the think-tank for the formation and development of South Africa's total strategy" (Frankel 1984: 46).

4 The one million estimate is that of Alistair Horne. The four million estimate is that of the ANC's Johnny Makatini, as noted in Chapter 3 of this book.

5 These ethical dilemmas are well developed in the political writings of *pied noir* Albert Camus.

6 The Shah's reign contained several indications of hesitant and even half-hearted behaviour. For example, in the period 1953-1954, in the face of growing communist influence and intense rivalry between the Shah and his Prime Minister Mossadeq, the Shah alternated between assertive and conciliatory behaviour, as well as considerable periods of indecision. This culminated in the Shah actually leaving the country, returning only under the protective umbrella of threatened United States and British military involvement. A similar period of indecision occurred in 1960 in a conflict between the Shah and Grand Ayatollah Borujerdi. The Hamlet-like behaviour of the Shah repeated itself for a third time in 1978-1979. Again it is important to note that the Shah left Iran of his own accord. Had he resisted

the forces seeking his overthrow in a more determined way, it is altogether possible that he may have succeeded. For a detailed description of particularly this last period, see Taheri, 1985.

7 The report of the working group on religion in the Human Sciences Research Council national research programme into Intergroup relations, *Religion, Intergroup Relations and Social Change,* provides an excellent introduction into the pattern of religious belief and observance in South Africa, as well as the interaction between religious belief and political attitudes and behaviour (Oosthuizen, 1985). John de Gruchy's *The Church Struggle* gives a good account of the role of the so-called English-speaking churches. Two documents, the *Kairos Declaration* (1985) and the *Lusaka Declaration of the World Council of Churches* (1986), illustrate the nature of this church grouping's support for resistance to apartheid. It is this group that most closely resembles the role played by some Ayatollahs in Iran. With regard to the Dutch Reformed community, two church documents, *Ras, Volk en Nasie* (1974) and *Ras en Gemeenskap* (1986), mark the changed relationship of this confession to apartheid concepts and practices. The least researched area is the syncretic, pietistic groupings commonly characterised as 'independent' churches. Vilakazi's (1986) study is useful. The most helpful general introduction to this subject is to be found in the paper commissioned for the South Africa Beyond Apartheid project and written by Richard Neuhaus.

8 In fact, though a very poor country at the time, Japan became the first nation to institute a compulsory mass education system, doing this in 1872.

9 Helen Suzman has argued cogently for the counter-productive nature of Western criticism, suggesting inter alia that it has been responsible for growing white support for the ruling party in recent times (Suzman, 1987).

10 Statutory job reservation persists only in the mining industry, and draft legislation ending racial bars on skilled and supervisory jobs in that industry has been published, and should be adopted in 1988.

11 For example, the eight development regions into which South Africa has been divided, and which are now central to growth strategies, cut across constitutional and racial boundaries.

12 It could be argued that an analogous competition did exist between the independent unions which re-emerged in the 1970s and state-sponsored (through legislation) works and liaison committees. However, the committees were the creature of management and not the state. They were also purely local in domain, and proved little impediment to the growth of unions.

313

APPENDIX I

Biographical notes
on the academic team

HERIBERT ADAM

Professor of Political Science at the Simon Fraser University, Vancouver, Canada. He is probably that country's foremost South African scholar. A German by origin, he has previously taught at the University of Natal and has published extensively on South Africa. Adam served as a member of the Buthelezi Commission.

PETER L. BERGER – PROGRAMME CHAIRMAN

Professor of Sociology at Boston University. An eminent sociologist, he has published extensively on the sociology of religion, the sociology of knowledge and more recently has been investigating patterns of development and modernisation in both South America and Asia. He previously taught at Rutgers University (New York) and has done work for the America Enterprise Foundation. His wife, Brigetta, holds the chair in Sociology at Wellesley College.

ANN BERNSTEIN

Policy Director: Urbanisation for the Urban Foundation in South Africa. She is a graduate of the University of the Witwatersrand and the University of California, Los Angeles. Previously, she was an intern at the United Nations Development Programme in New York, a Research Assistant to Helen Suzman, MP, a special Parliamentary Assistant to Colin Eglin, Leader of the Progressive Federal Party, and a senior research officer of the Urban Foundation. She has been a member of the National Executive of the South African Institute of Race Relations. Her published writings include 'Influx Control in Urban South Africa : An International and Empirical View' in *Up Against the Fences: Poverty, Masses and Privilege in South Africa* (H. Giliomee and L. Schlemmer, eds). She was nominated as one of the 'Women of our Time' by *The Star* in 1986.

VICKI CADMAN

Previously worked at the Indicator Project, University of Natal, Durban. She is presently working as a computer programmer.

JAKES GERWEL

Formerly Professor of Afrikaans literature and Dean of the Faculty of Arts at

314

the University of the Western Cape. He is now Rector and Vice-Chancellor of this university.

BOBBY GODSELL

Group Consultant, Industrial Relations and Public Affairs of Anglo American Corporation. He served on the Buthelezi and HSRC Intergroup Relations Project investigations.

RONALD GOLDMAN

Associate Dean at Boston University's College of Communication. For the past five years, he has concentrated upon developing relationships between American universities and South African educators. In 1983, Boston University, in conjunction with USSALEP (United States/South Africa Leadership Exchange Programme) conducted the first of a multiyear training programme for black journalists in South Africa. This programme represents a model of how American universities can help promote educational development in South Africa. Goldman will continue to work to promote such programmes.

SHELLEY GREEN

Worked as a research consultant on Africa and economic development. She recently completed a two year study on black entrepreneurship in the United States for Boston University.

DAVID HAUCK

Director of the South Africa Review Service of the Investor Responsibility Research Center in Washington, D. C. The Center provides research on social and public policy issues affecting United States companies and the institutional investors who invest in them. IRRC's work is supported by more than 300 institutional investors. Hauck has specialised in South African affairs, visits the country frequently and has published extensively on this country.

REUEL KHOZA

Managing Director of Co-Ordinated Marketing, marketing and management consultants to several major corporations. He is a patron of the Black Management Forum and sits on the Stancor and Stannic boards.

HELEN KITCHEN

Director of the African Studies Programme of the Center for Strategic and International Studies, Washington, D. C. She is one of America's leading analysts of Africa (from Cairo to the Cape) and of the United States policy-making process.

315

JAMES LEATT

Formerly Professor of Business Ethics at the University of Cape Town's Business School. A theologian by training, Leatt previously taught in the Religious Studies Department at the University of Cape Town, as well as at the Federal Theological Seminary in Alice. He is currently Deputy Vice-Chancellor of the University of Cape Town. He has published in ethics and political economy.

PIETER LE ROUX

Economist and Director of the Institute for Social Development at the University of the Western Cape. As Professor in Development Studies, Le Roux previously taught at the Rand Afrikaans University in Johannesburg. He has worked extensively on the second Carnegie Poverty Investigation and has also recently served as the Vice-Chairman of the Economics and Labour Work Group of the HSRC Intergroup Relations Investigation.

VINCENT MAPHAI

Senior lecturer in the Department of Political Studies, University of the Western Cape, specialising in Political Theory.

JOHN MARCUM

Professor of Political Science at the University of California (Santa Cruz campus). He has recently completed a term of office as the academic Vice-Chancellor of that campus. Marcum is a specialist in the regional politics of Southern Africa, having written the definitive history of the Angolan Civil War. He also chaired a USSALEP investigation into education in South Africa.

RICHARD NEUHAUS

Lutheran theologian and Director of the Rockford Institute Center on Religion & Society in New York City. He is the author of *Dispensations: The Future of South Africa as South Africans See It* (Eerdmans, 1986). In the South Africa Beyond Apartheid project he was responsible for examining the 'religion factor' as it pertains to the present and future of South Africa.

LAWRENCE SCHLEMMER

Director of the Centre for Policy Studies at the University of the Witwatersrand, Johannesburg, and one of the country's leading sociologists. Schlemmer was secretary to the Buthelezi Commission and an executive committee member of the recent HSRC Intergroup Relations Enquiry.

MICHAEL SPICER

Currently a Divisional Public Affairs Manager at Anglo American Corporation, he previously worked at the Royal Institute for International Affairs and at the South African Institute for International Affairs.

HELEN ZILLE

A journalist who served for a period of time as the political correspondent for the *Rand Daily Mail*. At present she is working as a freelance journalist and editor.

PAULUS ZULU

Senior Research Fellow at the Centre for Applied Social Sciences at the University of Natal, Durban.

APPENDIX 2

South African/American
Academic Research Project

1 PURPOSE OF THE SOUTH AFRICA BEYOND APARTHEID PROJECT

The South Africa Beyond Apartheid project seeks to identify and describe the aspirations, tactics and strategies of major actors, in America as well as in southern Africa, for a future beyond the political and economic system known as 'apartheid'. It seeks, secondly, to measure these aspirations, tactics and strategies against identifiable 'realities' of the South African issue as they operate on both continents. Thirdly, the project will outline a range of alternative strategic options for post-apartheid South African society.

2 SOUTH AFRICA BEYOND APARTHEID'S SPONSORS

This project is being sponsored and funded by a combined grouping of American and South African philanthropic foundations and corporations. The project is being overseen by the South Africa Beyond Apartheid Board of Trustees, representing these foundations and corporations.

3 SOUTH AFRICA BEYOND APARTHEID'S RESEARCH
PROJECT PARTICIPANTS

South Africa Beyond Apartheid's Board of Trustees have appointed a team of some twenty-five North American and South African academics and experts to conduct this project. This team, under the chairmanship of Professor Peter Berger of Boston University, has sole and exclusive responsibility for both the conduct of the research and the recording of the project's findings. The conclusions reached by the team will in no way be influenced by, nor will they necessarily reflect, the views of the Board of Trustees or sponsor organisations. A list of team members is given in Appendix 1.

4 PRESENTATION OF FINDINGS

The findings of the research project will be presented in book form and made available to the public. These findings may also be discussed in conferences or seminars with key actors likely to play roles in southern Africa beyond apartheid.

5 SOUTH AFRICA BEYOND APARTHEID'S TIMETABLE

It is hoped to conclude the South Africa Beyond Apartheid project within a two-year time frame, commencing in September 1985.

318

South Africa Beyond
Apartheid's sponsors

SOUTH AFRICAN
SABA FOUNDATION

Anglo American and De Beers Chairman's Fund
African Consolidated Investment
Ernest Oppenheimer & Son
First National Bank
A. E. Rupert

UNITED STATES
SABA FOUNDATION

Chemical Bank
General Motors
IBM
Johnson & Johnson
Mobil
Salomon Brothers

APPENDIX 4
Analytic scheme

The revised analytic framework is intended to provide a broad common framework aimed at guiding the research/writing to be conducted in the first phase of the project.

1 Who?
   Social and political location:
   Identification of the grouping in terms of standard social science categories (composition in terms of size, age, race/ethnicity, class, occupation, level of education).
   Identification of splits/cleavages and coalitions within and between groupings.
   Identification of the grouping in terms of the overall political spectrum in South Africa or the United States.
   History of the grouping.
   Patterns of leadership, organisation and recruitment.
   Vested interests of the leadership (acknowledged and unacknowledged).

2 Why?
   Long-range purposes:
   Identification of overtly stated scenarios for the future.
   Identification of implicit scenarios for the future.
   Normative presuppositions:
   – The stated norms/values of the grouping.
   Ideological location of these presuppositions:
   – The larger ethos within which they make sense to people in the grouping.
   Cognitive presuppositions:
   – The 'cognitive map' with which these people operate (How do they perceive themselves? How do they perceive the realities of South Africa, the United States, or the world at large?)
   – How do they perceive their putative antagonists and the aims, interests and values of the latter?
   – How do they perceive other actors in the situation?

3 How?

Strategies:

Identification of overtly stated strategies to realise the desired scenario.
Identification of implicit strategies – that is, strategies implied by the actions taken (and possibly not consciously perceived as strategies) rather than the rhetoric used.

Identification of obstacles as perceived by the grouping.

4 Are these strategies plausible?

Reality testing:

This is based on the team's common perception of reality and includes:

– An assessment of the cognitive presuppositions of the grouping.
– An assessment of the probable consequences and costs (political, social and economic) of the grouping's particular strategy, and of its chances of successful realisation.

Peter L. Berger: Suggested analytic scheme for the South Africa Beyond Apartheid project reality-testing

1 Internal critique

This means questions addressed to actors in terms of *their own* cognitive maps; in other words, here one tries to probe for weaknesses or inconsistencies within the several cognitive maps without suggesting that realism would require different cognitive presuppositions altogether.

(a) Factual errors on cognitive map.

E.g. Simple mistakes concerning economic or demographic data.

N.B. Such mistakes are only worth bringing up if they are relevant to the actor's strategic logic.

(b) Discrepancies between actor's goals and strategies.

E.g. The possibility or probability that announced goal A may not be attained by the strategic logic employed, but rather that unannounced and putatively undesired goal B may in fact be achieved.

(c) Discrepancies between actor's norms and strategies.

E.g. Pointing out that the strategy employed contradicts norms espoused by the actor.

N.B. Here no external norms, such as those held by the SABA interviewer, are introduced; rather, the actor's *own* norms are brought to bear on the strategic logic in play.

2 External critique

This means questions addressed to actors in terms of the *interviewer's* cognitive assumptions, thus suggesting that actors' cognitive maps may be empirically faulty. Depending on the sensitivity of the interview situation, this may be done directly ("I think that you are wrong here") or indirectly/ hypothetically ("Some people think that the situation is such-and-such – how would you respond to this?").

(a) Confrontation with an alternative cognitive map.

If the interview situation allows, the actor is here challenged by being asked to respond to a completely different interpretation of reality. If this is deemed to be too difficult, the following course can be taken.

(b) Confrontation with specific cognitive dissonances.

That is, rather than challenging the actor's cognitive map as a whole, specific parts of it are questioned in terms of the interviewer's (or, alternatively 'other people's') notions of reality. Four areas suggest themselves for this:

   (i) Unintended consequences of strategies.

      E.g. "You do this because you want to achieve that. Have you considered the possibility or probability that a completely different course of events may result?"

      N.B. This line of questioning is very similar to the one suggested above under 1(b), differing only in *degree* of unintended outcome.

   (ii) Unperceived economic costs.

      Put simply: "Have you figured out what your strategy will cost?"

  (iii) Unperceived political costs.

      E.g. "Have you figured out what this strategy will do to this particular political relationship?"

  (iv) Unperceived social costs.

      E.g. "Have you figured out what this strategy will do to the cohesion or social character of your constituency?"

   (v) Unperceived international costs.

      Simple enough.

3 Normative critique

This would mean questioning actors in terms of the norms relevant to the South Africa Beyond Apartheid project. Put negatively, is this particular strategy likely to impact destructively on:

(a) *the dismantling of apartheid*;

(b) *a democratic future for South Africa*;

(c) *the preservation of an economic base*;

(d) *the minimalisation of human costs?*

Bibliography

Adam, Heribert 1979: 'Survival Politics – in Search of a New 1979 Ideology' in Adam, H. and Giliomee, H. 1979: *The Rise and Crisis of Afrikaner Power.* Cape Town: David Philip.

Adam, Heribert 1987a: 'Exile and Resistance: ANC, Umkhonto, SACP and PAC'. Research paper prepared for the South Africa Beyond Apartheid project.

Adam, Heribert 1987b: 'The Ultra-Right in South Africa' in *Optima 35(1)*, March 1987. Published by the Anglo American Corporation and De Beers Group of Companies.

Adam, Heribert and Moodley, Kogila 1986: *South Africa Without Apartheid.* Berkeley: University of California Press (also Cape Town: Maskew Miller) (chapter 4).

Africa Analysis (12), December 1986.

Africa Confidential (28)5, 4 March 1987.

African National Congress: National Executive Council Statement of 16 December 1986.

African National Congress: National Executive Council Statement of 8 January 1987.

Afrikanerverbond, 10 October 1985.

Alexander, Neville 1985: *Sow the Wind: Contemporary Speeches.* Johannesburg: Skotaville.

Arnheim, M. T. W. 1979: *South Africa After Vorster.* Cape Town: Howard Timmins.

Arnheim, M. T. W. 1985a: in *Finance Week*, 7-13 November 1985.

Arnheim, M. T. W. 1985b: in *Finance Week*, 14-20 November 1985.

Baynham, S. J. 1985: 'The Military in Africa' in *Africa Insight 15(4)*: 277-282.

Bennett, Mark 1985: 'Countdown to the State of Emergency' in *Indicator S.A. 3(2)* Spring: 6-8.

Bernstein, Ann 1986: 'The South African Business Community'. A research paper prepared for the South Africa Beyond Apartheid project.

Bienen, Henry S. 1987: 'A New Policy – Selective Engagement' in *Orbis.* Philadelphia, Spring.

Black, A. 1986: 'Industrialization, Economic Crisis and the Question of Redistribution in South Africa'. *SAERT*, Amsterdam, December 1986.

Booysen, H. 1981: 'Die Behoud van Blanke Selfbeskikking'. Pretoria.

Booysen, H. 1985a: 'Dinamiese Konserwatisme'. Pretoria.

Booysen, H. 1985b: 'Boerevolkstaat Kort en Kragtig'. New Germany.

Boshoff, A. (ed) 1985: 'Die Afrikaner se Hoop Leef'. Pretoria: Afrikaner-volkswag Publication.

Boshoff, C. 1985a: 'Afrikanerkultuur in die Krisis'. Speech, Pretoria City Hall, 15 March 1985.

Boshoff, C. 1985b: 'Amerikaanse Liberalisme en Volkeverhoudinge in Suid-Afrika'. Volkskongres speech, 30 May 1985.

Botha, Pik 1986: Article in *The Citizen*, 7 February 1986.

Botha, P. W. 1986: Article in *The Star*, 8 February 1986.

Botha, P. W. 1987: Speech to parliament immediately after winning the 6 May 1987 white general election.

Bundy, Colin 1986: 'Schools and Revolution' in *New Society*, 10 January 1986.

Business Day, 12 November 1986.

Buthelezi Commission 1982: 'The Requirements for Stability and Development in KwaZulu and Natal'. Durban: H & H Publications (2 volumes).

Buthelezi, Mangosuthu 1985: Speech at the Youth Brigade Annual Conference.

Buthelezi, Mangosuthu 1986a: Memorandum presented at a meeting with Count Otto von Lambsdorff, February 1986.

Buthelezi, Mangosuthu 1986b: Speech to the European Democratic Group. Strasbourg, January 1986.

Buthelezi, Mangosuthu 1986c: Speech to the Department of Business Economics, University of the Witwatersrand, July 1986.

Cadman, Vicki 1986: 'The Homelands as Institutional Actors'. Research paper prepared for the South Africa Beyond Apartheid project.

Cadman, Vicki and Godsell, Bobby 1987: 'Inkatha'. Research paper prepared for the South Africa Beyond Apartheid project.

Campbell, Kurt M. 1987: *Soviet Policy towards South Africa*. London: Macmillan.

Cape Times, 11 October 1986.

Cape Times, 23 March 1987.

Chaliand, Gerard and Rageau, Jean-Pierre 1985: *Strategic Atlas: A Comparative Study of the World's Geopolitics and the World's Power*. New York: Harper & Row.

Citizen, The: Article on the State of Emergency, 19 March 1987.

Coetzee, P. J. 1981: 'Revolusionêre Oorlogvoering en Teeninsurgensie', in Hough, M. (ed): *Nasionale Veiligheid en Strategie met Spesifieke Verwysing na die RSA*. University of Pretoria, Institute for Strategic Studies (publication no. 10).

Commonwealth Eminent Persons Group on South Africa 1986: Mission to South Africa: the Commonwealth Report. Harmondsworth: Penguin.

Connor, Walker, 1978: 'A Nation is a Nation is a State is an Ethnic Group is a . . .'. Ethnic and Racial Studies 1(4): 319.

Cooper, Carole et al. 1984: Race Relations Survey 1983. Johannesburg: S.A. Institute of Race Relations.

Cooper, Carole et al. 1985: Race Relations Survey 1984. Johannesburg: S.A. Institute of Race Relations.

Cooper, Saths 1986: 'What Sort of Madness Is This?' in Frontline 6(5), September/October.

Crocker, Chester A. 1979: 'Current and Projected Military Balances in Southern Africa' in Bissell, Richard E. and Crocker, Chester A., 1979: South Africa into the 1980s. Boulder, Colorado: Westview Press.

Crocker, Chester A. 1987: 'A Democratic Future: The Challenge for South Africans'. Speech at the CUNY Conference on South Africa in Transition, White Plains, New York, 1 October 1987.

Davies, Robert 1987: 'Nationalisation, Socialisation and the Freedom Charter' in South African Labour Bulletin 12(2): 85-106.

Davis, Stephen M. 1987: Apartheid's Rebels: Inside South Africa's Hidden War. New Haven: Yale University Press.

De Gruchy, John W. 1985: 'Christians in Conflict: The Social Reality of the South African Church', in Journal of Theology for Southern Africa (51). June 1985.

De Klerk, F. W. 1986: Article in The Argus, 5 February 1986.

De Kock, Wessel 1986: Usuthu! Cry Peace! Cape Town: Open Hand Press.

Dreyer, J. P. and Brand, S. S. 1986: ''n Sektorale Beskouing van die Suid-Afrikaanse Ekonomie in 'n Veranderende Omgewing' in South African Journal of Economics. Paper delivered at the 1986 bi-annual conference of the South African Economic Society.

Du Plessis, F. J. 1985a: Persoonlike Besparings in Suid-Afrika: Staan Ons Tans voor 'n Krisis? Publication by the Potchefstroom University of a lecture delivered on 29 August 1985 at Potchefstroom University.

Du Plessis, F. J. 1985b: Die Vryemarkideologie in Perspektief. Publication by Potchefstroom University of a lecture delivered on 25 March 1986.

Du Toit, H. V. 1985: Book Review: 'Pretoria's Praetorians: Civil-Military Relations in South Africa' in Politikon 12(1): 64-68.

Edwards, Aiden 1987: Article in Business Day, 3 June 1987.

Financial Mail, 30 May 1986.

Frankel, Philip H. 1984: Pretoria's Praetorians: Civil-Military Relations in South Africa. Cambridge: Cambridge University Press.

Frankel, Philip H. 1986: 'The Security Forces as Political Actors', an unpublished paper, March 1986.

Furnivall, J. S. 1948: *Colonial Policy and Practice*. London: Cambridge University Press.

Geldenhuys, Deon and Kotze, Hennie 1983: 'Aspects of Political Decision-Making in South Africa' in *Politikon 10(1)*: 33-45.

Geldenhuys, Deon and Kotze, Hennie 1985: 'P. W. Botha as Decision-Maker: A Preliminary Study of Personality and Politics' in *Politikon 12(1)*: 30-42.

Geldenhuys, Deon 1986a: 'The South African Security Forces as a Political Actor', unpublished paper, Rand Afrikaans University, March 1986.

Geldenhuys, Deon 1986b: 'The Origins of South Africa's Present State of Security System', unpublished paper, Rand Afrikaans University, March 1986.

Geldenhuys, Deon 1986c: 'The Structure of the State Security System', unpublished paper, Rand Afrikaans University, March 1986.

Giddens, Anthony 1979: *Central problems in Social Theory: Action, Structure and Contradictions in Social Analysis*. London: Macmillan.

Giliomee, Hermann and Schlemmer, Lawrence 1985: *Up Against the Fences: Poverty, Passes and Privilege in South Africa*. Cape Town: David Philip.

Giliomee, Hermann 1983: 'The Botha Quest: Sharing Power Without Losing Control', in *Leadersip S.A. 2(2)*.

Giliomee, Hermann 1987: 'The Third Way', in *Sunday Times*, 2 August 1987.

Godsell, Bobby and le Roux, Pieter 1986: *Growth, Equity and Participation*. Pretoria: Human Sciences Research Council.

Godsell, Bobby 1987a: 'The Progressive Federal Party'. Research paper prepared for the South Africa Beyond Apartheid project.

Godsell, Bobby 1987b: 'The Role of the South African Security Agencies in the Process of Political Transformation'. Research paper prepared for the South Africa Beyond Apartheid project.

Godsell, Bobby 1987c: 'S.A. Trade Unions: An Update'. Research paper prepared for the South Africa Beyond Apartheid project.

Goldman, Ronald 1987: 'American Universities and South Africa'. Research paper prepared for the South Africa Beyond Apartheid project.

Goncharov, Victor 1987: 'Soviet Policy in Southern Africa' in *Work in Progress 48: 7*.

Green, Shelley 1987: 'Liberal and Conservative U.S. Activist Groups'. Research paper prepared for the South Africa Beyond Apartheid project.

Greenberger, Robert S. 1987: 'U.S. Trade Sanctions on South Africa Starting to Pay Long-Term Dividends', in *The Wall Street Journal*, 21 September 1987.

Grundy, Kenneth W. 1983: 'The Rise of the South African Security Establishment: An Essay on the Changing Locus of State Power'. Johannesburg: South African Institute of International Affairs (Bradlow Series No. 1).

327

Gurr, Ted Roberts 1970: *Why Men Rebel*. Princeton: University of Princeton Press.

Gwala, Z. 1985: 'Rebellion in the Last Outpost' in *Indicator S.A. 3(2)* (Political Monitor): 6-11.

Hanlon, Joseph 1984: *Mozambique: The Revolution under Fire*. London: Zed Publishers.

Hansard *(Debates of the House of Assembly)*, 1 February 1985. Cape Town: Government Printer.

Hansard *(Debates of the House of Assembly)*, 8 May 1985. Cape Town: Government Printer.

Hansard *(Debates of the House of Assembly)*, 27 March 1986. Cape Town: Government Printer.

Hartz, Louis 1984: *The Founding of New Societies*. New York: Harcourt, Brace and World.

Hauck, David 1987a: 'U.S. Businessmen and the Question of a Post-Apartheid South Africa'. Research paper prepared for the South Africa Beyond Apartheid project.

Hauck, David 1987b: 'U.S. Labour Unions'. Research paper prepared for the South Africa Beyond Apartheid project.

Hauck, David 1987c: 'State and Local Legislators and the Issue of South Africa'. Research paper prepared for the South Africa Beyond Apartheid project.

Hayes, J. P. 1987: *Economic Effects of Sanctions on Southern Africa*. London: Gower, for the Trade Policy Research Centre.

Haysom, Nicholas 1986: *Mabangalala: The Rise of Right-Wing Vigilantes in South Africa*. Johannesburg: Centre for Applied Legal Studies, University of Witwatersrand.

Heitman, Helmoed-Römer 1987: 'The Mean Machine' in *Sunday Times*, 5 July 1987.

Hirschman, Albert O. 1963: *Journeys toward Progress: Studies of Economic Policy-Making in Latin America*. London: Greenwood Press.

Hirschmann, David 1987: 'Changing Attitudes of Black South Africans towards the United States of America' in *Institute for Social and Economic Research (work paper No. 34)*: 22. Grahamstown: Rhodes University.

Horne, Alistair 1977: *Savage War of Peace: Algeria 1954-1962*. London: Macmillan.

Houghton, D. Hobart 1973: *The South African Economy*. 3rd ed. Cape Town: Oxford University Press.

Hutt, W. A. 1964: *The Economics of the Colour Bar: A Study of the Economic Origins and Consequences of Racial Segregation in South Africa*. London: Deutsch, for Institute of Economic Affairs.

International Institute for Strategic Studies 1986: *Military Balance 1985/6*. London: IISS.

328

Jenkins, Simon 1987: in *Times Literary Supplement*, 3 April 1987.

Kairos Document 1986: 'Challenge to the Church': A Theological Comment on the Political Crisis in South Africa. Johannesburg: Kairos Theologians.

Kane-Berman, John 1982: 'Inkatha: The Paradox of South African Politics' in *Optima (30)3*. Published by the Anglo American Corporation and De Beers Group of Companies.

Karis, Thomas G. 1986/87: 'South African Liberation – the Communist Factor' in *Foreign Affairs 65(2)* Winter.

Kemp, Koos 1984: 'Carel Boshoff en Sy Afrikanerdenke'. Pretoria: Oranjewerkers Promosies.

Khoza, Reuel 1987: 'The Black Professional and Business Class'. Research paper prepared for the South Africa Beyond Apartheid project.

Kitchen, Helen 1987: 'Washington Policy Community'. Research paper prepared for the South Africa Beyond Apartheid project.

Kühne, Winrich, 1986: *Sowjetische Afrikapolitik in der 'Ära Gorbatschov'*. Ebenhausen, Stiftung Wissenschaft und Politik.

Kuper, Leo 1965: *An African Bourgeoisie: Race, Class and Politics in South Africa*. New Haven: Yale University Press.

Kuper, Leo and Smith M. G. (eds) 1969: *Pluralism in Africa*. Berkeley: University of California Press.

Kurt, M. Campbell 1987: *Soviet Policy towards South Africa*. London: Macmillan.

Leatt, James 1987a: 'Education and Apartheid: A Decade of Resistance and Reform'. Research paper prepared for the South Africa Beyond Apartheid project.

Leatt, James 1987b: 'The Church in Resistance Post 1976'. Research paper prepared for the South Africa Beyond Apartheid project.

Leatt, James, Kneifel, Theo and Nürnberger, Klaus 1986: *Contending Ideologies in South Africa*. Cape Town: David Philip.

Le Roux, P. 1986: 'Die Uitdaging van die Demokratiese Sosialisme' in *Die Suid-Afrikaan, No. 6 Herfs*.

Le Roux, P. 1987: 'The State as an Economic Actor: A Review of Divergent Perceptions of Economic Issues'. Research paper prepared for the South Africa Beyond Apartheid project.

Lewis, Gavin 1987: 'Report on the Southern Rhodesia project', Urban Foundation (confidential).

Lijphart, Arend 1984: *Consociational for South Africa*. California Press.

Lijphart, Arend 1985: *Power-Sharing in South Africa*. Berkeley: University of California, Institute of International Studies (Policy Papers in International Affairs, No. 24).

Lipton, Merle 1985: *Capitalism and Apartheid: South Africa 1910-1984*. London: Gower.

Lodge, Tom 1983: *Black Politics in South Africa since 1945*. Johannesburg: Ravan.

Lodge, Tom 1984: 'State of Exile: The African National Congress of South Africa, 1976-1986' in *Third World Quarterly*, January 1987: 1-27.

Lodge, Tom 1986: 'Mayihlome!: Let Us Go to War: from Nkomati to Kabwe, the African National Congress, January 1984 - June 1985' in *South African Review (3)*. Johannesburg: Ravan Press.

Lombard, J. A. 1978: *Freedom, Welfare and Order: Thoughts on the Principles of Political Co-operation in the Economy of Southern Africa*. Pretoria: Benbo.

Lombard, J. A. 1981: *Socio Economic Prospects for the Eighties*. Bureau for Economic Policy and Analysis, University of Pretoria (BEPA Economic Papers No. 9).

Lombard, J. A. 1985: 'Inflasie en Lone' in *Buro vir Ekonomiese Politiek en Analise*, Universiteit van Pretoria. Pretoria: BEPA.

Lombard, J. A. 1986: 'Towards Economic Restoration' in *Indicator SA 4(1)*: 41-42.

Louw, Leon and Kendall, Frances 1986: *South Africa: The Solution*. Bisho, Ciskei: Amasi.

Lubbe, W. J. G. 1983: *Witman, Waar Is Jou Tuisland?* Pretoria: Oranje-werkers Promosies.

Mandela, Winnie 1986: *Sydafrika after Apartheid*.

Maphai, Vincent 1987: 'Resistance in South Africa: Azapo and the National Forum'. Research paper prepared for the South Africa Beyond Apartheid project.

Marais, J. 1983: *Waarheid en Werklikheid*. Pretoria: Aktuele Publikasies.

Marcum, John 1986a: 'Frontline States: The People's Republic of Angola'. Research paper prepared for the South Africa Beyond Apartheid project.

Marcum, John 1986b: 'Frontline States: The People's Republic of Mozambique'. Research paper prepared for the South Africa Beyond Apartheid project.

Maree, Johann 1986: 'The Past, Present and Potential Role of the Democratic Trade Union Movement'. York Conference Paper, Institute for South African Studies, September 1986.

Mbeki, Thabo 1984: 'The Futton Thesis: a Rejoinder' in *Canadian Journal of African Studies 18(3)*: 609-612.

Meer, Fatima (ed) 1985: 'Unrest in Natal'. Institute for Black Research, University of Natal. August 1985.

Metz, Steven 1986: 'The Anti-Apartheid Movement and the Populist Instinct in American Politics' in *Political Science Quarterly 101(3)*: 379-395.

Mkhatshwa, S. 1985: Keynote Address at the National Consultative Conference on the Crisis in Education organised by the Soweto Parents Crisis Committee. Johannesburg: University of the Witwatersrand.

Morris, Mike 1987: 'Choose Sides and Organise' in *Work in Progress 46*.

Moss, Glenn 1987: 'The Pan Africanist Congress: Alleged Guerrillas and Activists in Court' in *Work in Progress 47*, April 1987.

Muller, Edward 1979: *Aggressive Political Participation*. Princeton: Princeton University Press.

Ned, Temko 1987: *Christian Science Monitor*, 11 March 1987.

Nederduitse Gereformeerde Kerk: Algemene Sinode 1975: *Ras, Volk en Nasie en Volkereverhoudinge in die Lig van die Skrif*. Kaapstad: N. G. Kerk-Uitgewers.

Neuhaus, Richard J. 1986: *Dispensations: The Future of South Africa as South Africans See It*. Michigan: Eerdmans.

Neuhaus, Richard J. 1987: 'The Religion Factor'. Research paper prepared for the South Africa Beyond Apartheid project.

Nolutshungu, Sam C. 1983: *Changing South Africa: Political Considerations*. Cape Town: David Philip.

Nunn, Frederick M. 1976: *The Military in Chilean History: Essays in Civil Military Relations 1810-1973*. Albuquerque, New Mexico: University of New Mexico Press.

Nzimande, E. B. and Zulu, P. M. 1987: 'The Township Youth: From Civil Rights to Socialism'. Unpublished.

Nzo, Alfred 1986: Message on the occasion of the 65th anniversary of the SACP. 30 July 1986.

O'Dowd, Michael 1974: 'South Africa in the Light of the Stages of Economic Growth' in Leftwich, Adrian (ed) 1974: *South Africa: Economic Growth and Political Change with Comparative Studies of Chile, Sri Lanka and Malaysia*. New York: St. Martin's Press.

O'Dowd, Michael 1984: 'A Capitalist Approach to the Amelioration of Poverty'. Second Carnegie Inquiry into Poverty and Development, Cape Town.

Oosthuizen, G. C. et al. 1985: *Religion, Intergroup Relations and Social Change in South Africa*. Pretoria: Human Sciences Research Council.

Owen, Ken 1987: Article in *Business Day*, 8 May 1987.

President's Council 1987: *Report on the Technical Committee, 1983, and Related Matters*. Committee for Constitutional Affairs. Cape Town: President's Council, PC4.

Riekert Report 1979: *Report of the Commission of Inquiry into Legislation Affecting the Utilisation of Manpower*. (Excluding the legislation administered by the Department of Labour and Mines.) Chairman, P. J. Riekert. Pretoria: Government Printer.

Rhoodie, N., De Kock, Chris and Couper, Mick 1986: *Blanke Suid-Afrikaners se Persepsies van die Gedeeltelike Noodtoestand soos Afgekondig op 20 Julie 1985*. Pretoria: Human Sciences Research Council: 19.

331

Rupert, A. 1986: 'A plea for Co-existence'. Chairman's address delivered on 28 August 1986. Rembrandt Group Limited.

SABRA 1985: *'n Nuwe Grondwet vir die R.S.A.* Pretoria.

SAIRR (South African Institute of Race Relations) 1987, April 1987. Johannesburg: SAIRR.

SAIRR (South African Institute of Race Relations) 1987, July 1987. Johannesburg: SAIRR.

S. A. News Summary 1985: Second Quarter. Westville (Natal): Duncan Stuart.

Sampson, A. 1987: *Black and Gold: Tycoons, Revolutionaries and Apartheid.* London: Hodder & Stoughton.

Schlemmer, L. 1983: 'White Voter Preferences – Predictable Trends' in *Indicator S.A. 1(2)*: 11-13.

Schlemmer, L. 1987a: 'After Soweto and Sebokeng: The Elections of 1977 and 1987' in *Indicator SA 4(4)*: 9-11.

Schlemmer, L. 1987b: 'South Africa's National Party Government'. Research paper prepared for the South Africa Beyond Apartheid project.

Schlemmer, L. et al., forthcoming: *Report of the Working Group on Race: Ethnicity and Culture. National Investigation into Intergroup Relations.* Pretoria: Human Sciences Research Council.

Schreiner, G. D. L. et al. 1982: *The Buthelezi Commission* (Schreiner – drafter of the Main Report). Durban: H & H Publications.

Schwarz, Harry 1985: 'The PFP's Alternative Economic Democracy' in *Deurbraak*, May 1987: 7.

Seegers, Annette 1984: 'Dimensions of Militarization: Separate Development, State Structures and the Rise of the Military in South Africa'. Paper delivered at the conference on Economic Development and Racial Domination, University of Western Cape, 8-10 October 1984.

Seegers, Annette 1986a: 'An Assessment of the Scholarship of South Africa's Security Forces'. Unpublished paper, March 1986.

Seegers, Annette 1986b: Review article: 'The Military in South Africa: A Comparison and Critique'. *South Africa International 16(4)*: 192-200.

Shultz, George 1987: 'The Democratic Future of South Africa'. Speech at Business Council for International Understanding, New York, 29 September 1987.

Simkins, C. et al. 1985: 'Justice, Development and the National Budget'. Second Carnegie Inquiry into Poverty and Development in Southern Africa, Post Conference Series No. 6. Cape Town.

Sisulu, Z. 1986: Keynote Address at the National Education Crisis Committee, Durban.

Skocpol, Theda 1979: *States and Social Revolutions.* Cambridge: Cambridge University Press.

Slovo, Joe 1986: Speech at the 65th anniversary meeting of the SACP. London, 30 July 1986.

Smith, M. G. 1965: *The Plural Society in the British West Indies*. Berkeley: University of California Press.

Sorel, G. 1915: *Reflections on Violence*. New York: Peter Smith.

South Africa (Republic), Department of Defence 1986: *White Paper on Defence and Armaments Supply*. Cape Town.

South African Institute of Race Relations, *Race Relations Survey 1983*. Johannesburg, SAIRR.

Southall, Roger 1982: 'The Buthelezi Commission Report: Consolidation, Consociation, Collaboration'. Conference paper, *South Africa in the Comparative Study of Class, Race and Nationalism* held in New York, 8-12 September 1982.

Southern Africa Report 1987: Weekly newsletter of the South Africa Report Association. Johannesburg: Raymond Louw (editor and publisher), 6 February 1987.

Spicer, Michael 1986: 'The South African Development Co-Ordination Conference - SADCC'. Research paper prepared for the South Africa Beyond Apartheid project.

Spicer, Michael 1987: 'Europe as an Actor in the South African Issue'. Research paper prepared for the South Africa Beyond Apartheid project.

Stadler, Alf 1987: *The Political Economy of Modern South Africa*. Cape Town: David Philip.

Strijdom, A. J. 1984: *Die Anneksasie van die Volksiel*. Pretoria: Aurora Press.

Sunday Times, 31 May 1987.

Sunday Times, 7 June 1987.

Sunday Times, 5 July 1987.

Sunter, Clem 1987: *The World and South Africa in the 1990s*. Cape Town: Human & Rousseau/Tafelberg.

Suzman, Helen 1987: Speech entitled 'The Divided People' delivered on Mrs Suzman's behalf at 'The One People Oration' conference held on 7th July 1987 at Westminster Cathedral.

Swilling, Mark 1987a: 'Playing Rio Roulette' in *The Weekly Mail*, 20-26 March 1987: 11.

Swilling, Mark 1987b: 'Wrong, the Trend Is Left' in *The Weekly Mail*, 15-21 May 1987.

Taheri, Amir 1985: *Spirit of Allah: Khomeini and the Islamic Revolution*. London: Hutchinson.

Tambo, Oliver 1986: National Executive Council Statement delivered by Tambo on 16 December 1986, the 25th Anniversary of Umkhonto we Sizwe.

Taylor, Stan 1984: *Social Science and Revolution*. London: Macmillan.

Temko, Ned 1987: in *Christian Science Monitor*, 11 March 1987.

Terre'Blanche, E. 1984: 'Inleiding tot Emosie en die Stigting van die Afrikaner Volkswag'. Pretoria: Sigma Press. (Editor unspecified.)

Tomlinson, F. R. 1955: *Report of the Commission for the Socio- Economic Development of the Bantu Areas*. Pretoria: Government Printer (UG 61 of 1955).

Treurnicht, A. P. 1985a: in *Die Patriot* (Conservative Party's newspaper), September 1985.

Treurnicht, A. P. 1985b: Press release, 4 September 1985.

U. S. Department of State 1973: 'South Africa: Background Notes No. 8021'. Washington, D.C., July 1973.

U. S. Department of State 1987: 'A U. S. Policy towards South Africa'. *The Report of the Secretary of State's Advisory Committee on South Africa*. Washington, D. C., January 1987: 38.

Van der Merwe, Stoffel 1987: quotes in *Rapport*, 7 June 1987.

Weekly Mail, The, 9-15 January 1987.

Weekly Mail, The, 22-29 May 1987.

Weekly Mail, The, 29 May-4 June 1987.

Wickins, P. L. 1981: *Economic History of Africa from the Earliest Times to Partition*. Cape Town: Oxford University Press.

Wiehahn Commission 1979-1981: *Report of the Commission of Inquiry into Labour Legislation*, South Africa. (Chairman, Nicholas Everhardus Wiehahn.) Pretoria: Department of Manpower Utilisation 1-6.

Williamson, Craig 1986: 'Point, Counterpoint' in *Leadership S.A.* 5(1): 63-66.

Wittich, G. 1986: 'Research Priorities for Socio-Economic Planning in Post-Apartheid South Africa Manufacture (Parastatals)'. Paper delivered at the conference of the *SAERT*, Amsterdam, December 1986.

Yudelman, David 1983: *The Emergence of Modern South Africa: State, Capital and the Incorporation of Organised Labour on the South African Gold Fields, 1902-1939*. Westport, Conn.: Greenwood.

Zille, Helen 1986a: 'The Labour Party of South Africa'. Research paper prepared for the South Africa Beyond Apartheid project.

Zille, Helen 1986b: 'The Rightwing in South African Politics'. Research paper prepared for the South Africa Beyond Apartheid project.

Zulu, P. M. 1986a: 'Political Conflict and Unrest in African Townships: The Case of Natal', Maurice Webb Race Relations Unit, University of Natal. Unpublished.

Zulu, P. M. 1986b: 'South Africa's Reform Process: A Historical Perspective'. Maurice Webb, Race Relations Unit, University of Natal. Unpublished.

Zulu, P. M., Ngidi, S. and Booth, D. G. 1987: 'Political Resistance and Unrest in African Townships: Natal and the Eastern Cape 1984-86'. Research paper prepared for the South Africa Beyond Apartheid project.

Index

Academic boycott, 109-110
Activism: anti-apartheid, *see* Anti-apartheid activism; conservative, USA, 248; right-wing, 60, 90-94
'Actors', South Africa, 2-4
Adam, Heribert, 3, 4, 285, 314
Afghanistan, SACP on, 121, 122
African National Congress, 95-119; alienation problems, 159; allied organisations, 97; and PAC, 123-124, 128; and religion, 110-112; and SA Communist Party, 96, 97, 105, 117, 119; and women, 112-113; armed resistance, 31, 97, 97-103; attitude to whites, 97, 102, 103-104, 109, 116, 118; banning, 96; Commonwealth attitude to, 99; conflict within, 117; criminalisation, 95; founding, 127; Freedom Charter, 115, 128, 133, 135, 136, 137, 147, 221, 231; future vision and objectives, 113-118; infiltration by and of security system, 98; Inkatha, relationship with, 99; Kabwe conference, 97, 98, 105, 107, 112; legalisation, possible, 35; Marxist members, 117-118, 201; meetings of South Africans with, 7, 118-119, 173; military wing, 31, 97, 98, 101, 103; National Executive Committee, 97, 101; negotiation policies, 104-107, 237-239; nonclass alliance, 114; nonracial claims, 104; organisation, 96-97; police assessment of, 98; political

education, 107; self-restraint, 100; strategies, 102; support, internal, 95, 98-101; support, international, 95-96; SWAPO alliance with, 260-261; township presence, 130; Trotskyite criticism of, 215; underground activity, 98-101; USA, relations with, 95-96; Youth League, 127
African National Council, 270
African People's Organisation, 127
African socialist nationalism, 216-217, 220
African states, 260-264; and sanctions, 257-258; front-line, international aid to, 257; right-wing policies on, 81
Afrikaans culture, 24; ANC attitude to, 104; NP commitment to, 24: right-wing view, 69-70
Afrikaans language, 69
Afrikaanse Handelsinstituut, 22
Afrikaanse Protestantse Kerk, 68
Afrikaner, Die, 67
Afrikaner-Broederbond, 58, 62
Afrikaner nationalism, 43-44, 58, 63, 67
Afrikaners, 24-25; alliance with English-speaking South Africans, 24-25, 64, 65; and coloureds, 63; assimilation of other ethnic groups, 65; attitude to influx control, 22; CP/NP support, 57, 87; definition of, 24, 64; ethnic interests, 43-44; ideological

crisis, 68; NP commitment to, 24-25; resistance to change, 38-39, 76-77; support of partition, 75; survival crisis, 69
Afrikanervolkswag, 58, 62, 66
Afrikaner-Weerstandsbeweging, 59-61, 73, 81, 82, 89, 92, 93
Agriculture: homelands, 73; NP perspective on, 23, 170
Alexander, Neville, 215
Algerian analogy, 271
Alienation problems, ANC, 159
Alliance of Black Reformed Churches, 139
Alliance politics, 177, 180, 189, 194
Alliances, resistance, 97, 143-144, 177, 188
Amanzimtoti bombing, 103
ANC, *see* African National Congress
ANC Youth League, 127
Anglo American Corporation, 170, 207
Angola: aid to ANC and SWAPO, 260-261; Cuban forces in, 244; depleted by hostilities, 261; military spending, 31; right-wing view of, 82; SA intervention in, 82, 260-261; Soviet aid and influence, 261; USA involvement, 244
Anti-Americanism, 242
Anti-apartheid activism: external, 31, 97-103; African states, 240, 260-264; internal, 15-17, 125-163, 166, 177-178, 184; Soviet Union, 240, 258-260; United

States, 240, 241, 245-254;
Western Europe and Japan,
255-258
Apartheid: abolition versus
reform, 213-215, 295; as-
sumptions of, 289-291; black
perspectives, 7, 126, 137-139,
143, 145-146, 165; capitalism and, 287; Church and,
47, 139; connotations of,
213-214; criminalisation, international, 258; ethnic, 12;
historical origin, 7; incrementalists' perspective, 165;
institutions of, 213-215, 295-
296, 297-298; international
perspective, 240-266; legal
aspects, 154; legislation 10-
11, 12, 18, 127, 135, 154,
171, 183; reform, 8-14, 204-
206, 280; residential, 12, 50,
see also Group Areas Act;
right-wing perspectives, 66-
67, 68, 70, 74; territorial, 8-13,
44, 70; undermining of, 280-
281; victims of, 140, 143
Apartheid paradigm, 289-291,
295
Aquino, Corazon, 275
Armaments industry, 32
Arms embargo, 243
Army, see South African Defence Force
Arnheim, M. T. W., 77
Authoritarianism, 284
AWB, see Afrikaner-
Weerstandsbeweging
Azania News, 123
Azanian Confederation of
Trade Unions, 123
Azanian People's Organi-
sation (AZAPO), 101, 117,
123, 124, 137-138, 144, 153,
160, 214

Ball, Chris, 119
Banning, 16, 139, 154
Bantu Education Act of 1953,
149
Beck, Graham, 171
Beira corridor, 257
Berger, Peter, 3, 8, 314
Bernstein, Ann, 2, 4, 314

'Bi-communalism', 53
Bienen, Henry, 254
Biko, Steve, 141
Bill, Reverend Francois, 139
Bill of Rights, 147, 166, 188
Black, Anthony, 230
Black caucus (USA), 95
Black Consciousness Move-
ment, 16, 124, 137-138, 153-
154; and negotiation, 117;
attitude to whites, 138; community programmes, 141;
ideological alliances and differences, 144; origins, 129;
revolutionary militancy, 117;
role in youth resistance, 134;
socialist tendency, 124
Black Management Forum,
143
Blacks: and capitalism, 148-
149, 217; attitude to power-
sharing, 76-77, 79; attitude
to reforms, 40; black on
black violence, 102, 152,
159; churches, 139; collaborators, 138, 152; education,
132, 134-136, 149-151, 153,
224-225, 253-254; exclusion
from tricameral constitution,
130, 193; future visions,
113-118, 146-150, 176;
government meetings with
spokesmen, 39; labour, see
Labour; middle-class, 78,
158; mobilisation, 15-17,
157, 158; nonparticipation
strategies, 155, 160, 189; participation, 51, 166, 183, 189-
198; professional and business groupings, 141; radical,
78-80; status outside homelands, 10; unity, 194-195;
urbanisation, 154, 172; view
on disinvestment, 155; violence, control of, 79; wil-
lingness/unwillingness to
negotiate, 39-40, 104-107,
177, 237-239; women, 112,
173-174
Blanke Bevrydingsbeweging,
61, 84
Blanke Volkstaatparty, 60
Bloom, Tony, 209

Boesak, Alan, 138, 139
Booysen, Hercules, 62, 63,
64, 65, 66, 67, 71, 72, 73
Boshoff, Carel, 62, 65, 66, 67,
69, 85, 89
Botha, P. W., 'adapt or die'
statement, 37; defence force
background, 37; interpre-
tation of mandate, 13; rebuke
of A. Hendrickse, 184; reform policies, 204-206;
speeches, 13, 37, 76, 208, 209
Botha, Pik, 25, 106
Botswana, raid on, 106
Boycotts, 156, 276; academic,
109-110; bus, 156, 160; consumer, 135, 156, 161; criteria, 109; cultural, 109-110,
160; education, 152; election, 152; reasons, 155-156;
rent, 36; sport, 18; transport, 156, 160; see also Disinvestment; Nonparticipation;
Sanctions
Brain drain, 116, 265
Britain, see Commonwealth;
United Kingdom
British Anti-Apartheid Movement, 110
Broederbond, 58, 62
Buchner, Jack, 98
Bundy, Colin, 134
Bus stoning, 156, 160
Business reforms, 204-205
Business sector: future vision,
170-171, 191-192; mediatory
role, 173; meetings with
ANC, 118-119, 173; nature,
168-270; political role, 191-
192; sanctions debate, 173;
strategies, 171-173
Business sector, black, 19-23,
141-143, 209
Buthelezi, Mangosuthu, 107,
165, 176, 177, 178, 183, 269,
270-271
Buthelezi Commission, 21,
176, 177

Cadman, Vicki, 2, 314
Call of Islam, 110
'Call to prayer for an end to
unjust rule', 139

336

Dadoo, Y. M., 110
Deaths in political violence, 35-36
Debt crisis, 209
Defence, *see* Security; South African Defence Force
De Jonge, Klaas, 99
De Klerk, F. W., 25, 38
De Klerk, Willem, 39, 40
Democracy: Inkatha's concept of, 176; right-wing views, 72; social, 201; business sector views, 170
Democratic evolution, 216
Democratic socialism, 201, 216, 219
Democratic Turnhalle Alliance, 53-54
Democratisation, 292-295
Demonstrations, mass, 275-276
Dependency theory, 286-287, 288-289, 297
Destabilisation, neighbouring states, 260-263; townships, 161
Detainees' Parents' Support Committee, 35
Detente policy, 82
Detention, 35; children, 142; church leaders, 139
Deukmejian, George, 249
Disinvestment/Divestment, 18, 155, 206-207; resistance movements' view of, 155; right-wing perspective, 84; SA government response to, 18; *see also* Sanctions
Double standards, 80
Du Plessis, Barend, 106, 225
Du Plessis, Fred, 209, 212
Dutch Reformed churches, 47, 68, 298; black, 141
Du Toit, Z. B., 67, 68, 75, 76, 91, 93

East Asian example, 297
Eastern Cape, 54, 156
Economic Advisory Council, 212
Economic destabilisation, 155-156, 161
Economic exploitation, 145, 158

Economic independence policy, 18-19, 204
Economic integration, 43
Economic policies and visions: ANC, 113-119, 202; business sector, 168-170; government, 18-19, 202-204; incrementalists, 166; Inkatha, 176; Labour Party, 182; negotiation policy, 201, 202; PFP, 180; resistance movements, 148-149; revolutionary, 201; right-wing, 62, 81-85, 200-201; siege economy, 200-201, 203-204, 207-213; UDF, 135
Economic prospects, 200-239; and sanctions, 252-255; and USA involvement, 247, 252-255
Economic reforms, 204-206; right-wing views, 206-207
Economic relations, 204; United States, 247-254; Western Europe and Japan, 255-258; *see also* Investment, foreign
Economic resources: management of, 201, 296-297; redistribution, 208-209, 210-213, 225-227, 228-231
Economy: and sanctions, 209, 211-212; debt crisis, 209; management of, 201, 296-297
Education: ANC, 96; alternative, 136, 150, 151, 155; Black Consciousness role, 134; black objectives, 149-151; changes, 9, 132, 151; deracialisation, 9, 298; effect on resistance, 134; grievances, 132, 133, 134; nonracial, 172; people's, 136, 150, 151, 155; resistance, 129, 130, 131, 132, 133, 134, 136, 156, 161; right-wing view, 69; strategies, 153; UDF role, 136; USA funding, 253-254; *see also* Schools
Educational Opportunities Council, 255
Edwards, Aidan, 19

Eglin, Colin, 180
Elections, 55, 86, 180; pacts, 56, 180; postponement, 184
Emigration, white, 116, 265
Eminent Persons Group, 106, 107, 235, 256
Employment: homelands, 73; provision of, 209, 227-228: *see also* Unemployment
English-speaking South Africans: Afrikaner relationship with, 24-25, 64, 65; church activism, 141; NP support, 24-25, 47; right-wing attitude to, 64
Equal Opportunity Foundation, 255
Equality, definitions of, 148, 158
Ethnic apartheid, 12
Ethnic nationalism, 24, 65
Ethnicity: Afrikaner perspective, 24; black perspective, 104; coloured perspective, 181; NP perspective, 24
Europe: ANC support, 96; *see also* Western Europe
European Community, pressure on SA, 256
Evolutionary reform concept, 38; *see also* Change; Incrementalism, Reform
Exploitation, economic, 145, 158
Extra-parliamentary groups and organisations: black spokesmen associated with, 39; business sector, 168-173; external funding, 36, 208; in exile, 95-124; Inkatha, 173-178; internal resistance groups, 135-143; negotiating role, 39-40; right-wing, 58-61

Farmers, NP commitment to, 23
Fascism, 59
Federal concepts in NP policies, 13
Federalism: ANC attitude to, 104; PFP policy, 179
Federasie van Afrikaanse Kultuurverenigings, 62

338

Muslim movement, 110-111, 214
Muzorewa, Abel, 269, 270

NADEL, 142
NAFCOC, 117, 143
NAMDA, 142
Namibia, 29, 244
Natal: Afrikaans-English coalition in, 24; joint executive authority, 10; Kwa-Zulu-Natal Indaba, 21, 53, 54, 176, 177; Kwazulu-Natal unity issues, 10, 21, 283
Natal Indian Congress, 127, 160
National African Federated Chambers of Commerce, 117, 143
National Association of Democratic Lawyers, 142
National Convention Alliance, 194
National Council, statutory, 38, 50
National Council Bill, 12
National Education Crisis Committee, 136, 150, 156, 167, 175
National Educational Union of South Africa, 142
National Executive Committee, ANC, 97, 101
National Forum, 117, 133, 136-137, 139, 160
National Intelligence Service, 29
National Medical and Dental Association, 142
National Party: Afrikaner orientation, 24-25; caucus, 40, 46; congresses, 18; English-speaking support, 24-25, 47; government, see Government, South African; ideological positions, 25, 40-41; military support, 33; policy declarations, 13; policy reforms, 9-12, 44; power sharing, commitment to, 37; racist orientation, 48; socio-economic distribution of

support, 20, 40; support base, 19-28
National Security Management System, 81
National state, white, 58, 61, 74, 94
National states, see Homelands
Nationalisation, 148; ANC attitude, 115; Marxist-Leninist objectives, 216
Nationalism, African socialist, 216-217, 220; Afrikaner, see Afrikaner nationalism; right-wing, 63-65
Native Representative Council, 127
Native Trust and Land Act, 127
Naudé, Beyers, 138, 139
Nazism, 59
NECC, 136, 150, 156, 167, 175
'Necklacing', 102, 152
Nederduitsch-Hervormde Kerk, 68, 139
Nederduitse Gereformeerde Bond, 68
Nederduitse Gereformeerde Kerk, 47, 68, 139
Negotiated settlement: economic system compatible with, 218-235
Negotiation, 17, 46, 47, 107, 160, 201, 202; ANC perspective, 104-107, 237-239; black views, 39-40, 106; business sector's role, 192; economic factors, 201, 202, 218-239; government and, 46, 47, 160, 201, 202, 235-237; Inkatha strategies, 37-38, 46, 47, 177; suspension of violence and, 106
Neo-conservative reform, 204-206
Neuhaus, Richard, 3, 316
New Republic Party, 86, 180
New Unity Movement, 160
Newly Industrialising Countries, 255, 256
Nkomati Accord, 244, 262-263

Nkomo, Joshua, 270
Nkosi Sikelel'i Afrika, 110
Nolan, Albert, 139
Nonparticipation strategy, 155, 160, 189
Nonracial tradition, 297-298
Nothnagel, Albert, 27

O'Dowd, Michael, 219
Open areas, 12, 49, 50
Opposition party, official, 55, 85, 178-179; see also Conservative Party; Progressive Federal Party
Oranjewerkers, 58, 62, 74-75, 89, 94
Organisation for African Unity, 123
Owen, Ken, 28
Own Affairs and General Affairs, 13

Pan Africanist Congress, 122-124; and ANC, 123-124; military wing, 31; white membership, 123
Parallelism, 44
Parliament, 11, 38, 76, 130, 131, 181, 183, 193
Parliamentary Standing Committee, 11
Participation policies, 166, 183, 189-198
Partition: right-wing proposals, 57, 61, 70-76, 89
Pass laws, 171, 204
Personnel Practitioners' Association, 143
Philippines, 275
Plural society concept, 42, 285
Pluralist democracy, 292
Pokela, John, 122
Police, 28, 32; ANC infiltration, 98; and extra-parliamentary groups, 17; attitude to economic strategy, 210; black municipal, 32; powers conferred on, 210; relationship with blacks, 100; right-wing support, 81
Political objectives: ANC and

affiliates, 113-118; black resistance, 146-149; business sector, 170-171, 191-192; government, 13-14; incrementalist, 164-168; right-wing, 61-62

Political parties: multiracial membership, 10; voter bases, 20, 40, 57, 174, 179, 181

Political prisoners, release of, 171

Population Registration Act, 12

Populism, 114, 117

Poqo, 31, 124

Post-apartheid institutions, 295-296

Post-apartheid vision, *see* Future vision of South Africa

Power-sharing, 11, 37, 49-50, 292-295; P. W. Botha's statements, 76-77; right-wing views, 76-77, 79

Power transfer, 237

Praetorianism, 33

President's Council, 11; meetings of black spokesmen with, 39-40

Pressure, external, 240-266, 280; African states, 240, 260-264; exiled South Africans, government's response to, 14, 17-19; Soviet Union, 240, 258-260; United States, 240, 241-254; Western Europe and Japan, 255-258

Pressure, internal: government's response to, 14-17, 19; internal groupings, 125-163; right-wing, 38-39; *see also* Resistance

Private ownership, 151, 297; *see also* Capitalism; Nationalisation

Private Sector Council on Urbanisation, 172

Professional groups, black, 141-143

Professional organisations: resistance, 133

Progressive Federal Party, 178-181; economic policies, 180, 220, 223; election results, 86; future vision, 179-180, 196; participation strategies, 195-196; relations with ANC, 186; strategies, 180-181, 195-196

Prohibition of Political Interference Act, 10

Protest, 275-276; Labour Party, 184

Protest politics, 166

Provincial government, 10, 11

Psychological liberation, 138

Race federation, 13, 53

Racial conflict, 290-291; USA compared with South Africa, 271-273

Racism: ANC perspective, 104; assumptions of, 289-291; black, 104; right-wing views, 65, 78-79

Radicalism, black, right-wing views on, 78-79

Raids into neighbouring states, 106, 184

Reconstruction, attempts at, 156

Redistribution, 162, 208-209, 210-213, 225-227; and economic growth, 228-231

Referendum (1983), 179

Reform: black perspective, 40; business sector's role, 191-192, constitutional, 11, 38, 76, 130, 131, 181, 189, 193, 197; constraints on, 38-39, 76-77; economic, 204-206; education, 9; extra-parliamentary, 284; government motivation, 49-50; incrementalist perspective, 165-166, 186-189; initiatives for, 37-38, 48, 49-50; method of, 186-189; multistrategy approach, 188; neo-conservative, 204-206; policy changes, 9-13; right-wing opposition to, 76-78, 206-207; strategic, 204-206; *see also* Change; Changes

Regional development policy, 9, 10

Regional Services Councils, 10, 48, 54; Inkatha rejection of, 193

Religion: ANC and, 110-112; right wing and, 66-69; *see also* Churches

Relly, Gavin, 173

Rembrandt, 207

Rent boycott, 36

Rent crises, 130, 132-133

Representation of Natives in Parliament Act, 127

Residential integration, 50

Residential segregation, 12, 50; *see also* Group Areas Act

Resistance: alienation problems, 159-162; coercion, 162; control of, 45, 54; nature of, 144-145; policies, 151-152; political costs, 159-161; social costs, 161-162; strategies, 152-155; tactics, 155-156

Resistance to change, 12, 38-39, 76-79; violent, 90-93

Resources: distribution of, 148, 201; management of, 296

Revolution: analysis of, 16, 77; economic considerations, 201; incrementalists' perspective, 165; PFP rejection of, 186-187; reform and, 77-78, 186, 295

Revolutionary approach, 213-218

Rhodesia, *see* Zimbabwe

Right wing, 55-94; Afrikaner support, 87; Christianity, 66-68; culture, 69-70; economic policies, 62, 82-85, 200-201, 206-207; election results, 55; foreign policy, 79-80; military and police support, 81-82; nationalism, 63-65; opposition, methods of, 85-93; opposition to reform, 38-39, 76-78; organisations, 56-61, *see also* specific organisations; partition policy, 70-76; resistance, violent, 90-93; security forces, support from, 81-82; view of economic reforms, 206-207

Rural areas: Labour Party support in, 181